Contents

Section Five Disasters Database

Section Six Red Cross Red Crescent

World Disasters Report

1998

International Federation
of Red Cross and Red Crescent Societies

Oxford University Press
1998

Oxford University Press, Great Clarendon Street, Oxford OX2 6DP

Oxford New York

Athens Auckland Bangkok Bogota Buenos Aires Calcutta Cape Town Chennai Dar es Salaam Delhi Florence Hong Kong Istanbul Karachi Kuala Lumpur Madrid Melbourne Mexico City Mumbai Nairobi Paris São Paulo Singapore Taipei Tokyo Toronto Warsaw

and associated companies in Berlin Ibadan

Oxford is a trade mark of Oxford University Press

Published in the United States
by Oxford University Press Inc., New York

© International Federation of Red Cross and Red Crescent Societies, 1998

Illustrations, photographs and maps © International Federation of Red Cross and Red Crescent Societies, 1998, unless otherwise indicated

British Library Cataloguing in Publication Data: Data available

Library of Congress Cataloging in Publication Data: Data available

ISBN 0-19-829456-5

Typeset by Pictos S.A., Geneva, Switzerland

Printed in Great Britain on acid-free paper by The Bath Press, Bath, Somerset, UK

The opinions expressed in this publication do not necessarily represent the official policy of the International Federation of Red Cross and Red Crescent Societies or of individual National Red Cross or Red Crescent Societies. Maps and the designations used do not imply the expression of any opinion on the part of the International Federation or National Societies concerning the legal status of a territory or of its authorities.

Acknowledgements

The *World Disasters Report 1998* was edited by Nick Cater and Peter Walker.

Design: Nikki Meith, *Maximedia.* Layout: Daniel Ruffieux. Production manager: Sue Pfiffner.

Principal contributors: Chapter 1, David Satterthwaite, IIED. Chapter 2, Angela Astrop and Goff Jacobs, Transport Research Laboratory; Boxes 2.1 and 2.2, Nick Cater. Chapter 3, Mette Sonniks, IFRC Reference Centre for Psychological Support; Jean-Pierre Revel, IFRC; and Gerard Jacobs, American Red Cross; Box 3.1, Wendy Smith, IFRC. Chapter 4, Philip Wijmans, Lutheran World Federation; Box 4.1, Susan Purdin, Sphere Project; Box 4.3, Cyrus Mechrat and Hossein Sarem-Kalali; Box 4.4, UNHCR. Chapter 5, Peter Walker; Susan Purdin, Sphere Project; Ian Levine, Amnesty International; and John Mitchell, British Red Cross; Box 5.3, Jim Bishop, InterAction; Box 5.4, Sarah Davidson, People in Aid. Chapter 6, Tony German and Judith Randel, Development Initiatives; Box 6.2, OECD/DAC; Box 6.4, Terry Jeggle, UNIDNDR. Chapter 7, Susan Viets, IFRC. Chapter 8, Nick Cater. Chapter 9, John Sparrow, IFRC. Chapter 10, Walter R. Cotte, Colombian Red Cross. Chapter 11, Theophilos A. Argitis, New Europe; Chapter 12, Centre for Research on the Epidemiology of Disasters; PIOOM, Leiden University; US Committee for Refugees. With thanks to all those who assisted contributors during travel and research, including Helene Berman; Terry Cannon; Anne Eyre; Eric Falt; Eric Hoskins; Dinesh Mohan; Peter Pellett; Derek Summerfield; Ronald Swatzyna; Tony Taylor; and Ben Wisner.

Contact details

International Federation of Red Cross and Red Crescent Societies
17, chemin des Crêts, P.O. Box 372,
1211 Geneva 19, Switzerland
Tel: (41)(22) 730 4222
Fax: (41)(22) 733 0395
E-mail: secretariat@ifrc.org
WWW: http://www.ifrc.org/

Editing

Nick Cater
Words & Pictures
Tudor St Anthony, Muchelney,
Langport, Somerset TA10 0DL, UK
Tel: (44)(1458) 251 727
Fax: (44)(1458) 251 749
E-mail: cater@ifrc.org

Contents

Section One Key Issues

Section Two Methodologies

Section Three Quality of Aid

Section Four The Year in Disasters 1997

Tackling future city risks

Each year the *World Disasters Report* highlights the issues for the future of disaster response and considers the lessons learnt over the past year. 1997 did not witness any major new crisis of the type that dominated the international news in previous years. Instead the humanitarian community had to concentrate on the growing challenge of continuing to service protracted disasters in the Democratic People's Republic of Korea, Bosnia and Herzegovina, the African Great Lakes and other areas. In many of these smoldering crises, the humanitarian community, both local and international, is running what amounts to a welfare support service. And increasingly this support is being provided in urban areas.

Research and predictions suggest that this will be typical of humanitarian work in the future, particularly as global economic changes and demographic shifts start to have an impact upon the types of disasters the world faces.

Within the next generation, most of the world's population will live in urban areas. Yet most disaster response practice and experience to date is with rural people and rural disasters.

So how well will we cope with the new urban challenge? Findings highlighted in this year's *Report* focus on the critical role of good governance in the urban setting. Effective and accountable local authorities are the single most important institution for reducing the toll of natural and human-induced disasters in urban areas. An increasingly urbanized world actually holds the potential to reduce greatly the number of people at risk from disasters, but only if urban governments become more accountable to all their citizens. And it is not the mega-cities that will dominate the urban future, indeed many of them have started to shrink in size over the past decade. Rather, it is the small- and medium-sized towns that hold the key, often spreading beyond their original boundaries to include hazardous land, the mixing of shanty towns and industrial complexes, the uncontrolled growth of road traffic and the inadequately serviced squatter camps. In these cities the potential for disaster, particularly for the poor, is high and will remain high without a drastic change in the approach of those who govern and plan.

Within the profile of future urban disasters one killer is often overlooked: the motor car. Traffic accidents have already claimed 30 million lives worldwide this century; in 1990, they were estimated to be the ninth biggest cause of death. By the year 2020, traffic accidents will be the third largest cause of death and disability in the world, way ahead of war, HIV and other infectious diseases. Most of this increase will take place in the cities of the developing nations, and, as with war and many other disasters, it is the innocent who suffer. Pedestrians, not motorists are the main victims of crashes. Changes in road design and vehicle safety can make a difference, but for cash-strapped governments, investment in road safety awareness and first aid training may provide a better payoff.

Increasing death tolls from urban disasters, including road accidents, are preventable. The future may be urban, but it is not set in stone. As economic globalization becomes a reality, and as the debate surrounding the role of civil societies evolves, opportunities are presenting themselves to government and to other forms of civic action, to reduce risk and plan for a safer future.

George Weber
Secretary General

Chapter

Meeting the challenge of urban disasters

As many cities grow to ten or more million inhabitants and close to half the world's population lives in urban areas, is the world more at risk from disasters? Will the death toll from "natural" disasters – floods, cyclones, earthquakes – grow as larger cities develop on sites at risk? Since most factories are in cities, are industrial accidents going to kill more people? With so many people concentrated together, will epidemics run out of control? And will other environmental problems grow with the increasing concentration of people and industry?

The answer to all these questions is an emphatic no, if good practice in environmental policy and disaster prevention, mitigation, preparedness and response is applied within a framework of good urban governance. This should bring sharp falls in disaster-related deaths and injuries, and a dramatic decline in premature death, illness and injury from other environmental hazards. The answer is yes, however, if there is poor practice, and weak and ineffective urban governments. Disaster prevention can also be hindered by "undemocratic" local communities, which lack the communication processes available in open, democratic societies.

By concentrating people, enterprises, all their wastes and their motor vehicles, cities are often hazardous places to live and work. But this concentration brings opportunities. There are economies of scale in reducing risks from floods, earthquakes or cyclones, and in responding rapidly and effectively to disasters. There is generally a greater capacity among city dwellers to help pay for such measures, if costs are controlled and the risks well communicated. Community-driven solutions may be possible even if local or national authorities are indifferent or weak.

Higher population densities mean much lower costs per household and per enterprise to provide clean, piped water, disposal of waste, comprehensive storm and surface water drainage, most forms of health care and education, and emergency services, such as fire-fighting and 24-hour hospital and ambulance services. The concentration of industries reduces unit costs for pollution control, disposal of hazardous wastes, and checks on plant, equipment and occupational health and safety.

The demand for land relative to population could be reduced by concentrating populations. This would allow homes and businesses to avoid the most hazardous sites, such as landslide-prone slopes, or for these sites to mix hazard mitigation and everyday use, as flood management systems do with parks and recreational lakes. Even in cities where hundreds of thousands of people live on sites at risk from floods or landslides, the problem is not so much a shortage of

---

Box 1.1 Adapting to low-income life on the flood line of an Indian shanty

Many low-income communities in Indore, India, see flooding as a natural, seasonal event and take steps to limit damage. Most at risk are those on land near the city centre next to small rivers which act as storm drains, but these locations offer economic and social advantages.

Families are close to jobs, markets and sources of waste, from which many earn a living, and have easy access to health services, schools, electricity and water. Land is cheap and, because it is in public ownership, evictions are less likely. Most residents have strong community, family and kinship ties, and some feel children are safer because cars cannot use the narrow streets.

A study by the London School of Hygiene and Tropical Medicine found that households and small businesses make both temporary and permanent flood adaptations. These include raising floors, paving courtyards, choosing furniture less likely to be washed away, keeping trunks to carry valuables, and fixing shelves and electric wiring above expected water levels. Roofing may be unattached so it can be removed if the house is at risk of being swept away.

Residents have evacuation contingency plans, and flood prediction and protection systems. In Shekha Nagar settlement, the first response of residents to the threat of floods is to move the old, young and animals to higher ground. Then they move electrical goods, followed by other valuables and cooking utensils. Clothes are moved last as they are easier to replace and not damaged by flooding. Established residents know how to use the state system of flood damage compensation, an unintended incentive to build houses in high-risk areas.

land as that lower income households cannot afford safer sites and governments do too little to help them find alternatives.

Increasing urbanization reflects both economic and political changes. The main economic change is the more than fourfold increase in the size of the world economy since 1950, with the scale of urban-based economic activities growing more rapidly than agriculture and other rural activities. Political changes have also helped to underpin urbanization, especially decolonization and – at least until some recent retrenchment – the increased role of the state.

An increasing proportion of people live in large cities. By 1990, a sixth of the world's population lived in cities of a million or more. There were 12 cities of more than 10 million. The average size of the largest 100 cities has climbed from around 700,000 in 1900 to 2.1 million in 1950 and 5.1 million in 1990. Exceptional circumstances – civil strife or drought – may cause rapid city growth without economic growth, but increasing urbanization is usually a positive symptom of change, associated with a stronger and more diversified economy and a higher national per capita income. The world's larger cities are concentrated in the largest economies.

Many governments have tried to present the problems of management of urban change as being related mainly to the rate of growth. Yet the growth rates for large cities in the South in recent decades are not unprecedented. Many of this century's fastest growing cities have been American; few major cities in the South have grown more rapidly than Los Angeles, Dallas, Phoenix and Miami since 1900.

Rather than growth rates, the problems of cities in most low or middle income nations – fast expansion of informal settlements, overcrowding of declining tenement districts, failure of city authorities to ensure sufficient water supply,

---

Box 1.2 **Why half the world's population does not live in a city**

There are many myths about cities and urbanization, including:

Myth 1. *Cities in the South are growing at unprecedented rates:* There are, in fact, both historical and contemporary precedents for the speed with which cities in the South have grown or are growing. Similar precedents exist for the rate at which the level of urbanization within countries worldwide is increasing; in this century, for instance, Dallas, Los Angeles, Phoenix and Miami, all in the USA, are among the world's fastest growing cities.

Myth 2. *Much of the world's urban population is concentrated in mega-cities:* In 1990, the last year for which relatively reliable statistics were available, less than 3 per cent of the world's population lived in mega-cities with 10 million or more inhabitants. Many of the world's mega-cities were also growing slowly.

Myth 3. *Large cities are mushrooming everywhere:* Most of the world's largest cities are concentrated in the largest economies. In 1990, 11 of the 12 largest cities in the world were in its 25 largest economies (with half in its five largest economies). In this same year, 30 per cent of the world's "million cities" were in the world's five largest economies. Most of the world's "million cities" have long histories as cities; they are not recent phenomena.

Myth 4. *People are flocking to the largest cities:* Many of the world's largest cities had more people moving out than moving in during the 1980s – including not only northern cities such as London, New York and Chicago, but also Rio de Janeiro, Mexico City, Buenos Aires and Calcutta.

Myth 5. *Half the world lives in cities:* While close to half the world's population live in "urban centres", thousands of urban centres are market towns or administrative and service centres that are too small to be considered cities. There is no agreed international definition of what constitutes an urban centre or when urban centres become cities. The proportion of the world's population currently living in urban centres is best considered not as a precise percentage (i.e., 45.2 per cent in 1995 according to UN estimates), but as being between 40 and 55 per cent, depending on the criteria used to define an "urban centre".

---

sanitation, waste collection, health care and more – are far more related to the failure of governments to change their institutional basis for managing an increasingly urban society. Few international agencies have supported changes in governance for urban areas.

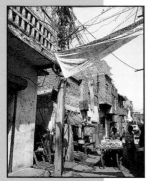

Charles Page/ International Federation

During the 1980s, new urban trends became evident which imply a future less urbanized and less concentrated in large cities than predicted. Recent census data show slower than expected urbanizing rates in many nations in Africa, Asia and Latin America, largely because debt crises and stagnation reduced the economic advantages of moving from rural to urban areas. Many wealthy nations or regions also stopped urbanizing because more companies started in rural areas or relocated there. Rural-urban distinctions are becoming unclear: many rural households have "urban" lifestyles, commute to urban jobs and use infrastructure once considered urban, from piped water to telephones.

The populations of many of the world's largest cities grew relatively slowly during the 1980s; some even fell as smaller cities attracted more new investment. What is evident in most wealthier nations has became apparent elsewhere. Mexico City, Calcutta, Rio de Janeiro, Sao Paulo and Buenos Aires were among the cities with more people moving out than moving in during the 1980s.

This tendency for large cities to lose some economic dominance has been partly counteracted by globalization, which enhanced the role of some centres of worldwide financial markets, for example, while others attracted major offices of multinational corporations. But the key nodes within the global economy include many smaller cities, such as Singapore or Zurich.

Disaster risks

"Mega-cities" of ten million or more people – sizes unprecedented historically – hold a daunting prospect for disaster prevention. Many of the world's largest cities are at risk from both natural disasters and the concentration of industries with technological hazards. However, by 1990, less than 3 per cent of the world's population lived in mega-cities and far more urban dwellers lived in small towns and district centres. The trend towards more decentralized urban systems suggests that fewer mega-cities will develop and their populations will stabilize at sizes smaller than predicted.

Disasters are exceptional events which suddenly kill or injure large numbers of people or cause major economic losses. As such, they are usually distinguished from common or constant environmental hazards, be they road accidents or air pollution. This useful distinction has its limitations. Far more urban dwellers die of easily preventable illnesses arising from environmental hazards in their food, water or air than from disasters, yet disasters often get greater attention.

If 1,000 people are killed by a flood, earthquake or industrial explosion in a large city, such a disaster is reported around the world. Yet the annual death in the same city of 1,000 people from traffic accidents, or 10,000 children from easily preventable diseases are not considered disasters. However dramatic and tragic, disasters make a relatively small contribution to all deaths, illness and injury.

In a similar way, distinctions between "natural" and "human-induced" disasters in an urban context may be unhelpful, when earthquakes can help start fires and hurricanes can rupture tanks of toxic chemicals. Most natural disaster deaths and injuries happen because of inadequate human attention to disaster

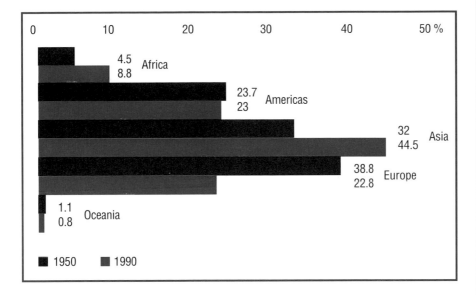

Figure 1.1
In 1950, 40 per cent of the world's urban population lived in Europe, with Asia and the Americas (North and South) providing just over 50 per cent together. By 1990 the pattern had changed dramatically. Asia now accounts for nearly 45 per cent of the world's urban population, and Europe, with its old cities and tight urban planning regulations, is home to less of the world's urban than the Americas.
Source: IIED.

prevention, mitigation and preparedness, from poor building controls to the lack of early warning systems. Almost all urban deaths and injuries from floods, landslides and fires, and most of those from tropical cyclones and earthquakes, could and should be prevented. So should deaths and injuries from industrial accidents.

The difference between disasters and other environmental hazards becomes even less clear as the latter become particularly serious. For instance, gradually worsening air pollution reaches certain levels, it may be characterized as a disaster, bringing in special countermeasures, such as vehicle controls. South-east Asia's forest fire air pollution in 1997 affected tens of millions of people, but it was not a new problem. What made it a disaster was its scale and severity.

Integrating an understanding of disasters within other environmental hazards exposes the human-natural linkages, highlights vulnerability, and shows how far human intervention can cut risks. Most illness and premature death in cities in Africa, and much of Asia and Latin America, are caused by easily preventable or curable infectious and parasitic diseases. Most injuries are preventable because they are largely the result of inadequate housing, poor traffic management or low standards for occupational health and safety. Good quality health care and emergency services would also greatly reduce the damaging health impact of injuries. Similarly, while many disasters have natural triggers that cannot be prevented, their impact can often be enormously reduced by understanding who is vulnerable and acting to reduce this vulnerability before the disaster occurs.

There are also important overlaps between "the culture of prevention" for everyday hazards and for disasters. A city with good sewers, drains and rubbish collection is also much better able to cope with flooding. Well-designed and well-built homes greatly reduce risks from physical hazards, and from earthquakes, floods or cyclones. Good emergency services – fire, police, ambulance – can also serve as the basis for rapid and effective disaster response.

In assessing urban risk, it is clear that many cities are built on, or contain, disaster-prone sites, for three main reasons. First, cities were founded on

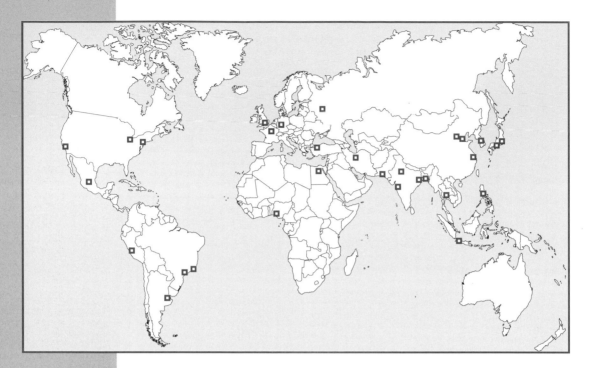

hazardous sites because at that time the site's advantages outweighed the risks. Initial development of many cities in flood-prone river valleys or deltas was linked to available fresh water and fertile soil. Many cities also developed on coasts or rivers because of the economic, political and military importance of ports and water transport.

Second, city development was not guided by a disaster-prevention culture. Construction of any city involves massive modifications to the natural site, usually without measures to minimize hazard risks. Exploitation of forests and soils for food, fuel and materials often disrupts watershed management. Exposure of soil for building allows erosion, increasing silt loads which block drains, raise river beds and exacerbate floods. Groundwater extraction can cause serious subsidence and interfere with drainage systems, increasing the flood risk. Expanding built-up areas increases surface water runoff from storms. Potential measures to reduce all these risks are often executed inadequately or not done at all.

Third, cities outgrew what were originally relatively safe sites. Most of the world's major cities were founded centuries ago, many on sites that were originally safe and convenient. When these cities were relatively small, there was no need for urban development over hazardous sites. As they grew, the population could no longer be accommodated in safe areas, or all the safe, well located sites became too expensive for low income groups.

Why does a city on a dangerous site – or one outgrowing its safe site – not stop growing, allowing new urban investments to go elsewhere? One reason is the scale of existing investment and the multiplicity of vested interests which ensure an inertia against changes to a new location, or a focus on taking measures to reduce the site's risk. Since poorer communities bear most hazard costs, powerful groups have less interest in change. Wealthy households and

Urban agglomeration	Population (thousands 1990)	Annual average increment in population 1980-1990 (thousand)	Annual average growth rate 1980-1990 (%)
Tokyo	25,013	316	1.4
New York	16,056	46	0.3
Mexico City	15,085	120	0.8
Sao Paulo	14,847	275	2.1
Shanghai	13,452	171	1.4
Bombay	12,223	416	4.2
Los Angeles	11,456	193	1.9
Beijing (Peking)	10,872	184	1.9
Calcutta	10,741	171	1.8
Buenos Aires	10,623	72	0.7
Seoul	10,558	228	2.5
Osaka	10,482	49	0.5
Rio de Janiero	9,515	73	0.8
Paris	9,334	40	0.4
Tianjin	9,253	199	2.4
Jakarta	9,250	327	4.4
Moscow	9,048	91	1.1
Cairo	8,633	178	2.3
Delhi	8,171	261	3.9
Manila	7,968	201	3.0
Karachi	7,965	294	4.7
London	7,335	- 41	- 0.5
Chicago	6,792	1	0.0
Istanbul	6,507	211	4.0
Lima	6,475	204	3.9
Essen	6,353	2	0.0
Teheran	6,351	128	2.3
Lagos	c. 5,900	152	3.0
Bangkok	5,894	117	2.2
Dhaka	5,877	267	6.2

*Figure 1.2
The map opposite shows where the world's largest urban agglomerations (1990) are situated. Cities in the developing world, especially Asia, showed the highest growth rates from 1980 to 1990.*
Source: United Nations, World Urbanization Prospects: the 1994 Revision, Population Division, New York, 1995, (updated figures for Lagos reflect more recent census data).

prosperous businesses on risky sites often have the advantage of insurance to help them balance short-term advantage against longer-term risks.

In most disasters – from floods to fires or epidemics – members of low income groups are killed or injured disproportionately. This is also true for most other environmental hazards. Only when urban authorities act on the needs of politically and economically less powerful inhabitants does this bias against low income communities lessen. One of the most relevant measures of "good governance" in cities is the extent to which urban authorities reduce risk disparities between low- and high-income groups.

Disasters have a greater impact on poorer groups in many ways. Their communities usually lack the good housing, infrastructure and services that can reduce the human effects of disasters. Despite the dependence of city economies on the cheap labour provided by those living in illegal settlements, and on the products of their informal enterprises, public agencies may use the lack of land rights to refuse infrastructure and services to those in shanty towns.

Figure 1.3
Where are the
cities growing?
The last forty
years have seen
tremendous
shifts in the
pattern of city
dwelling in the
world. Africa
has nearly
quadrupled its
million-plus city
number. Today
45 per cent of
the world's
urban
population
living in
million-plus
cities are in
Asia. Europe
now only
houses twice
Africa's city
population,
reflecting the
move away from
city life to small
town
commuting as
well as the more
global shifts in
population
distribution.
Source: IIED.

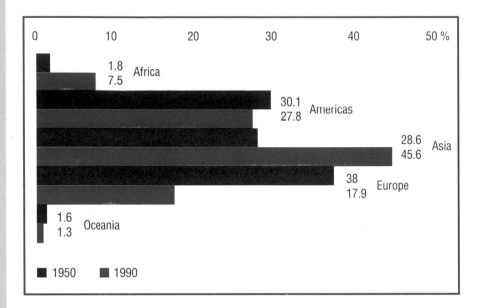

When their homes are destroyed by a disaster, poor families lose their most valuable asset and often their working tools and materials, leaving few resources for recovery. They are generally not able to take time off to recover from injury because they cannot survive the loss of income and are unable to obtain health insurance. Poorer groups' needs are generally least served by post-disaster action. Relocation by authorities or aid agencies may mean losing jobs and social networks – family, friends – important for coping mechanisms and finding work.

Enormous variations in death tolls from comparable disasters in different places or times are spurring a growing interest in understanding who is vulnerable to death, injury or property loss, why they are vulnerable, and what can be done to reduce vulnerability. The vulnerability of an individual, household or community reflects their capacity to anticipate (and avoid) a disaster, limit its impact and cope with and recover from its consequences. Analyses of vulnerability show how much is linked to income level and how much vulnerability can be reduced by competent and effective urban authorities.

People can be vulnerable in at least four ways, by being:

■ in places at risk (for example, living in flood-prone sites, in buildings not designed to withstand earthquakes, or in places with poor infrastructure, such as a lack of drains);

■ more affected by the hazard, such as older people less able to move when a flood happens;

■ more affected by the lack of rapid response from, say, slow or ineffective emergency services; and

■ less able to cope with the consequences, such as losing all capital assets.

Such distinctions show why low income households are generally the most affected by disasters and options to cut vulnerability. For example, vulnerability in a flood-prone settlement may be reduced by:

■ limiting the risk of flooding, perhaps through better watershed management upstream;

- offering people a safer site and support in moving;

- helping make their homes and area better able to cope, through improved storm drains;

- developing an effective early warning system;

- ensuring that emergency services can respond rapidly; and

- having ready the assistance families will need to cope with losses.

Vulnerable groups often get the least help. For instance, the response to the 1997 Acapulco hurricane concentrated on hotels and tourist areas, rather than on the service workers' hillside settlements, which had been ravaged by floods and mudslides.

For cities, the single most important hazard reduction factor should be an authority making the best possible use of local knowledge and resources to reduce risks. This implies acting on many fronts:

- ensuring that all public agencies – including those responsible for education, health, planning, building control, and emergency services – take appropriate disaster prevention and preparedness measures;

- enforcing regulations on industrial plant safety and waste disposal;

- integrating the above into broader tasks, including reducing risks from other environmental hazards;

- working with other local authorities (for instance, in upstream watershed management), as well as with the national Red Cross or Red Crescent society and non-governmental organizations (NGOs);

- ensuring effective communication with local people; and

- representing the priorities of its people in negotiations for funds with higher levels of government.

The effectiveness of urban authorities can be judged not only in what they do but also in what they encourage. This means supporting the efforts of households, community organizations, NGOs and private enterprises. Much can be achieved when all such groups work together to reduce hazards. But urban authorities can only do this if their inhabitants recognize their legitimacy and feel that their interests are being represented. This means supporting and responding to community-directed hazard identification, vulnerability analysis

---

Box 1.3 From smog to AIDS and 'quakes, the hazards of Los Angeles

Physical, biological, technological and social hazards in greater Los Angeles are many and interact in surprising combinations.

Air pollution affects infants, the elderly and people living with AIDS more strongly than other people. Earthquakes cause natural gas and refinery fires. Floods can distribute hazardous waste across wide areas.

The desert wind known as the Santa Ana can clear air pollution out of valley neighbourhoods but can also whip up wild fires that threaten suburban homes.

These many, interacting hazards are neither class nor colour blind. Those most at risk from earthquakes are low income Hispanics living in thousands of non-reinforced brick and masonry apartment houses. Age is also a factor. Thousands of homeless youths on the streets are vulnerable to HIV infection, violence, malnutrition, exposure and fires in abandoned buildings. The rich are not immune: storms, landslides and subsidence affect their costly homes, as do fires that race through narrow valleys.

Figure 1.4
Causes and
effects: The
bigger the
economy, the
bigger the cities.
It may be that
economic
growth in the
developing
world needs
urban centres
for effective
industry,
services and
trade.
Source: IIED,
1996.

The number of cities with populations of	10m+	5m+	1m+
Worldwide	12	33	281
In the world's five largest economies	6	11	103
In the next ten largest economies	5	11	67
In the next ten largest economies	0	4	34
In the rest of the world	1	7	77

and action programmes. In most urban centres, it implies a new relationship with the groups who are most vulnerable to disasters, and developing "solutions" with them, not for them.

The complex mix of factors which determine vulnerability, and the many different points of intervention to reduce it, have encouraged more use of community-based hazard mapping and participatory discussions about how best to tackle them. Accurately mapping vulnerability must have the full involvement of local inhabitants to incorporate an understanding of the advantages of the hazardous site. Community-based processes can identify and build on qualities, resources and skills that will reduce vulnerability. In Cali, Colombia, local mitigation workers – preventionistas – have been trained to work with people in illegal settlements to map hazardous areas and regulate further building.

The very high costs of reducing vulnerability become more affordable if they are spread over time and among different groups. A study of a low-income settlement in Delhi found that over 20 years, 90 per cent of the buildings could incorporate earthquake-resistant features, but programmes needed to be tailored to existing building and upgrading processes, largely through masons, unskilled labourers and self-help.

Low-income households will also invest their time, effort and funds in reducing vulnerability, if confident they will not be evicted. In one flood-prone area of Georgetown in Guyana, a community-based organization coordinated drain-digging, maintenance and bridge construction work, and encouraged local people to improve their house design. But the scope for more effective action was limited by their uncertain legal status on the land.

Effective urban government

Many urban authorities remain weak, ineffective and undemocratic, and face external constraints on their performance, from fragile national economies to extreme inequalities. Attracting new investment in an increasingly competitive world economy may hamper a city's efforts to reduce hazards. National authorities may be reluctant to permit city and municipal authorities the power and resources to act effectively in disaster preparedness, prevention and mitigation.

In the absence of effective urban governments, there are measures that low income communities can themselves take to reduce their vulnerability. Such direct action also helps them organize to make demands on the state. But the scope for community action is limited, if faced with hostile or indifferent urban authorities.

Effective and accountable local authorities are the single most important institution for reducing the toll of natural and human-induced disasters – and other environmental hazards – in urban areas. An increasingly urbanized world holds the potential to greatly reduce the number of people at risk from disasters. This can only be achieved in well-managed cities which make basic services available to all and respond to the needs of vulnerable groups.

Chapter 1 Sources, references and further information

Blaikie, P., Cannon T., Davis I. and Wisner B. *At Risk: Natural Hazards, People's Vulnerability and Disasters.* London: Routledge, 1994.

Cannon, Terry. "Vulnerability analysis and the explanation of 'natural' disasters" in Varley, Ann (ed.), *Disasters, Development and Environment.* Chichester: John Wiley and Sons, 1994.

Carfax. *Urban Studies.* Journal published by Carfax Publishing Ltd., PO Box 25, Abingdon, Oxfordshire OX14 3UE, UK. ISSN: 0042-0980.

International Decade for Natural Disaster Reduction (IDNDR). *Cities at Risk: Making Cities Safer...Before Disaster Strikes.* Geneva: IDNDR, 1996.

International Institute for Environment and Development (IIED). *Environment and Urbanization* Journal published by IIED, 3 Endsleigh Street, London WC1H ODD, UK. ISSN: 0956-2478.

Kishore, Kamal. *Seismic safety of informal housing in urban areas.* Paper presented at the IDNDR and QUIPUNET Internet Conference, 1997.

Pelling, Mark. "What determines vulnerability to floods; a case study in Georgetown, Guyana", *Environment and Urbanization,* Vol.9, No.1, pp. 203-226, 1997.

Sassen, Saskia. *Cities in a World Economy.* Thousand Oaks, London, New Delhi: Pine Forge Press, 1994.

Satterthwaite, David. *The Scale and Nature of Urban Change in the South.* IIED paper, London, 1996.

Stephens, Carolyn, Patnaik, Rajesh and Lewin, Simon. *This is My Beautiful Home: Risk Perceptions towards Flooding and Environment in Low Income Urban Communities: A Case Study in Indore, India.* London: London School of Hygiene and Tropical Medicine, 1996.

UNCHS. *An Urbanizing World: Global Report on Human Settlements 1996.* Oxford and New York: Oxford University Press, 1996.

Varley, Ann (ed.). "The exceptional and the everyday. vulnerability analysis in the International Decade for Natural Disaster Reduction" in *Disasters, Development and Environment.* Chichester: John Wiley and Sons, 1994.

World Health Organization (WHO). *Creating Healthy Cities in the 21st Century.* Background paper prepared for the Dialogue on Health in Human Settlements for Habitat II. Geneva: WHO, 1996.

World Bank. *The Urban Age.* Journal published by the World Bank.

Web sites

Carfax: http://www.carfax.co.uk/urs-ad.htm

IIED: http://www.iied.org/human/env_urb.html

In many developed countries, death rates on the roads are coming down as a combination of better-designed cars, good roads, stricter standards for driving and policing all add to safer journeys. Not so in the cities of the developing world where investment in car maintenance, road safety and driver skills is a low priority. Vehicles in Southern cities now pose a significant threat to life, particularly for the pedestrian.
© Christopher Black. Peru, 1998.

Chapter

2 Must millions more die from traffic accidents?

From the moment's inattention that risks tragedy to the driver deliberately flouting speed and drinking laws, traffic accidents are both an everyday part of life and a worsening global disaster destroying lives and livelihoods, hampering development and leaving millions in greater vulnerability.

In this century of road death – the world's first pedestrian death was in 1896, the first driver died in 1898 – the car has claimed an estimated 30 million lives. By 1990, traffic accidents were assessed to be the world's ninth biggest cause of death, killing at least 500,000 people a year, though some put the fatality figure as high a million, and injuring around 15 million.

Assessing the long-term impact of accidents and taking full account of the impact of injuries, a major study of the "global burden of disease" forecast that by 2020 road crashes will move up to third place in the world league table for death and disability, just behind clinical depression and heart disease but ahead of respiratory infections, tuberculosis, war and HIV.

Road safety campaigns, driver training, better vehicle care, seat-belt legislation and traffic management measures have been cutting crash deaths in the North for 30 years despite rising vehicle numbers. The death toll has shifted strongly south into the developing world, whose estimated 70 per cent share of global road fatalities is rising fast.

Like many other disasters, traffic accidents affect particular groups – such as the poor and the young – and leave many more vulnerable in their wake. The impact on the economically active also shows a resemblance to the AIDS pandemic. In adults aged 15 to 44, traffic accidents are the leading cause of death for men and fifth most important for women.

Charles Page/
International Federation

And just as civilians today make up the vast majority of victims of conflict fuelled by the global trade in small arms, those least able to defend themselves on the road – pedestrians and bicyclists – make up a large proportion of the casualties of the car.

Box 2.1 Transport trends put world on a collision course into 21st century

While there are some major differences in transport use between different countries, economies and cultures, large similarities exist and the long-term trends and links between traffic and incomes are very clear.

For example, European cities are usually far denser in population than American ones, which means the vast majority of all US trips are by car and very few by foot, bicycle or any mass transport system, whereas 40 to 50 per cent of European trips are by foot or bicycle and around 10 per cent by mass transport.

Urban densities in Asia can be up to three times that of Europe, limiting city car use.

Investments in present technologies and the existing trends in vehicle use and incomes worldwide imply a substantial and sustained growth in motor transport into the 21st century, and thus a rising toll in lost lives and livelihoods for decades, even if accident reduction strategies are increasingly taken up in the developing world.

Studies by the Massachusetts Institute of Technology (MIT) and the International Institute for Applied Systems Analysis (IIASA) have suggested that from European cities to African villages – with a few exceptions – people spend a remarkably similar amount of time travelling: a cluster of figures between 60 and 90 minutes that make an average of 1.1 hours a day.

The figures for transport spending are also fairly predictable. In developing countries with few cars, people spend 3 to 5 per cent of their income on transport; this percentage rises to stabilize at 10 to 15 per cent once car ownership reaches one per family.

As incomes rise and travellers move from foot and bicycle to car, train and plane, the kilometres travelled and speed of travel increases. But a growing number of developing world cities are seeing gridlock, from Manila, where average car speeds are around 11 kph, to Bangkok, where the typical vehicle spends the equivalent of 44 days a year stuck in traffic.

Faster growth and rising car sales in developing countries mean that their proportion of the world's traffic volume will rise in relation to developed nations.

MIT/IIASA studies estimate that global traffic volume will more than double from 23.4 trillion passenger kilometres in 1990 to 53 trillion in 2020, and then almost double again by 2050 to 103 trillion. Just under half that figure, 51 trillion, will be in the developing world, up from only 22 per cent in 1960.

Significant progress in traffic safety will be required in the developing world if that is not to mean very large human and financial costs from higher morbidity and mortality.

Crash cost

Traffic accidents can be measured in grief, pain and gross national product. Extrapolating from 1990 figures derived by the UK Transport Research Laboratory (TRL), they hamper growth and progress by costing developing countries around US$ 53 billion a year, roughly the level of all international aid.

Combining tangible costs, such as vehicle damage, medical treatment, and assessments of lost output, with attempts to quantify the intangible costs of suffering, the impact of crashes is significant and long term: one study suggested that more years of life are lost from traffic accidents in Thailand, for example, than tuberculosis and malaria combined.

Despite growing efforts in safety, the far greater human impact in the developing world of traffic accidents is expected to worsen. Work by the Dutch Road Safety Institute suggests fatality rates are closely linked to the rate of change in traffic volume, with a time lag of about a decade as societies adjust to their "motorization".

Global traffic forecasts show car, bus and truck numbers climbing fast and vehicle use increasing rapidly in developing countries which have limited health facilities and road environments already busy with pedestrians, bicyclists and animals.

However, the true scale of the problem is unclear, and limited information undermines efforts to identify and tackle traffic problems. Research suggests at

---

Box 2.2 **Emission efficiency fails to keep pace with growth of pollution**

Deaths and injuries from traffic are not just the result of accidents; the potent cocktail of pollution from exhaust fumes and what they can become in the atmosphere can cause a range of illnesses, from asthma to lead poisoning.

There is concern in both the developed and developing world about the impact of vehicle emissions, despite the large improvements in engine efficiency, exhaust treatments through catalytic converters and cleaner fuels.

The American Lung Association estimates that approximately 100 million US citizens live in cities where ozone levels go above national standards. The British Road Commission on Environmental Pollution has said vehicle exhausts are causing up to 10,000 deaths a year. In Africa, according to recent research by the University of Michigan, 90 per cent of children in some cities are affected by lead poisoning.

As many countries reduce lead pollution, Africa's share of the global burden has risen from 5 per cent in 1980 to 20 per cent in the mid-1990s, almost all caused by mining, smelting and traffic, with traffic the largest cause in cities. Highest African lead polluters are South Africa at 4,542 tonnes a year, Algeria at 2,932, Egypt 2,124 and Nigeria 1,729.

African fuels have the world's highest lead content to boost performance, sometimes as much as one gram a litre, more than three times European levels and 20 times those of the US.

Lead concentrations in the blood of 100 micrograms per litre or more can cause neurological harm, bringing reduced IQ, loss of short-term memory, impaired hearing, coordination difficulties and learning problems.

Studies in Cairo showed lead levels in breast milk could be linked to traffic densities where mothers lived.

Child newspaper vendors in Cape Town had about 300 micrograms of lead if they worked on main streets, while those on quieter streets had lower levels.

After the US introduced unleaded petrol in the 1970s, mean lead levels in children aged one to five fell 77 per cent in ten years.

While phasing out leaded fuel will address one important health issue, the global problem of fumes will almost certainly get worse. The growth in vehicles numbers and kilometres travelled is expected to outpace any likely improvements in vehicle emissions.

---

least a 20 per cent under-reporting of developing world road fatalities for a range of reasons, including poor accident recording systems.

Injury under-reporting is probably even greater, since a study of road accident victims in hospitals in seven developing countries found a strong over-representation of 16 to 45-year-old men, probably because health costs and lost earnings mean the economically active are often the only crash victims taken to hospital.

Though complicated by questions of demographics and evidence of poor reporting of child road deaths and injuries, children under 15 in developing countries account for around 15 per cent of fatalities, against 6 per cent in developed countries. This may be linked to limited school safety education, and to the higher proportion of deaths among developing world pedestrians.

According to analysis by TRL, pedestrians in developing world cities are at greater risk than in the UK, because most journeys are by foot and people are therefore on the street much more than in developed countries. Pedestrian fatalities are around 30 per cent of all road deaths in South-east Asia and South America, 40 per cent in many Asian, African and Caribbean countries, 50 per cent in the Middle East, and around 20 per cent in Europe and the US.

In many developed countries, fewer pedestrian and bicyclist casualties reflect a retreat from the street; for developing world families with no car, this move away from the street is not always possible. As well as preventing children from playing in the street, the number of English seven- and eight-year olds walking to school fell from 80 per cent in 1971 to 9 per cent in 1990 because of their parents' fear of traffic.

Those less able to make this retreat, even in the developed world, have higher accident rates, one Scottish study suggests. People living in Edinburgh's poorest areas, where 70 per cent of families had no car, were far more likely to be injured or killed than those from the richest neighbourhoods, where family car ownership was close to 90 per cent. The risks for the poor from walking were at least double for all ages, but the excess casualties were largest among children and young people aged 5 to 16, with risks at least eight times higher.

Death rates

Analysis of traffic accident figures uses a range of rates for deaths and injuries, vehicle numbers and traffic volume. Fatality rates – usually expressed as injury accidents per year per million vehicle kilometres – are often used to compare national road deaths, especially in the developed world. Because of limited vehicle-use information in developing countries, an alternative is deaths per 10,000 registered vehicles, although this may understate fatalities because vehicles no longer in use may remain on registers.

On this basis, national differences are striking. In Nepal and Bangladesh, recent fatality rates are 82 and 76.8 deaths per 10,000 vehicles respectively, compared to 1.9 for Australia and Japan. Even within the developing world, there are wide variations, with Ghana and Ethiopia among the highest, at 111 and 191.6.

But statistics can also tell another story. When some external experts wonder why developing countries do not take more action on safety, others point to the difference between the number of fatalities as a proportion of total population. The US per capita fatality rate, for example, is 15.5 per 100,000, while next door Mexico's is the significantly lower 5.7 per 100,000.

Many developing countries are seeing large increases in vehicle numbers, such as India, where four-wheel vehicles increased by 23 per cent to 4.5 million between 1990 and 1993, and it has been forecast that 267 million vehicles will be on the roads by 2050.

The impact of those increases can be seen in Viet Nam, where between 1995 and 1996 the number of cars and motorcycles rose 17 per cent, while accidents increased by 22.7 per cent to approximately 19,638, deaths by 3.8 per cent to 5,962, and injuries by 26.5 per cent to 21,718.

Accident analysis by Viet Nam's police traffic department blamed 32.4 per cent on speed, 28.7 per cent reckless overtaking, 11.3 per cent drunkenness. Human error was cited in 85 per cent of crashes, and mention made of pavement hawkers, lack of traffic signs or lights, limited policing and low investment affecting road quality, with 40 per cent of the 140,000 km of road described as poor.

Of all accidents in Viet Nam, approximately 60 per cent involve motorcycles and 30 per cent cars, buses or trucks, though police analysis showed that in Hanoi, taxis made up just a 60th of the car fleet but were involved in a third of the city's traffic accidents. Across the country, taxis were involved in a high proportion of accidents, deaths and injuries. The government has announced new action to enforce existing rules on taxi driver qualifications, as well as updated traffic laws, safety checks on all vehicles and improved police training.

Viet Nam, like all countries in Asia, is showing a steep rising curve in figures for vehicle sales. While the region's recent economic problems may curb new purchases and imports, that will encourage drivers to keep older and potentially less safe vehicles on the road. But long-term forecasts of the global expansion of traffic volume for all forms of transport show a four-fold increase by 2050, with the developing world proportion reaching just under 50 per cent.

Road accidents are generally classified as being fatal if the victim dies within 30 days of the accident. Whatever the other factors, poor medical facilities contribute to higher death levels; a TRL study suggests developing world fatality rates are linked to per capita hospital bed and nurse numbers.

Box 2.3 A five-year national safety plan to reduce vehicle accidents

A strategy for governments to cut accidents has been developed by the Transport Research Laboratory. Fiji, Viet Nam and Botswana are among the countries to adopt it. Once political and administrative responsibilities for road safety have been determined, it is useful to set up a permanent body, such as a national road safety council (NRSC).

These are typical stages in developing a road safety programme:
- define the nature and scale of problem;
- set up a working group to examine problem;
- define role and funding of NRSC;
- develop legislation for NRSC;
- establish NRSC;
- provide technical and financial support;
- establish coordinating bodies;

- devise a programme of urgent short-term activities; and
- implement priority action plan and develop five-year programme.

A typical action plan has three phases. Phase 1 defines the problem and raises awareness. Phase 2 develops the national five-year plan or other strategy, implements urgent actions and improves data collection.

In phase 3, the five-year plan is implemented, with these factors: coordination and administration, infrastructure improvements, data systems, urban actions, funding, vehicle roadworthiness, legislation, medical services, enforcement, research, education, monitoring, training, testing.

While any improvements in medical facilities could help reduce the number of people injured in road accidents who subsequently die, some needs are time limited, as so often in sudden-impact disasters. Road accident victims stand a greater chance of survival if they get attention within the "golden hour" after the accident by having good first aid, ambulance and paramedic services, a costly option for large and mainly rural developing countries.

In France, for example, the Samu emergency service takes specialist medical staff – such as anaesthetists and resuscitators – to serious accidents so they can stabilize patients before their transfer to hospital, especially if time may be lost cutting victims free from wreckage, as happened in the case of Diana, Princess of Wales.

Even when victims reach hospital, hidden injuries may go untreated because of the complexity of crash effects, which involve multiple impacts: vehicle against other objects; body against the inside of the vehicle; internal organs against the rest of the body. For pedestrians, similar impacts occur: vehicle against body; body against whatever it is thrown into; and again internal organs hitting the inside of the body.

As seat belts, air bags and other safety measures reduce immediate fatalities, and doctors become more skilled at saving lives, attention in the North is shifting to disabling injuries, such as damage to legs and feet. Aiding that process has been the use of computer simulations of accidents, such as those carried out by the National Crash Analysis Center at George Washington University, which suggest that floor padding might significantly reduce leg injuries, for example.

Other research in the US shows risk factors for vehicle types, individual brands and accident combinations, which reveals not only the higher dangers of certain sports cars but also the way larger and heavier vehicles are safer, but only for their occupants. Smaller and lighter vehicles – and their occupants – come off significantly worse in collisions with larger vehicles; an unfortunate result, given pressures for fuel efficiency and lower pollution.

Although their numbers are growing, cars are a far smaller part of the accident profile in the developing world, and other vehicles have a far greater impact: in the UK, buses are involved in 3 per cent of accidents, while the figures in Pakistan, India and Sri Lanka are at least six times larger.

Planning priorities

From health budgets to vehicle damage and police time, traffic accidents cost nations millions of dollars. TRL analysis suggests that road accidents cost a minimum of 1 per cent of any country's gross national product, which allows crude estimates for developing world costs.

In large countries such as Mexico and India, road accidents may well be costing $2.5 to 3.2 billion a year. In countries such as South Africa and Pakistan, costs may be $0.5 to 1 billion. In smaller countries, such as Zimbabwe and Kenya, costs could be $55 to 70 million annually. With average GNP per capita under $3,500, all these countries are within the World Bank definition of a developing country, and they can ill-afford such avoidable costs.

To help traffic safety take an appropriate place within national budgets, a range of systematic methods of determining road accident costs and the value of preventing them are available, although none is perfect. Whatever the system and however broad the estimates, cost figures must be made on a comparable basis with other sectors needing scarce funds. Good figures will also ensure that the most cost-effective safety improvements can be introduced.

A survey in Cyprus suggested that for serious casualties the lost output, medical costs and property damage are each of a similar order, and together comprise 96 per cent of total costs, excluding any allowance for suffering. The survey estimated that output losses made a road death 20 times the cost of a serious accident. Health elements in crash costs are important not just for themselves, but for the substantial opportunity of treatment denied to others in need.

High and worsening levels of traffic accidents in the developing world are not inevitable, and cost-effective action is possible on many fronts, but safety strategies and priorities may not transfer well from developed countries. The US or UK of the mid-1960s, when death rates began to fall even though vehicle numbers and traffic volume were still rising, are very different from today's developing world in income, traffic mix, health facilities and more.

Annual UK road safety spending is about UK£ 1 billion at 1980 prices; a figure almost as much as the cost of accidents. It is a cost-effective use of resources: between 1965 and 1994, the number of vehicles registered almost doubled yet road accidents fell by over 50 per cent. Detailed evaluations of individual schemes in the UK, particularly low-cost engineering work, show very high economic rates of return. Evidence is beginning to emerge that some measures can also achieve substantial results in the developing world.

A recent TRL assignment showed that in a small country with an annual estimated cost of road accidents of $32 million, a five-year programme of investment in safety engineering, education, training and traffic law enforcement costing a total of $800,000 would cut road accident costs by 5 per cent each year. Annual savings of $1.6 million would be a benefit:cost ratio of about 10:1. Road safety projects produce particularly high rates of return.

Assuming effective targeting of road improvement expenditure, developing world accident costs justify major investments. Given the high initial returns likely in countries where little had previously been achieved, 10 per cent of estimated crash costs would suggest typical expenditure levels ranging from the Philippines at $220 million and Indonesia at $137 million to Pakistan at $53 million, Cameroon at $10 million, and Ghana, Nepal and Malawi at $7 million, $3 million and $2 million.

Box 2.4 **When each fatality loses a family 25 years of working life**

Accidents have a significant economic effect through loss of working lives. Though not necessarily representative, the following nations indicate the scale of impact. The figures show the number of working years lost for each road accident fatality.

- Argentina (1990) 23.5
- Costa Rico (1989) 25.9
- Mexico (1991) 28.9
- Mauritius (1992) 22.2
- Puerto Rica (1991) 24.9
- Trinidad and Tobago (1991) 25.7

The impact of injuries is harder to show but, in surveys carried out in hospitals in 1997 victims were asked to estimate how long they would be away from work.

This necessarily vague snapshot found that the proportion expecting to be off work for four weeks or more was 40 per cent in Ghana, 35 per cent in Zimbabwe and just 4 per cent in Peru. A large proportion of those questioned were wage earners, suggesting a substantial impact on household economies.

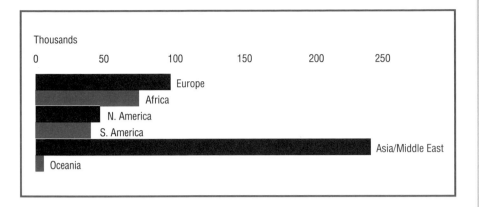

Figure 2.1
Less is more:
number of road
accidents by
region
(1992/1993).
Relative to
population,
economic size
and geographic
area, developing
economies have
fewer vehicles
and less roads
but far more
accidents and
fatalities than
developed
economies.
Source: TRL.

Given the long time frames, there are few studies which show the "before" and "after" success of safety measures in accident levels, but some measures look promising, and priorities for action are becoming clearer.

Engineering forgiveness

On the whole, engineering – from car design to street lights – is far more effective than efforts to change driver behaviour. Engineering and planning improvements can make human errors less likely, or be more "forgiving" when they occur, through good design on new road schemes to prevent accidents and remedial measures to cut existing accident rates.

Despite significant North-South differences, there are simple steps relevant almost anywhere, from highlighting accident "black spots", removing roadside objects and separating different traffic types to shifting from junctions to roundabouts. Some measures can be too forgiving, since drivers compensate for better surfaces, wider lanes or clearer markings by increasing speed. Even traffic lights may do more to change the type of accidents than reduce overall levels. As one safety expert commented: making conditions idiot-proof encourages idiots.

Success with very low-cost measures, such as road signs and markings, is less likely in countries with higher levels of road user risk-taking or limited police enforcement. TRL research has shown that dangerous behaviour – such as ignoring red stop lights or crossing "no-overtaking" lines – is not due to lack of knowledge. Studies in Jamaica, Zimbabwe, Cameroon, Pakistan and Thailand suggest that the one real knowledge gap concerns safe stopping distances.

Drinking and driving has been the subject of tight legislation, close enforcement and high-profile campaigns in many developed countries to the extent that influential public opinion and peer pressure is strongly against drink-driving, which also often carries the ultimate penalty (for motorists): loss of the driving licence. However, surveys of drivers or the victims of accidents in Trinidad, Zimbabwe and Papua New Guinea suggest this remains a far greater problem in many developing countries.

The benefits to individual road users of better vehicle design and the use of seat belts and helmets is likely to be similar in different countries, and many more improvements are expected, such as side-impact and roll-over airbags. However, these may have little impact on overall fatality rates in developing countries, where only a small percentage of total road users are in four-wheel vehicles.

Depending on the legislation in an importing country, safety features, such as seat belts, may not be fitted to vehicles sold to developing countries.

Safety risks

Indeed, just as more roads appear to lead to more congestion, vehicle safety seems to bring more danger, especially for those already most vulnerable, such as pedestrians and bicycles. Some studies suggest safety measures, from seat belts to vehicle design and road construction, lead people to compensate by taking more risks, driving faster and following other cars more closely.

One key factor in such behaviour is that most motorists are men, who score far higher in all forms of risk-taking, accidents and violent deaths. Another factor is the illusion of control in the increasingly cocooned car environment of air conditioning, music and comfortable seats; passengers in trains, boats or planes would not accept the same level of risk.

Resistance to certain safety measures, such as the low seat-belt use in many countries, or their failure, encourages development of automated systems, such as air bags, which in turn encourage yet more risky behaviour. Since the developing world has a far greater proportion of vulnerable road users still using the streets, this could suggest that greater vehicle "safety" may have little impact on – or potentially even increase – overall death and injury rates.

Differences in accident patterns, victim demographics, education systems and resources make it uncertain whether developed country safety education methods and materials can be easily transferred. But it is clear that safety education should start as early as possible. In developing countries, where child pedestrian accident rates are generally higher, a study of children's road crossing knowledge indicated that they were less likely to receive advice from parents, teachers or the police than in the UK.

Only half of a sample of developing countries include road safety as a mandatory curriculum subject, and TRL research – including the development of classroom resources in Ghana – showed 50 per cent or fewer schools in Botswana, Pakistan and Zimbabwe teaching the subject, and a strong unmet demand for educational materials. Outside schools, community programmes are also important in the developing world, since far fewer children go on to secondary education, school attendance rates may be low, and illiteracy rates – especially among women – can be high.

Box 2.5 Counting car crashes in grief, pain and gross national product

The economic costs of road accidents can place a severe financial strain on a country's resources. It has been calculated that the cost is equivalent to approximately 1 per cent of a country's gross national product (GNP). Based on this calculation, the figures below give an indication of regional accident costs in 1990:
- Europe $77,200 million
- Africa $4,200 million

- North America $71,900 million
- South America $11,100 million
- Asia and Middle East $60,000 million
- Oceania $4,000 million

The world bill for road accidents amounted to $230 billion in 1990; of that sum, developing countries paid $36 billion, resources they can ill afford.

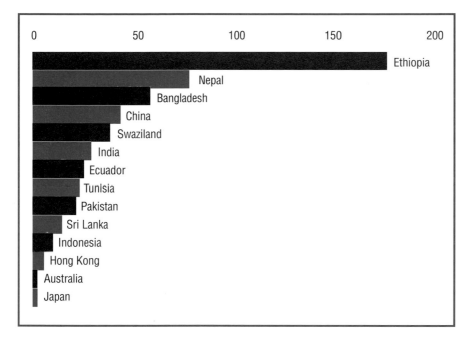

Figure 2.2
Fatalities per
10,000 licensed
vehicles per
year. While
these figures do
not indicate the
distances
covered per
fatality or factors
such as road
conditions, the
variation
suggests there
are many
possible
measures to
save lives and
cut costs
through simple
steps in vehicle
checks, driver
training, safety
campaigns,
seat-belt laws
and much more.
Source: TRL.

In developing countries – where police attribute up to 17 per cent of accidents to vehicle defects – expensive networks of vehicle testing centres are far less useful than low-cost random roadside checks using simple equipment. Visual checks alone, for example, would identify worn tyres, which can substantially increase accident risks.

Enforcing existing rules, such as limits on bus passenger numbers, could make a useful difference, while improvements in traffic police training and deployment can help cut accident levels, such as the 6 per cent fall after highway patrols began on inter-city roads in Pakistan and even higher figures in Egypt found by some studies.

Ensuring observance of speed limits is crucial. Cars are getting faster, with increased acceleration and higher top speeds. For pedestrians, traffic speed is a life or death issue. At 32 kph a car will kill 5 per cent of pedestrians it hits; at 64 kph, it kills 85 per cent. Speed also significantly increases the risk of accidents, especially serious ones.

UK transport ministry research in the early 1990s showed that in vehicles up to three years old, two in 10,000 standard cars – accelerating to 96 kph in over 10 seconds – were involved in a fatal crash in a single year, while nearly five in 10,000 high performance cars (0 to 96 kph in under 10 seconds) were in a lethal accident. Into these faster cars, evolving technology brings both benefits and hazards for vehicle safety, as drivers are expected to handle many more information messages and controls at higher speeds within a more complex road environment.

Mobile telephones and other forms of wireless communications offer automated collision notification, immediate contact with emergency services, in-vehicle information on roadway conditions, as well as greater driver security and the ability to report congestion, crashes and drunk drivers. But use of mobile telephones – which is spreading fast in the developing world – may also create similar crash risk levels as driving with blood alcohol over the US legal limit, according to one 1997 study published in the New England Journal of Medicine.

Other developments may offer more immediate safety progress for developing countries, such as research on sustainable transport systems at the Indian Institute of Technology's Transportation Research and Injury Prevention Programme (TRIPP). India reflects the developing world realities of a very different traffic mix and victim profile: 60 per cent are killed by buses and trucks, while in New Delhi 75 per cent of those killed are pedestrians, bicyclists and motorcyclists; only 5 per cent are in cars.

Work is underway on "less aggressive" bus and truck bumpers, better brakes for bicycles and rickshaws, improved safety in locally manufactured vehicles, separation of different vehicle types, speed reduction through traffic calming, and the design of cheaper helmets with better ventilation for hot climates, in the knowledge that only when all motorcyclists wear helmets can much take-up be expected among bicyclists or rickshaw drivers.

Importantly in a country of limited street lighting where vehicle lights may be poor, TRIPP takes a close interest in making vulnerable road users more visible, through use of yellow paint on rickshaws and motorcycles, laws to make motorcycles use headlights at all times, or development of a brightly coloured shopping bag that instantly converts into a safety vest.

Few other disasters have quite the close everyday relationship of the car crash with its victims: familiarity truly breeds contempt as the individually rare collision becomes a global tide of road kill with a multi-billion dollar price tag.

This is not an unseen virus, a seismic event beyond prediction, or even a cheap weapon in the hands of a fearful soldier; it is the unintended and preventable effect of actions by peaceful fellow citizens that threaten innocent victims caught in the wrong place at the wrong time.

As the world enters its second car century, transport and safety experts see many ways in which the rising curve of traffic's human and financial toll can at least be slowed, such as "pedestrian friendly" vehicle front panels, post-accident driver retraining, separating vulnerable road users into increasingly car-free city areas, better educational materials, and even incentives for crash-free drivers.

In tackling the traffic disaster, everyone has a role, from governments, which may need to assume politically tough choices about different groups' rights to mobility and safety, to manufacturers, who must be aware of the needs of those vulnerable road users becoming victims of their profitable products.

For communities themselves and organizations working closely with them, the challenges are clear: identify risks and raise awareness, promote preventive action, foster public opinion and peer pressure for safety, and help victims defend themselves through education on first aid, traffic risks and safety measures.

For international agencies, the imperative for action is also clear. On the eve of a massive growth in developing world traffic, crashes already cost the South almost as much as all the aid they receive. Traffic accidents damage progress by killing and injuring the economically active, seek out the most vulnerable, and are forecast to do more harm through death and disability than many of the health threats presently given greater priority for assistance.

Chapter 2 Sources, references and further information

Downing, A.J. and Sayer, I.A. *A preliminary study of children's road-crossing knowledge in three developing countries.* TRL Supplementary Report 771, Transport Research Laboratory, Crowthorne, Berkshire, UK, 1982.

Euromonitor . *International Marketing Data and Statistics.* London and Chicago: Euromonitor, 1995. ISBN: 0-86338-5680; ISSN: 0308-2938

Faith, Nicholas. *Crash; The Limits of Car Safety.* London: Boxtree, 1997. ISBN 0-7522-1192-7.

Ghee, C., Silcock. D., Astrop., A and Jacobs, G. *Socio-economic aspects of road accidents in developing countries.* TRL Report 247, Transport Research Laboratory.

Hills, B.L. and Elliot, G.J. *A Microcomputer Accident Analysis Package and its use in developing countries.* Crowthorne: Transport Research Laboratory, 1986.

Hills, B.L., Baguley, C.J. and Jacobs, G.D. *Engineering approaches to accident reduction and prevention in developing countries.* CODATU V11 Conference, February 1996.

HMSO. *Road Accidents Great Britain: The Casualty Report.* London: HMSO, 1995. ISBN: 0-115-18495.

International Road Federation. *International Road Federation Year Book.* Geneva: IRF, 1993.

Jones-Lee, M.W. et al. *The value of preventing non-fatal road injuries: Findings of a willingness to pay national sample survey.* TRL CR330, Transport Research Laboratory, 1993.

Kirby, H.R. (ed.). "Personal Travel Budgets". *Transportation Research* special issue, Part A, Vol. 15, No. 1, January 1981.

Marchetti, C. "Anthropological Invarients in Travel Behavior" in *Technological Forecasting and Social Change.* Vol. 47, No. 1, September 1994.

McShane, Clay. *Down the Asphalt Path; The Automobile and The American City.* Columbia University Press, 1994.

Pucher, J. "Urban Passenger Transport in the United States and Europe; A Comparative Analysis of Public Policies" in *Transport Reviews.* Vol. 15, No. 2, 1995.

Sayer, I.A. and Palmer, C. *Pedestrian accidents and road safety education in selected developing countries.* CODATU V11 Conference, February 1996.

Sayer, I.A. and Downing, A.J. *Pedestrian accidents and road safety education in selected developing countries.* TRL Report 227, Transport Research Laboratory, 1996.

Sayer, I.A. and Hitchcock, A. *An analysis of police and medical road accident data: Sri Lanka 1977-1981.* TRL Supplementary Report 834, Transport Research Laboratory, 1984.

Schafer, A. and Victor, D.G. "The Future Mobility of the World Population" in *The Cooperative Mobility Program,* Discussion Paper 97-6-4, Centre for Technology, Policy and Industrial Development, MIT 1997.

Scientific American. "The Future of Transportation". October 1997 special issue.

Transport Research Laboratory. *Road Accidents in Europe and North America (1995).* Overseas Road Note 10, 1996.

United Nations. *Statistics of Road Accidents in Europe and North America.* Geneva: UN, 1995. ISBN: 92-1-016295-1.

Web sites

International Road Federation: http://web.eunet.ch/irf

Scientific American: http://www.sciam.com

Rebuilding cities after war is not just a matter of buildings and infrastructure. Shattered lives have to be rebuilt, too. Psychological support for those who have suffered trauma, lost everything, witnessed or committed acts that will scar them for life must become a key component of restoring normality.

© Christopher Black, Bosnia and Herzegovina, 1996.

Chapter

3 Reaching out with psychological support

Disasters are not only physical events that take lives and damage property. When disaster strikes a community, people experience powerful emotions. These psychological effects are not so visible or obvious as the destruction of homes, for example, yet recovering from the psychological and emotional consequences may take far longer than dealing with the material losses.

Psychological support in the aftermath of crisis is increasingly being brought into relief operations alongside programmes for shelter or food. A growing range of agencies involved in emergencies are addressing issues of disaster mental health, including the World Health Organization (WHO), the United Nations High Commissioner for Refugees (UNHCR), the United Nations Children's Fund (UNICEF), Médecins sans Frontières, Care International and the International Federation of Red Cross and Red Crescent Societies.

The work may range from helping communities affected by destructive natural hazards, such as flooding, to supporting women sexually assaulted during conflicts, or addressing the special needs of families fearful of the future in the wake of the Chernobyl nuclear disaster.

In every disaster, there are degrees of impact and a range of effects which require varied responses, yet the greatest assistance is given not by outsiders but by the local community and near neighbours. This may be even more true when considering psychological assistance. Members of the same community share similar values, understand what is appropriate behaviour and literally "talk the same language".

Because of this, and the time often required for psychological support – even with professionals, there are no "quick fixes" – volunteers are vital. Little of this chapter is about mental health professionals treating clients with severe conditions, such as post-traumatic stress disorder. Instead it will highlight the psychological impact of disaster, focus on post-disaster psychological support by volunteers and examine how the simple interpersonal work of non-professionals can prevent long-term problems.

Lars Schwetje/ International Federation

What causes the needs?

Psychological suffering as a result of disaster is linked with the feeling of grief and loss. The deaths of relatives and friends as well as material losses will affect the sustainability of people's lives. But not everyone is affected in the same way or as deeply, and given all the types of disasters – fast or slow onset, costly in lives or in property, high death toll – no two disasters have the same psychological impact.

Box 3.1 **Making time for aid workers to acknowledge their stress**

You are lying face down on the office floor, closely examining the dust, while a man has his foot on your back and a gun close to your left ear. The safe is being systematically emptied into a blue sports bag. Your agency's money, a cash box, envelopes of staff valuables...

Movie thriller, bad dream or reality in a once-secure state where life is suddenly uncertain? The aid worker who survived this incident still has flashbacks and cannot bear to look at bank notes.

Mention stress and the questions come: Why is there more stress today; does talking about stress encourage people to feel it; is stress actually real? Some people claim: "I've worked in disasters for 20 years without stress."

Modern life certainly has more pressure, from insistent communications to travelling laptops. For aid workers, there is also the work context of distress and instability, job insecurity and demands for high performance, and not least the murder of colleagues in recent years. A well-developed International Federation strategy helps delegates recognize and

acknowledge their own stress, accept responsibility to seek support and continue with care until fully recovered. The biggest change has been in other delegates – those claiming stress-free lives – seeing what is needed to acknowledge a colleague's distress, and how they can be returned to wholeness.

Mission end is a special time when each person needs a listening ear, recognition of their work, space to digest events, and the chance to be with friends and family before setting out again.

This is a time when a national Red Cross or Red Crescent society plays a key role in allowing the delegate to express pent-up tensions publicly and privately. Radio interviews, meeting presentations and reunions with other delegates are individually beneficial and boost National Society credibility.

Such outpourings will help the public understand that aid missions are not foreign adventures, but mean long hours of demanding physical and mental effort, and – very often – real dangers.

Flooding disasters usually affect the most vulnerable who cannot afford either to live in safe zones or to protect themselves efficiently. Recurrent flooding further increases vulnerability factors and may result in fatalistic behaviour and resignation.

Similar feelings may be found among people living in areas subject to hurricanes or cyclones, while trauma is also possible in disasters as different as fires – which can leave people feeling helpless as the fires spread out of control – and epidemics of disease, which may raise a range of fears and phobias.

Earthquake survivors frequently mention their fear of sudden death as the earth shook and the feeling that the once-reliable ground could no longer be trusted. This may result in frequent, but slow and unorganized migrations of population after an earthquake. For those who cannot leave, prolonged depression seems to be more prevalent.

In "man-made" disasters, outbreaks of violence and civil unrest created by socio-economic disturbances may cause even more physical and psychological suffering for the destitute living in these communities. In some cases, it is striking to see young members of these communities destroying their own environment.

Box 3.2 **Responding to the long-term needs of flood victims**

In 1993, a long series of spring and summer rainstorms in South Dakota followed a winter with unusually heavy snows. Nearly half the state was flooded, including areas never flooded in recorded history. Most of the flooding was standing water, and in some areas it remained in place for more than a year. Although South Dakota is very sparsely populated, more than 5,000 families were affected.

Mental health response in the emergency phase of the disaster was provided by a collaboration of both established community mental health centres and the American Red Cross. Mental health professionals were located in all evacuation shelters and service centres where families applied for assistance. Most communities also had local crisis telephone numbers.

South Dakota used a US federal government grant to provide a broad crisis intervention programme to respond to the floods. Unlicensed mental health providers were hired and given 40 hours of training in disaster mental health. The providers were supervised by three licensed mental health professionals, who also provided some direct services for the most affected families and individuals. A free statewide hotline was established. Mental health staff appeared on radio and television programmes to discuss peoples' reactions to traumatic events and the mental health services available. Advertisements for services were run in newspapers and magazines.

Services were offered primarily by telephone, with outreach services provided in 793 private homes and in community buildings across the flood area. All

5,000 affected families were contacted by telephone, offered mental health services, and sent periodic newsletters. Referrals for more traditional mental health services were made for 640 individuals or families. Community mental health centres, as well as schools and child centres, were offered staff training and brochures. In addition, all medical facilities, nursing homes and senior citizen centres were contacted.

Several patterns of responses were identified:

- South Dakota's residents struggle in a difficult environment and depend on each other to survive. Those affected by the flooding responded to the offer of services politely, accepted printed information, but generally denied any need. Nearly a year later, a bitter winter storm was the factor which overwhelmed the coping skills of many people, who then turned back to the information they had received and called the hotline for help.
- The tension of dealing with the floods revived the traumatic emotions of many who had experienced sexual and physical abuse as children.
- Officials at many levels experienced significant stress in dealing with the disaster.
- Neighbours who escaped the effects of flooding often had significant "survivor guilt".
- Mental health providers felt significant cumulative stress after months of helping those affected by floods. Two licensed mental health professionals were hired to provide support to the flood counsellors for several hours each week.

On a larger scale, the psychological suffering can be horrific when entire countries – such as Liberia, Rwanda or former Yugoslavia – turn to conflict, civil war or genocide. The violence of South Africa left its legacy in large numbers of children deeply affected by their brutal experiences on the front line of the battle against apartheid.

Many disasters produce temporary or permanent displacement, while millions become refugees by crossing a border in fear. US and UK studies suggest a high proportion of the refugees who emerge from conflicts can have mental health problems from both their negative experiences and their loss of a supportive community.

In many cases the reconciliation and healing processes, when a clear commitment to initiate them is made, will take years if not decades because the resulting trauma may be transferred from generation to generation. A major challenge for the 21st century is to try to address these enduring results of trauma before they develop into new outbreaks of violence.

Who is affected?

When most people think of disaster victims they imagine those directly affected: families picking through the rubble of a home destroyed; children who stare into the camera with the blank expressions of loss; those bloodied in the aftermath of an earthquake. But disasters can psychologically affect a wide range of people:

- those directly affected;

- those indirectly affected, as observers, witnesses or bystanders, or through interaction with those directly affected, such as family, friends or colleagues; and

- helpers and rescue workers.

The pain of those directly affected by these events is felt and shared by their families and friends. Those who witness these conditions and situations, even through television coverage, may also be significantly moved. This is especially true of children, whose cognitive developmental level often makes it difficult to understand the images they see.

Many young children in the United States saw unedited television coverage after the bombing in Oklahoma City in 1995. The bombed building had included a child care centre; there were many pictures of the bloodied bodies of children being rushed from the building. Hundreds of children all over the country were terrified to return to their child care centres in the days that followed. These kinds of psychological impact are collectively known as "secondary stress".

The media can clearly have an aggravating effect by heightening impact through immediate live reports, repeating particular sequences, and bringing potentially traumatic events to a larger – sometimes global – audience.

Individuals are affected when they can empathize with the pain of those directly affected, when they can imagine themselves or their loved ones in the place of those affected, and when they simply care about the welfare of other people. The psychological effect of disasters is often described as spreading like ripples from a stone cast into water.

How do rescuers cope?

Few realize the impact that disasters can have on the helpers trying to feed people in a famine or search through the rubble of collapsed buildings. Depending on the situation encountered by relief workers, they may experience traumatic stress, or find it difficult to continue their work. In some cases, the tough ethos of the rescue organization may make it difficult for individuals to acknowledge their problems without feeling stigmatized.

Box 3.3 Crucial volunteers in the response of Red Cross and Red Crescent

Dedicated to providing humanitarian assistance to victims of conflicts and disasters wherever they strike, the International Red Cross and Red Crescent Movement is the largest voluntary organization in the world, with 175 National Societies and many millions of volunteers.

For decades, the focus was exclusively on giving material assistance. In recent years, however, many National Societies have led the way in highlighting disaster mental health needs and then developing programmes to alleviate psychological suffering among both crisis-hit communities and aid workers.

Beyond the direct relief of suffering, the rationale behind the Psychological Support Programme (PSP) is that psychological suffering hampers proper disaster assessment and decision making. Good disaster management will reduce suffering, shorten the relief phase and accelerate rehabilitation.

Implementation of PSP is done locally within the cultural framework of each National Society. It tries to cover psychological support within three programmes: disaster preparedness, first aid and social welfare.

As a mainly volunteer-based support programme to help reduce victim suffering and perhaps prevent the need for later professional care, the PSP does not include treatment of severe trauma. Some basic points are common to all programmes developed so far:

■ Psychological needs and support are best expressed and implemented within the victims' cultural set of values; support should take account of existing mechanisms by which suffering can be expressed.
■ Psychological support is not treatment. It is provided by volunteers who have received adequate training from dedicated professionals who are willing to provide further supervision and guidance.
■ Time is critical to the successful management of psychological problems. Large numbers of trained volunteers can provide both immediate and long-term support.
■ Relief workers may also suffer from stress-related problems, which can result in serious psychological disorders. The needs of staff, volunteers and expatriate delegates must be addressed from the early stages.

There are support programmes for victims in Bulgaria, Spain and the United States, as well as in the contaminated areas around Chernobyl. In Australia, Bangladesh and Belgium, support programmes for volunteers and/or delegates are being developed. Now the challenge is to take PSP into tough disasters, such as Rwanda, former Yugoslavia, DPR Korea, and as many other National Societies as possible.

The PSP focuses on training volunteers to train their peers, who can then provide direct support to affected populations; a comprehensive approach is possible through the International Federation, its National Societies and the Copenhagen-based Reference Centre for Psychological Support.

Hosted and funded by the Danish Red Cross, the Reference Centre was set up in 1993 to build mental health programmes and support for victims of disaster.

The Reference Centre prepares guidelines for National Societies to develop and implement a PSP, holds a database on National Society programmes, and distributes information, practical knowledge and experiences to all National Societies through its *Coping with Crisis* newsletter.

An increasing number of National Societies have started a psychological first aid programme, and are involving local professionals to ensure the cultural context of the National Society has a high priority in the programme. Evaluation, support and supervision are all important for the programme continuity.

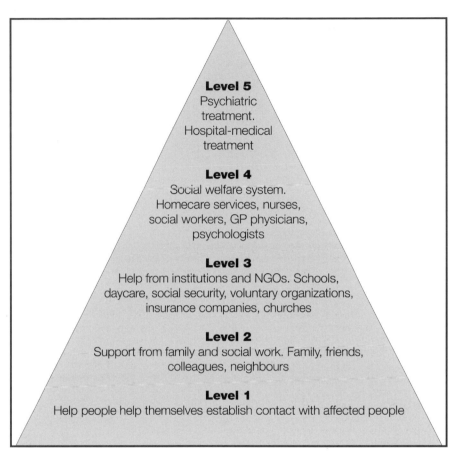

Figure 3.1
This disaster mental health "pyramid" shows the different levels of support possible after a disaster, suggests how each level builds on and supports others, and shows the importance of communication and cooperation between professional and non-professional support systems.
Source: International Federation Reference Centre for Psychological Support.

More emphasis is now being placed on training people to cope by understanding how they may react in emergencies, and offering them proactive ways to prevent and address the longer-term effects of stress.

The International Federation acknowledges that stress is a major cause of illness among relief workers and, if unrecognized, cumulative stress can lead to serious illness.

The International Federation has a network of support available for relief workers and includes sessions on stress management in workshops and training courses. Psychological support and counselling is available in Geneva before and after missions and increasingly, as national Red Cross and Red Crescent societies recognize the need for this kind of assistance, they are instituting psychological support on a national level.

What are the reactions?

People's feelings in disasters are ordinary reactions to extraordinary situations. When people experience high levels of stress, they respond with very individual patterns of predictable reactions. It is not entirely clear whether these reactions are universal, or whether they vary from culture to culture. Many psychologists believe that internal reactions are universal, while external reactions are modified by cultural norms. Reactions fall into four categories: cognitive, emotional, behavioural and somatic.

Cognitive reactions include recurring dreams or nightmares about the disaster; reconstructing the events surrounding the disaster in one's mind, in an effort to make it come out differently; difficulty concentrating or remembering things; questioning spiritual or religious beliefs; and repeated thoughts or memories of the disaster, or of loved ones who died in the disaster, which are hard to stop.

Common emotional reactions include feeling numb, withdrawn, or disconnected; experiencing fear and anxiety when things remind the individual of the disaster, particularly sounds and smells; feeling a lack of involvement or enjoyment in everyday activities; feeling depressed much of the time; feeling bursts of anger or intense irritability; or feeling a sense of emptiness or hopelessness about the future.

Behavioural responses may involve being overprotective of one's own and one's family's safety; isolating oneself from others; becoming very alert at times and startling easily; having problems getting to sleep or staying asleep; avoiding activities that remind one of the disaster, avoiding places or people that bring back memories; having increased conflict with family members; keeping excessively busy to avoid thinking about what happened; and being tearful or crying for no apparent reason.

Box 3.4 **Beyond the radioactivity is Chernobyl's psychological fallout**

Twelve years after the Chernobyl explosion, the health consequences are still being assessed but the number of people with psychological effects appears to far exceed the number who have developed physical illnesses, and the psychological effects are increasing over time.

That may be the result of far more than the disaster itself. It was followed by the political break-up of the Soviet Union – which left many feeling stranded in their own country – and the substantial negative impact for millions of people of economic changes for which they were not prepared.

The International Federation's humanitarian response began in 1991, when psychological needs were already being mentioned as an area for investigation, but it took several years before a pilot project on psychosocial rehabilitation began in Belarus, the most affected country.

The Chernobyl Humanitarian Assistance and Rehabilitation Programme (CHARP) has been based on mobile diagnostic laboratories (MDLs) that travel out to the most remote communities. They collect data on radioactivity levels in the environment and people, provide a full medical examination and immediately offer the results to the individual, and deliver "clean food" – non-contaminated milk powder,

micronutrients and multi-vitamins – to children of school age.

In 1996, the International Federation's second evaluation recommended starting a pilot programme to reduce stress related to ignorance of the situation by delivering clear, simple, reliable and easily understandable information on radioactivity, its health consequences and the best coping methods.

A psychosocial delegate and her counterpart, both based at the Minsk regional delegation, helped identify people in each MDL team willing to become trainers for all MDL staff. MDL staff were identified as the priority target group because they deliver information about radioactivity and health directly to affected populations. They are also most directly affected by secondary stress.

Local specialists in mental health and psychological support helped organize a first workshop in 1997. Training sessions have since been organized in the area by the "trained trainers" and supervised by the psychosocial delegate and her counterpart. There have been calls to transform the pilot project into a full programme and extend it to all affected oblasts in Ukraine and the Russian Federation.

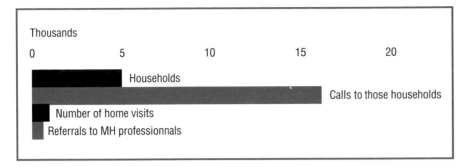

Thousands

| 0 | 5 | 10 | 15 | 20 |

Households

Calls to those households

Number of home visits

Referrals to MH professionnals

Figure 3.2
Good communications allowed a comprehensive provision of mental health services during and after the South Dakota flooding, including an average of more than three telephone calls to each family.

Somatic reactions may include insomnia, headaches, stomach aches, muscular tensions, increased heartbeat, and fluctuating body temperature, all of which may worsen as stress accumulates, culminating in acute illness.

Some researchers have tried to suggest why reactions vary so much between people affected by the same disaster, including identifying a triad of protective factors for children: support figures outside the family, support within the family and the individual characteristics of the child. And there are claims that strong belief systems – from the religious to the political – may also help people resist or better endure some psychological effects.

Who can give support?

Psychological support can be defined as the psychosocial help anyone can give to other people in stressful, critical, traumatic or life-threatening situations. This support is provided mainly by being present, to care and to listen to the person, and sometimes by talking to give the person struggling with the event the space and time to explore and process the painful experience. The purpose of this support is to create safety, security and hope for the person suffering.

This definition of psychological support clearly indicates that the assistance can be provided by almost anyone able to feel and show empathy by understanding the experience of those affected by traumatic events, and seeing the world through their eyes. Empathy is also the capacity to listen carefully and ask clarifying questions. "Active listening" is a very basic skill. It requires that the helper listen carefully and show the person respect, to create space for the person to talk and react to the disaster. This process takes time.

Friends and family provide most psychological support. Many countries use semi-professionals or "para-professionals," caring individuals with a limited amount of focused training. This requires well-qualified supervisors and a clear system of referrals to professional institutions and resources. A small percentage of affected individuals may be served by mental health professionals.

Psychological support can achieve:

- immediate relief to some degree;

- reduced risk for long-term psychological problems resulting from the stress; and

- more effective response to the physical and material needs confronting individuals and their families.

Psychological support is based on common sense and the human characteristic of wanting to help. In order for this concept to be genuinely useful, it is best to define the most effective structure for the support so that it will become a valuable tool for the helper. It is important to remember that good support and help can come from many directions, and that victims can benefit from the caring presence and active listening of other people to help and guide them in the first chaotic phases of the disaster. The most important tool a helper can provide is empathy.

Depending on the nature and stage of the disaster, there may well be much that a community can still do for itself, and it is clear that effective techniques for coping with crisis are based on the affected person's interaction with their community and environment.

Psychological response

After fire swept her neighbourhood and destroyed scores of homes, Californian psychologist Roxane Cohen Silver conducted a series of surveys of those who lost their houses. She found that many had plenty of positive emotions because of the help they had received from family and friends.

The "positives" needed far less counselling than those who had found the event traumatizing for months or years. The traumatized could also be identified easily: they had experienced the most "temporal dislocation" – being unsure of the day and feeling disconnected to past or future – immediately following the fire.

Disasters do not necessarily render victims helpless and inactive, and even in sudden-onset events, few people panic. This has implications for planning based around the psychosocial resources available within the community which may greatly enhance communities' indigenous capacity to cope.

The US Federal Emergency Management Authority has identified five trends in psychosocial responses to disaster which highlight the capacity of communities to help themselves as well as indicating priorities for responding personnel.

First, victims are not left helpless by disaster, and are often active rather than passive in their response. Emergency managers should anticipate and plan for goal-directed behaviour.

Second, most victims will reflect typical stress symptoms, at least in the short term, but many will recover with the support of family, friends and community networks.

Third, particular social groups, especially women and children, may be more vulnerable to the psychological and social effects of disaster.

Fourth, a common feature is the emergence of networks of social support, both formal and informal, in which victims participate following a disaster. Such "therapeutic communities" are characterized by a rise in informal and volunteer help, increased community morale and increased altruistic behaviour. By nurturing the rise of therapeutic communities after disaster, emergency managers can facilitate the growth of an effective healing environment.

Fifth, successful community-based and participatory approaches to disaster management often recognize local human capacity as well as vulnerability. Empowering those most affected by disaster through a role in decision making, planning and response can have psychosocial and practical benefits.

People exposed to disaster may have come close to death, which could shake their belief in themselves and their values to the foundations. Life may be perceived as chaos, decreasing their ability to react adequately to the new situation, manage their lives and meet basic needs. Rebuilding the foundation will create meaning from chaos, and much of the foundation in life is built on human relations.

It is important that victims know that the reactions they experience in an emergency are not unique, and that they are ordinary reactions to extraordinary situations. Without this reassurance, victims may feel they are "going crazy" or becoming incapable.

How to help?

Psychological support offers ways to help those affected by disaster. Helpers examine their abilities and ways of dealing with the emotional aspects of disaster, and then use and teach methods to help victims cope with the aftermath of disaster and support those attempting to recover from its impact.

Good support can come from many directions and it does not require a close relationship between those affected and the helpers. Just by being present with those struggling towards recovery, the helper provides support. The helper must learn to be present as a person – rather than as an expert or figure of authority – to help a victim. "How to be present" is most important, not necessarily what is done.

Psychological effects should be dealt with during the acute phase of disaster response, when support of physical needs is being provided. Immediate psychological support can reasonably be seen as a preventive programme. In the acute phase of a disaster, psychological support provided by either trained or untrained volunteers might stop many victims from developing severe traumatic problems which will require professional treatment.

The potential value of that has been shown by recent research by the US Centers for Disease Control. It identified an increasing number of suicides among disaster victims even years after the event. Suicides increased by 62 per cent in the year after an earthquake, by a third in the two years after a hurricane and by 14 per cent in the four years following a flood. The overall rise in suicides over four years following a disaster was 13.8 per cent.

The researchers suggested that as well as the stress of personal losses and negative experiences, the figures may reflect issues of employment, disaster-related loan repayments and the long-lasting disruption in the community's social fabric and routine.

These persistent effects and the different timings of their greatest impact imply that psychological support efforts should continue to help those in need, or at least be available in case of need, for months if not years. Volunteers will therefore be an essential part of any long-term strategy.

Psychological support is growing as a tool in many disasters around the world, with its practitioners building its knowledge base and their experience in working with both communities in crisis and the aid staff sent to help. Its importance is being underlined by new studies that show the impact of disasters on long-term suicide rates and the deep psychological needs of refugees.

It is clear that psychological suffering affects many people in often complex ways, with symptoms that can last for years or even lead to suicide. Yet with a range of simple techniques, such as active listening, local volunteers can play an important and very cost-effective front line role in psychological support, preventing future traumatic problems.

There is work to be done in the field of psychological first aid to enable communities at risk of disasters to hold themselves together and support their members. The psychological effects of disasters are also of growing concern to aid agencies and rescue organizations in terms of their staff health, safety and effectiveness as relief operations get closer to the centre of conflicts and take on other tough assignments.

There are simple lessons to be learned in the role that psychological support can play as a key part of disaster preparedness, response and recovery.

Chapter 3 Sources, references and further information

Anderson, Mary B. *Develop-ment and Social Diversity.* Development in Practice Readers. UK and Ireland: Oxfam Publications, 1996.

Berthold, S. Megan. *Violence Exposure and Resilience Among Khmer Adolescents: Implications for Practice.* Cali-fornia State University, 1998.

Commins, Stephen. *Deve-lopment in States of War.* Development in Practice Rea-ders. UK and Ireland: Oxfam Publications, 1996.

Danieli, Yael, Rodley, Nigel S. and Weisæth, Lars. *Inter-national Responses to Traumatic Stress.* New York: Baywood Publishing Company, Inc., 1996.

Danish Red Cross. *Psycho-logical first aid and other human support.* Copen-hagen: Danish Red Cross, 1993.

Danish Red Cross. *Psykolo-gisk Førstehjælp og medmenneskelig støtte.* Copenhagen: Danish Red Cross, 1997. Available in English from May 1998 from the Reference Centre for Psy-chological Support, Danish Red Cross, 27, Blegdamsvej, P.O. Box 2600, DK-2100 Co-penhagen Ö, Denmark. Tel. +45 35 25 9200. Fax: +45 35 25 9292. E-mail: mette-sonnicks@redcross.dk

Figley, Charles R, Ph.D. *Compassion Fatigue: Coping with Secondary Traumatic Stress Disorder in Those Who Treat the Traumatized.* New York: Brunner/Mazel Publishers, 1995.

Newburn, Tim. *Disaster and After: Social Work in the Aftermath of Disaster.* London: Jessica Kingsley Publisher Ltd, 1993.

Summerfield, Derek. "Making a drama out of trauma" in *The Health Exchange,* October 1997.

Gwotzyng, Ronald J. *Disaster Mental Health Approach to Post-Traumatic Stress.* Arlington: University of Texas, 1998.

"Refugee children may need a lot of psychiatric help", in *British Medical Journal,* No. 7134 Volume 316, March 1998.

Web sites

Australasian Journal of Disaster and Trauma Studies: http://www.massey.ac.nz/~trauma/

Disaster Mental Health Institute, University of South Dakota: http://www.usd.edu/dmhi/

Emergency Services and Disaster Relief Branch, US Center for Mental Health Services: http://www.mentalhealth.org/emerserv/index.htm

International Electronic Journal of Innovations in the Study of the Traumatization Process and Methods for Reducing or Eliminating Related Human Suffering: http://rdz.stjohns.edu/trauma/trau-maj.html

International Society for Traumatic Stress Studies: http://www.istss.com/

Mental Health for Children and Youth in Armed Conflict: http://www.xs4all.nl/~mtrapman/

My Heart's In Bosnia: http://rdz.stjohns.edu/trauma/Bosnia_home.html

Operation Green Cross: http://www.fsu.edu/~gcp

PILOTS (Published International Literature on Traumatic Stress), US National Center for Post-Traumatic Stress Disorder: http://www.dartmouth.edu/dms/ptsd/PILOTS.html

Post Traumatic Stress Resources Web Page, PTSD Program, Department of Psychiatry, Carl Hayden Veterans Affairs Medical Center, Phoenix, Arizona, USA: http://www.long-beach.va.gov/ptsd/stress.html

Trauma links at the Disaster Center: http://www.disastercenter.com/trauma.htm

Trauma Information Pages http://www.trauma-pages.com/

It is not just a bit of plastic draped over a few sticks. It is a home, a refuge from violence, a place of privacy, a shelter from the weather. Good shelter can greatly enhance people's chance of survival. Bad shelter – which only serves to keep the rain out – may, through short-sighted neglect, actually contribute to suffering and higher death rates.

Christopher Black/International Federation. Democratic Republic of the Congo, 1997.

Chapter

Shelter solutions beyond sticks and plastic sheets

One of the most basic needs of individuals, families and communities is for safe and comfortable living space. For many years, shelter as an emergency item was seen simply as a logistical problem, but this is not enough. A shelter is a home. A home is security, safety, privacy, protection from the environment. Homes make up a community, be it a street in a village or a row of tents in a camp. These broader needs are as important in planning and providing shelter as are the requirements for square metres of living space and access to water.

Strategies in humanitarian assistance

Three possible scenarios dictate the basic shelter needs of disaster victims. The type of disaster, the numbers of people involved, the politics surrounding the disaster and the ability of the community to cope with the disaster: all determine which scenario people will be forced to follow.

Scenario A - People stay at home: Communities that are displaced by natural disasters, such as earthquakes or cyclones, want to stay in or near their homes. Even if their homes are destroyed or damaged, assistance to people "where they are" is much more sustainable and allows normality to be restored more quickly than assistance which encourages people to move away in search of temporary shelter. Aid goes directly into the area where people live, where they know each other, where social structures can keep going, where life remains as normal as possible.

In the extreme emergency phase, people may need temporary lodging in schools, churches or even large tents, but one member of the family will often stay on the family plot to guard property and land. If government and aid agencies handle this scenario well, there is a very real possibility that the emergency will be short-lived and normality will quickly return.

Scenario B - People are displaced and stay in host communities: During civil strife, and after some natural disasters such as extensive flooding, whole communities may be forced to flee their homes and region. Often they will leave most, if not all, of their possessions behind. They are sometimes helped with transport, but more usually move on foot, taking with them only items they can carry and the clothes they wear. In this situation, it is much better if displaced populations are absorbed into a local host community, possibly with family members or people who share historical, religious or other ties. Governments and agencies need to provide assistance to the entire population according to need, since both resident and displaced people are, in effect, disaster-affected.

Box 4.1 Looking for new standards for housing through the Sphere Project

Set up in July 1997, the Sphere Project draws on the expertise and experience of individuals and agencies worldwide to set agreed minimum standards to improve the quality of humanitarian response and accountability to beneficiaries and donors. This chapter is based on a preliminary study concerning shelter and site selection. Along with the International Federation, NGOs led by the Steering Committee for Humanitarian Response, InterAction, VOICE and ICVA, UN agencies and certain donor governments collaborate on the project.

The minimum standards stem from Sphere's humanitarian charter, which is based upon international humanitarian, refugee and human rights law and reaffirms humanitarian agencies' commitment to provide for the basic needs of people affected by calamity and conflict. The project will in future focus on ensuring that the humanitarian community is aware of the standards, and integrates them into field practice during humanitarian assistance operations. The complete text of the Sphere document will be available in autumn 1998, but basic information and progress reports can be accessed through the International Federation's website at http://www.ifrc.org/pubs/sphere

---

Ironically, helping both displaced and host communities is often cheaper in the long run than simply providing for the needs of victims. Security issues, long term effects on the environment, the possibilities to share shelter, clinics, schools and shops all favour an integrated approach to assistance, and can have lasting positive effects on the host communities even after the disaster victims have returned home.

In the late 1980s and early 1990s, Mozambican refugees were integrated into the communities close to the border in Swaziland. They even went back to Mozambique to work on their farms, which was at times belittled by aid workers, even though it meant the refugees were not only producing extra food, but also preparing for their return home. But the local Swazi community, who so generously looked after the Mozambican refugees, was not assisted. This led to continuous problems for aid agencies and, even worse, for the displaced people themselves.

Scenario C - People are displaced and stay in clusters: Sometimes, despite the best intentions of assisting agencies, displaced people end up in the least preferred scenario - that of the refugee or displaced people's camp. There are many potential difficulties: the displaced communities may be too large for the local population to absorb; the displaced may fear persecution and violence from elements within their own or the host community; security or political problems may arise.

The host government - or the displaced themselves or the first assistance agency to arrive - has often selected the site of the camp, usually around water and sanitation points. But now, more permanent and suitable sites sometimes need to be set up, leaving the old one as a transit camp, or abandoning it altogether. Ideally camps should be planned and the infrastructure installed before people settle but this rarely happens. If there are no alternative sites for a new camp, the initial site may need reorganizing to meet minimum standards as laid down by United Nations High Commissioner for Refugees (UNHCR) or in the new Sphere standards (see chapter 5).

Scenario implications

Herding people into isolated camps is, of course, the least preferable scenario, but probably the one most people associate with emergencies. The implications are daunting: the displaced become dependent on external aid; the host community suffers from the strain on the local economy and environment; and increased health hazards, perceived and real, can become an issue.

Even host governments cannot force local communities to accept displaced people, but an efficient and honest aid programme to the entire population may encourage them to do so. The early arrival of aid agencies, and provision of water, shelter, food and sanitation, can make a big difference and prevent bad management of the camp system.

Whichever scenario is played out, there are key issues which need to be addressed for all displaced people. The provision of clothing, household items and shelter are common to all, whilst the selection of site, and camp management, are most relevant to scenario C.

Site selection and planning should produce the best living conditions possible under the circumstances. A good site will provide the displaced with a suitably healthy environment, where they and their families can lead a peaceful, dignified existence and where they can benefit from efficient help.

Camps close to existing communities offer many advantages; displaced populations can profit enormously from the infrastructure already in place: roads, bridges, warehousing, communications facilities, and services such as health, electricity, security (police) and waste management. In addition, the displaced may find work and opportunities to trade locally.

In the past, mass population movements often led to extensive damage of the host environment. Prevention is always better than cure, but particularly so when it comes to the environment (see also chapter 9, box 2).

*Charles Page/
International Federation*

The initial choice of locations for future camps and settlements will determine the type and degree of subsequent environmental damage. It is useful, if possible, to carry out an environmental impact assessment, tapping the expertise from various sectors: resource management, forestry, site planning, water supply, land use planning, etc. Several points in particular need to be considered: How much and what sort of energy sources are available in the area? Are there any environmentally sensitive areas such as parks or game reserves nearby? Does any local expertise in the field of environment management exist?

During the emergency phase, when attention is usually focused on saving lives, effective environmental assessment and planning will be decisive in determining the quality and overall cost of environmental intervention over the entire duration of the relief action.

Topography, or the shape of the landscape, plays a special role in determining the suitability of sites.

Is water available, or is there at least a good prospect of being able to access water, for households, agriculture and sanitation? Is it possible to pipe water in or will water-tankers be needed?

Water also needs to leave a site. Drainage of sanitation and surface water is critical. A minimum 2 per cent gradient is needed for good surface run-off. More than 6 per cent and soil erosion sets in. If the site is not at least 3 metres above the water table in the rainy season, the ground water may become polluted. Soil type and vegetation also affect the potential for soil erosion: areas covered with grasses, scrubs and trees provide for shade and resist erosion.

Sites should be secure and easily accessible for logistical reasons. Ideally, the site should be less than five kilometres from an all-weather road, but at least 50 kilometres from national borders in refugee situations and, of course, well away from potential military targets.

Land rights must be firmly established before occupying the land. Water rights, and the right to use other natural resources – wood, stone, sand – should be arranged immediately before or upon site selection.

Camp layout

Once an accessible and secure site has been chosen and the displaced move in, the camp will gradually turn into a community. Whether this process is easy or difficult will depend on the actual layout of the camp. There should be sufficient space for family household areas, mostly for public health reasons, and the layout should enable effective, efficient provision of services.

Best practice today suggests the following criteria for good site layout:

■ A minimum of 30 square metres per person, but excluding any land for agriculture (crops and livestock).

■ The total camp size should be between 20,000 and 50,000 people allowing for the inevitable compromise between the efficient utilization of services and the social and physical impact on local people and environment.

■ Living areas or village groups should be clustered, leaving empty land for future expansion, graveyards, wood lots and, separately, space for children to play.

■ Firebreaks, 50 metres wide, every 300 metres, especially in high-density camps, provide a key safety feature.

■ Different graveyards may be required for different groups in a camp. Graveyards should be situated at least 30 metres from water sources (further away in fractured rock formations like limestone), and at least two metres above the water table. No run-off water from the graveyard should enter the camp.

The impact of displaced people on the environment can be immense. This will not always be immediately visible, but long-term damage can take decades to rectify. Taking more water from an aquifer than flows into it causes a lowering of a water table. Using all wood available to obtain fuel increases soil erosion. In complex environments such as tropical forests, species particularly valuable for building and furniture construction may disappear altogether, either used locally or traded out of the area.

Some degradation of the environment is inevitable, but uncontrollable pressure can be avoided. Effective assistance and protection of the environment do not have to be mutually exclusive. Refugee camps can cause environmental damage to globally important natural features, as well as repercussions on the livelihood of local inhabitants. Analysing the short- and long-term costs and benefits helps decisions on camp location and size. The equations are difficult, however, when

Box 4.2 Key problems that affect the search for better shelter

1. Agencies now help much larger numbers of people than in the past.
2. More disaster victims today are found in cold climates.
3. More agencies are now involved in shelter provision than in the past. Coordination, capacity and competence are becoming critical.
4. The lack of space for people to settle and the poor siting of settlements is putting an increased strain on local populations and the environment. A lack of privacy, reduced human dignity, loss of social structures and increased dependency are all on the increase.
5. Servicing larger populations leads to specific logistical problems. Often it takes too long for materials to arrive on the site of the emergency.
6. Finance versus media. Large refugee situations make good television, but the necessary finances, often generated through publicity, are needed in the long term as well as the immediate disaster.
7. More people needing urgent shelter and more people trying to provide it have led to widely varying standards in the provision and use of shelter materials.
8. Security problems are on the increase particularly amongst large populations of displaced people.
9. There is too little involvement of beneficiary and local populations in the planning, provision and servicing of temporary shelter.

humanitarian considerations are weighed against environmental and economic ones.

In an effort to reduce the scale of environmental damage associated with mass population movements, agencies often focus on reducing camp energy consumption. The simplest and probably the most cost-effective way to achieve reduction in energy consumption is to get displaced people themselves to implement economy measures, encouraging them to take steps which will reduce their own energy demands.

Women and camp security

Security in a displaced people's camp is often a problem. External security is important, but internally there can be serious security problems as well. There is usually much frustration due to events which caused the displacement, and a lack of individual, psychological and social fulfilment. Violence, including rape, may be hazards for many people within the displaced population. Latrines on the edge of a camp can force people, especially women and children, to leave the camp at night. If possible, isolated, rarely frequented places, should be avoided.

Women often keep the family together. Husbands may be involved in fighting, or may have migrated out of the area to find work, or may be staying at home to

---

Box 4.3 Liberia's post-conflict reconstruction after displacement

The years of civil war in Liberia completely devastated the country causing the displacement of more than 50 per cent of the population (1,500,000 people). Shortly after the peace agreements, Liberia is now a country without government and public services, with basic infrastructures destroyed. Education, health, administration, road infrastructure, water supply systems, trade, and residential properties have all suffered devastating losses. According to a recent estimate, 30,000 settlements were completely destroyed during the fighting.

For the Liberian people, the priority has to be:
- consolidation of the new civil capacity on the national territory;
- the demobilization of ex-servicemen;
- the reinstatement and rehabilitation of the displaced populations returning to the country; and
- work programmes intended to ensure minimal services and food self-sufficiency for the population.

In assisting Liberia rebuild, the international community, through the NGOs, the International Red Cross and Red Crescent Movement and the UN has adopted a strategy based on the implementation of fast-impact micro-projects, aimed at restoring and ensuring a minimum level of subsistence of the population, or on urgent, long-term programmes. For example, demobilized combatants are engaged in micro-projects relating to maintenance of roads, public buildings and water supply systems.

UN Operations (UNOPS) is organizing the repair and maintenance of roads and damaged bridges, to restore access throughout the country. International NGOs have established food-for-work programmes to engage ex-serviceman in civilian projects, are distributing food to schools and other vulnerable groups, and, in cooperation with the Food and Agriculture Organization, are engaged in the distribution of seeds and agricultural tools, intended in particular for returning refugees of rural origin. The International Labour Office and the UN Development Programme have initiated a capacity-building operation to set up short-term professional training programmes, while UNICEF, in collaboration with some NGOs, is working on a countrywide water-supply programme.

But rebuilding old systems and structures must not be seen as an end in itself. It cannot be limited to actions aimed at the simple short-term reconstitution of the situation as it was before the war. It can help development by promoting prevention, stimulating the process of construction of peace and creating the capacities necessary for its realization.

---

guard property. The women look after the children and provide for food, water and even shelter when men are absent.

Life in camps is often disproportionately harsh for women. During mass movements, social structures collapse, and women's social position and support mechanisms become endangered. Not only does the family place more demands on women, but their safety is reduced because of the threat of rape and theft.

In camps, therefore, special attention must be given to women and their security. Both female heads of households – and there are many in camps – and single women could be grouped together in the same part of the camp, with latrines not too far away and sufficient lighting at night. If possible, the camp should be patrolled, especially at night, by the local police force.

All of the above can be better understood and organized when a camp leadership committee is rapidly established and women are well represented, but it may sometimes be necessary to establish a separate committee to concentrate on women's concerns.

Protection from the elements

Shelter needs are determined by the expected duration of stay and prevailing local climatic conditions. Shelter can mean anything from plastic sheeting, suitable for short-term protection in moderate climates, to more permanent structures – even brick buildings – if the displaced stay for a long period of time in a cold climate.

Using existing housing is always the best short-term solution and, if not available, sheets, tents, Rub-halls (tented warehouses), temporary structures made of wood and iron sheeting, structures made of mud bricks, or burnt bricks or, better still, cement bricks can be utilized.

Priority should be given to repairing people's own existing structures or to improving or enlarging host families' shelter facilities.

Displaced people should have sufficient family shelter to reduce casualty and sickness and to enhance security, human dignity and privacy, without harming the environment. Families need security (both physical and psychological), privacy and protection from the weather.

Single-family units are always better than communal housing. Even where several families are housed in one large tent, living space can always be divided into single-family sections. Respect for human dignity and family property dictates that people need space to call their own.

Key indicators of best practice in shelter include:

- At least 3.5 to 4.5 square metres of living space per disaster-affected person. This is a World Health Organization and UNHCR standard, but depends largely on the climate and the make-up of the family. In a cold climate, people will spend more time inside and therefore need more space inside the covered area. In hot climates, people stay outside most of the time and only come in for sleeping. Older people generally spend more time inside the covered area, especially when it is cold.

- In temperate and tropical climates, sheets of plastic with support materials (wood, plastic poles or hard paper tubes) can provide durable solutions for up to two years. Material for walls can often be found locally but roofing needs to be provided. Support materials need to be provided to avoid local deforestation.

■ An average family of five people should receive at least a 4 metre by 5 metre sheet of plastic, with roof supports for their temporary shelter. This should provide an average of 4 square metres covered space per person but, as part of the plastic will be used for the walls, space inside the house will be reduced. Most families are not average families – there may be fewer or more people, with elderly people as well as children. All this affects the amount of material needed.

■ Tents, not plastic sheeting, should be provided in cold climates where there is the urgent need for shelter from cold winds and driving rain. Tents need to be able to withstand at least one year's cycle of weather changes. Where heating is necessary, larger multi-family tents may be preferable, as long as possibilities exist for separating living space into individual family sections inside.

■ In cold climates, beds or bed-mats and mattresses need to be provided.

■ Local materials (e.g., grass for roofs, bamboo structures) can be used if available without environmental damage. In areas with large displaced populations, materials should be "harvested" carefully to avoid waste and environmental damage.

■ A small, separate shelter for cooking should be provided with any temporary housing. This is especially important in cold climates, or where wood fires are used, as smoke from the fire can cause respiratory diseases, especially in children.

■ In the longer term, more permanent structures need to be put in place. Plastic sheeting and tents have a limited life span and need to be replaced often on an annual basis.

■ Nothing lasts for ever. All equipment needs to be replaced and/or repaired over time.

Cooking and clothing

Very often, displaced people do not have enough clothing. Perhaps they never had much in the first place, or were unable to carry it with them as they fled from danger. All their belongings may have been lost or damaged in a sudden disaster such as an earthquake or flash floods.

Appropriate clothing should be provided for women, children and men, and climatic and cultural issues need to be assessed. In cold climates, several layers of clothing or blankets insulate better than fewer thick layers.

Women need specialized clothing for reasons of hygiene and personal dignity:

■ Displaced women over 14 years old should receive two full sets of clothing including new underwear and a supply of sanitary napkins.

■ Sanitation facilities should provide privacy for women to wash and dry personal clothes.

Families displaced from their homes need to have access to utensils for household work and soap for personal hygiene.

The basic household items each family needs include: a fuel-economic stove, three different sizes cooking pots with lids, a bucket, a basin, a machete, a jerrycan and two wooden spoons. In addition, each person should receive a plate, a spoon and a mug.

Help them help themselves

People displaced for more than a few weeks need to be able to help themselves. Agricultural work, for example, allows them to improve their diet, have a healthy occupation and become more self-reliant. In some cases, skills can be learned that will help the displaced on their return home.

With a few simple tools – hoes, axes, shovels, watering cans and some vegetable seeds – displaced communities can start small-scale agricultural production. Agencies should try to make sure that there is sufficient land for kitchen gardens and consider setting up agricultural and nutritional training programmes.

Box 4.4 Guidelines on the protection and care of refugee children

Children are particularly vulnerable when homes and houses are destroyed. UNHCR's guidelines for the protection and care of refugee children are equally applicable to children within internally displaced populations.

Shelter: Ensure the availability and an adequate standard of shelter and environment, with particular concern for space, privacy and security. Increasingly the shelter and spatial environment imposed on refugees, particularly when families are forced into shared facilities, is minimal and crowded so as to violate all humane standards; conditions are so low that families cannot maintain a normal family life and are without a minimum of privacy.

Playgrounds and space: The general refugee camp layout should have enough space for playgrounds and other needs for children. The availability, distribution and location of shelter, playgrounds, water points, health centres and recreational facilities all affect the safety and well-being of refugee children. They should be planned in such a way that children are protected from accidents, away from heavy traffic, canals, garbage (rubbish) dumps, etc.

The camp should be laid out in community entities and groups of entities. Each group should have, to the extent possible, all communal basic facilities for the children. This will ensure that the children are close to all basic facilities and are provided with protection. Keep in mind the need to take into account the overall camp layout, cultural factors and the roles and daily tasks of mothers and children, especially girls.

Lack of space for play may force children away from their parents into remote places and streets. In certain refugee situations where refugees are concentrated and marginalized, refugee children may suffer from social isolation and slip into antisocial activities.

Urban areas: Give particular attention to material needs, water, sanitation and shelter needs of refugee children living in urban areas. Refugee families increasingly seek refuge in towns and cities and, due to extreme poverty and other difficulties related to their refugee status, may live in situations which put children's health at great risk. Overcrowding and lack of space often create problems affecting children such as, for example, very limited possibilities to play.

Camp settlement character: Maintain the civilian and humanitarian character of refugee camps or settlements. The presence of armed resistance fighters in or near refugee camps or settlements increases security challenges and other problems.

Location: Locate camps or other accommodation at a safe distance from the border of the country of origin or conflict areas to minimize the danger of armed attacks, harassment or military recruitment.

Safe living environment: Promote safe living arrangements for refugee children and their families. Provide living facilities that offer families and communities the most opportunities to protect children. Consider the needs for privacy, adequate space, spatial configuration of camps, lighting at night and special security arrangements.

Source: *Refugee Children: Guidelines on Protection and Care. Geneva 1994.*

Along with water, food and medical care, shelter is a critical determinant of survival in the initial stages of a disaster. Yet the development of accepted standards and an understanding of the diverse needs of disaster victims lags far behind similar developments in other areas such as the provision of food, or basic medical care. Shelter is still seen too often as simply a matter of tents and plastic sheeting, yet it is far more complex than that.

Through the effect good shelter can have on people's state of mind, their resistance to disease, their protection from the environment, their ability to sustain family life, it can dramatically increase people's chances of survival.

If this is true, so is the corollary. Bad shelter shortens people's lives and increases their exposure to disease, violence and despair.

Chapter 4 Sources, references and further reading

Aysan, Y. and Oliver, P. *Housing and Culture After Earthquakes: A Guide for Future Policy Making on Housing in Seismic Areas.* Oxford: Oxford Polytechnic, 1987.

Aysan, Y. and Davis, I. *Disaster and Small Dwellings: Perspectives for the UN IDNDR.* London: James and James, 1992.

Barakat, S., (guest editor). "War and aftermath: rebuilding war-torn societies" in *Disaster Prevention and Management,* Volume 4, Number 1, MCB University Press Limited, West Yorkshire, 1995.

Chalinder, A. *RRN Good Practice Review number 6: Temporary Human Settlement Planning for Displaced Populations in Emergencies.* London: ODI, January 1998.

Cuny, F.C. *Disaster and Development.* Oxford: Oxford University Press, 1983.

Davis, J. and Lambert, R. *Engineering in Emergency: A Practical Guide for Relief Workers.* London: RedR, 1995.

Disaster Management Center, University of Wisconsin. *New Approaches to New Realities.* Proceedings of the First International Emergency Settlement Conference. Madison: University of Wisconsin, 1995.

Maskrey, A. *Disaster mitigation: a community-based approach.* Oxford: Oxfam, 1989.

Nimpuno, K. *Emergency Settlement: Unsustainable Development.* Delft: Disaster and Emergency Reference Center.

UNCHS. *Planning for Human Settlement in Disaster-Prone Areas.* Nairobi: UNHCS (HABITAT), 1983.

UNHCR. *Shelter and Infrastructure and Camp Planning.* Geneva: UNHCR PTSS, 1994.

Web sites

Relief and rehabilitation network: http://www.oneworld.org/odi/rrn

UN Department of Humanitarian Affairs (UNDHA) International Decade for Natural Disaster Reduction (Solutions for Cities at Risk, Internet Conferences): http:/www.quipu.net/risk/

UN Centre for Human Settlements (Habitat): http://www.undp.org/un/habitat/

UNDHA Reliefweb: http://www.reliefweb.int

UNHCR: http://www.unhcr.ch

The relationship between aid agencies and aid recipients is changing. More emphasis is being placed upon quality assurance and compliance with internationally recognized standards. Aid agencies feel more accountable to their beneficiaries, but critical questions over how that accountability is to be exercised still have to be answered. Agencies want to demonstrate greater accountability, but do they have the systems in place to allow this to happen?
Christopher Black/International Federation. Haiti, 1996.

Chapter

5

Setting standards for a changing world of risk

The profound economic and political changes of the past decade have inevitably affected the business of humanitarian response. Governments are being pressured by the triple constraints of growing public indebtedness in many states, international trade liberalization and the changes in technology, particularly communications and computing, to function increasingly as regulators and facilitators of markets. States are being forced to retreat from their role as key employers and service providers. Welfare services, once seen as a state duty, are now subject to the same market forces as vehicle production. Some states have been able to manage this change, in others it has been catastrophic. For humanitarian agencies, these changes have had three critical consequences:

■ "Downsizing" state welfare exposes many more people to risk, poverty and suffering, bringing sharp rises in humanitarian assistance, for example across the former Soviet Union.

■ Independent humanitarian agencies are expected to be alternative service providers, sub-contracting former state roles in competition with companies and each other.

■ As trade becomes the substance of politics, issues of international standards, accountability and regulation-based control will reach into many fields, including aid.

Christopher Black/
International Federation

Humanitarian agencies can no more resist these changes than states, and will become subject to more regulation, particularly as they compete for sub-contracted state or international activities. They will be expected to perform to recognized standards and will be held more accountable, not only to those who supply them with resources, but also to those who provide the regulatory framework within which they work, and to those who receive services.

Change is inevitable, but how it is introduced is not. Humanitarian agencies can shape their regulatory framework to ensure it promotes their long-standing principles of impartiality, universality and service to the most vulnerable. This chapter outlines how, at the field, national and international level, agencies are trying to shape that new system of regulation, with its standards, codes and accountability, to guide their work into the next millennium.

Deliverance

The *Code of Conduct for the International Red Cross and Red Crescent Movement and NGOs in Disaster Relief,* on which the *World Disasters Report* has reported regularly, is gaining ground. The *Code* and its principles of ethics and behaviour are entering the aid lexicon, and some 149 independent humanitarian agencies had registered their support by the end of 1997. Government donors, such as the UK and Sweden, see the *Code* and its implementation as integral to the promotion of quality assistance.

As *Code* use grows, agencies see the need to go further and create practical standards for the competence and quality expected at the core of assistance. The project to develop these minimum standards in humanitarian response is dubbed "Sphere". This international, inter-agency project follows a cooperative, collaborative process to develop a humanitarian charter for people affected by disaster, and an associated set of minimum standards in the four essential areas of humanitarian response: water and sanitation, nutrition and food security, shelter and site management, and health services.

The Sphere Project is undertaken in collaboration with the International Red Cross and Red Crescent Movement; non-governmental organizations (NGOs) led by the Steering Committee for Humanitarian Response, the US InterAction network and the VOICE group of agencies working with the European Union;

United Nations (UN) agencies; and interested donor governments. The Sphere humanitarian charter and set of minimum standards are to be published in 1998.

Effective field implementation of standards needs three actions: adoption, training and accountability.

Adoption: The standards should be adopted by operational agencies worldwide. Adoption will be advanced by early acceptance of the standards by the many agencies involved in their development. A major share of assistance worldwide is distributed by members of the Steering Committee for Humanitarian Response and InterAction.

From headquarters to field offices, staff of these agencies have been developing the standards and humanitarian charter, and should be prepared to be held accountable to them. As these agencies begin using Sphere standards in operating policies and procedures, the momentum will carry recognized standards into the practices of other humanitarian agencies.

Training: A humanitarian system which aims to reach established international standards in delivering goods and services demands staff trained in those

---

Box 5.1 Checklist of the *Code of Conduct for Disaster Response Agencies*

The ten points of the *Code of Conduct for the International Red Cross and Red Crescent Movement and NGOs in Disaster Response* are:

- The humanitarian imperative comes first. The right to receive humanitarian assistance, and to offer it, is a fundamental humanitarian principle which should be enjoyed by all citizens of all countries.
- Aid is given regardless of the race, creed or nationality of the recipients and without adverse distinction of any kind. Aid priorities are calculated on the basis of need alone.
- Aid will not be used to further a particular political or religious standpoint. Humanitarian aid will be given according to the need of individuals, families and communities.
- We shall endeavour not to act as instruments of government foreign policy. Non-governmental humanitarian agencies (NGHAs) are agencies which act independently from governments. We therefore formulate our own policies and implementation strategies and do not seek to implement the policy of any government, except in so far as it coincides with our own independent policy.
- We shall respect culture and custom. We will endeavour to respect the culture, structures and customs of the communities and countries we are working in.
- We shall attempt to build disaster response on local capacities. All people and communities – even in disaster – possess capacities as well as vulnerabilities. Where possible, we will strengthen

these capacities by employing local staff, purchasing local materials and trading with local companies.
- Ways shall be found to involve programme beneficiaries in the management of relief aid. Disaster response assistance should never be imposed upon the beneficiaries. Effective relief and lasting rehabilitation can best be achieved where the intended beneficiaries are involved in the design, management and implementation of the assistance programme.
- Relief aid must strive to reduce future vulnerabilities to disaster as well as meeting basic needs. All relief actions affect the prospects for long-term development, either in a positive or a negative fashion. Recognizing this, we will strive to implement relief programmes which actively reduce the beneficiaries' vulnerability to future disasters and help create sustainable lifestyles.
- We hold ourselves accountable to both those we seek to assist and those from whom we accept resources. We often act as an institutional link in the partnership between those who wish to assist and those who need assistance during disasters. We therefore hold ourselves accountable to both constituencies.
- In our information, publicity and advertising activities, we shall recognize disaster victims as dignified humans, not hopeless objects. Respect for the disaster victim as an equal partner in action should never be lost.

standards, best practices and implementation strategies to advance a standard accountability   methodology.

Standards' training courses should be offered to field staff at regional sites around the world. Multi-agency, field-based training will model and foster collaboration in practice. In addition, people wishing to do humanitarian work need training before deployment, such as through universities offering courses in public health. Providing coherent pre-service and in-service training will enhance the capacity of all humanitarian agencies to offer consistent, high quality services for people affected by disasters.

Accountability: The standards developed by the Sphere Project are based on a humanitarian charter drawn from international law and re-affirming the rights of people affected by disaster. Humanitarian agencies signing the standards are stating their commitment to deliver essential goods and services in support of these rights. The agencies hold themselves accountable to their beneficiaries, members and donors. Within the agencies that developed the standards, this commitment acts as an ethical base for accountability in practice. Inter-agency "peer pressure" also compels compliance with agreed standards.

Sudan experience

Where the Sphere Project aims for global effect by drawing on broad experiences, other field-based initiatives offer wide lessons from single crises. As in many countries with internal conflicts, Sudan's decades of war have been characterized by human rights abuses on all sides; denial of access to civilians in need; abuses of humanitarian assistance; and constant insecurity for relief staff.

Operation Lifeline Sudan (OLS), a consortium of UN agencies and over 30 NGOs, has been providing humanitarian assistance on all sides of the conflict since 1989. It works from Khartoum and Nairobi on the basis of negotiated access, rather than – as happened in Somalia – a UN Security Council resolution.

OLS has faced a series of moral, political and legal dilemmas, including:

■ erosion of respect for values affecting both aid staff and civilians, especially the displaced;

■ threats to humanitarian action's independence, as it is often a substitute for political action;

■ unclear humanitarian mandates with respect to other agendas, for example military and political;

■ questioning traditional principles – such as neutrality and impartiality – because of the political causes of humanitarian crises;

■ fears that humanitarian aid strengthens war economies and prolongs conflict;

■ uncertainty over international politico-legal responses to sovereignty and access issues; and

■ problems of legitimacy in areas beyond government control.

The dilemmas reveal a fundamental question: Amid extreme violence, can humanitarian agencies create an environment in which to achieve their objectives – delivering aid effectively and accountably – and does that mean confronting how warring parties create the disaster?

Box 5.2 The A to Z list of sponsors and signatories to the Code of Conduct

The agencies sponsoring the *Code* are:

International Federation of Red Cross
and Red Crescent Societies
International Committee of the Red Cross
Caritas International
Catholic Relief Services
International Save the Children Alliance
Lutheran World Federation
Oxfam
World Council of Churches

By March 1998, the following humanitarian organizations supported the *Code of Conduct* and endeavoured to incorporate its principles into their work:

Argentina	Fundación Evangélica "El Buen Pastor"
Australia	Care Australia
Austria	Austrian Relief Programme (ARP)
Austria	Association for Afro-Asian Affairs
Bangladesh	Youth Approach for Development and Cooperation (YADC)
Belgium	Agora - Vitrine du Monde
Belgium	Care International
Belgium	Centre International de Formation des Cadres du Développement (C.I.F.C.D.)
Belgium	ICA - ZAGREB (Institute of Cultural Affairs International)
Belgium	Médecins sans Frontières (International)
Belgium	Oxfam
Benin	Conseil des Activités Educatives du Bénin
Canada	Adventist Development and Relief Agency (ADRA)
Canada	Canadian Feed the Children
Canada	Family to Family
Canada	Oxfam
Congo, DR of	Humanitas, Corps de Sauvetage
Congo, DR of	Oxfam
Côte d'Ivoire	ADRA

Croatia	ADEH International
Croatia	Pax Christi (Germany)
Denmark	ADRA
Denmark	Dan Church Aid
Denmark	Danish Refugee Council
Dominica	Brisin Agencies, Ltd.
Dominica	Dominica Christian Council
Dominica	Society of St Vincent de Paul
Ethiopia	Selam Children's Village
Finland	Save the Children
France	ADRA
France	Enfants du Monde
France	Enfants Réfugiés du Monde
France	Médecins du Monde
Germany	ADRA
Germany	Johanniter-Unfall-Hilfe e.V.
Greece	Institute of International Social Affairs
Guinea	Commission Africaine des Promoteurs de la Santé et des Droits de l'Homme (CAPSDH)
Hong Kong	Oxfam
India	ADRA
India	Ambiha Charitable Trust
India	ASHA (Action for Social & Human Acme)
India	Centre for Research on Ecology, Environmental Education, Training and Education (CREATE)
India	Federation of Interfaith Orphanage and Allied Educational Relief Technical Training Institutions
India	Global Forum for NGOs for Disaster Reduction
India	Institute for Youth and Disaster Preparedness
India	Joint Assistance Centre

India	Mahila Udyamita Vikas Kalya Evan Siksha Sansthah
India	Tear Fund India Committee on Relief and Rehabilitation Service (TFICORRS)
Ireland	Concern Worldwide
Ireland	Express Aid International
Italy	Associazione Amici dei Bambini
Italy	Centro Internazionale di Cooperazione allo Sviluppo C.I.C.S.
Italy	Comitato Collaborazione Medica (CCM)
Italy	Comitato di Coordinamento delle Organizzazioni per il Servizio Volontario
Italy	Comitato Internazionale per lo Sviluppo dei Popoli (CISP)
Italy	International College for Health Cooperation in Developing Countries (CUAMM)
Italy	Movimondo
Italy	Reggio Terzo Mondo (R.T.M.)
Italy	Volontari Italiani Solidarietà Paesi Emergenti (V.I.S.P.E.)
Japan	Association of Medical Doctors of Asia (AMDA)
Laos	ADRA
Lebanon	Disaster Control Centre
Luxembourg	Amicale Rwanda-Luxembourg
Myanmar	ADRA
Netherlands	Caritas Nederland
Netherlands	Disaster Relief Agency
Netherlands	Dorcas Aid International
Netherlands	Dutch Interchurch Aid
Netherlands	Memisa Medicus Mundi
Netherlands	Netherlands Organization for International Development Cooperation (NOVIB)
Netherlands	Tear Fund
Netherlands	Terre des Hommes
Netherlands	ZOA Refugee Care

New Zealand	Oxfam
New Zealand	Tear Fund
Norway	Norwegian Organization for Asylum Seekers
Norway	Norwegian Refugee Council
Philippines	ADRA
Portugal	Instituto Portugues de Medicina Preventiva (I.P.M.P.)
Russia	ADRA, Euro-Asia Division
Sierra Leone	Association for International Development and Services (AID-SL)
Spain	Intermón
Spain	Radioaficionados Sin Fronteras
Sri Lanka	ADRA
Sri Lanka	Consortium of Humanitarian Agencies
Sri Lanka	The Family Rehabilitation
Swaziland	Save the Children Fund
Sweden	International Aid Sweden
Sweden	PMU Interlife
Sweden	Qandil Project
Sweden	SAMS (Scandinavian African Mission Sweden)
Sweden	Swedish Fellowship of Reconciliation (SWEFOR)/Kristna Fredsrorelsen
Sweden	Swedish Organization for Individual Relief (SOIR)
Switzerland	Ananda Marga Universal Relief Team (AMURT)
Switzerland	Association for the Children of Mozambique (ASEM)
Switzerland	Commission Internationale Catholique pour les Migrations
Switzerland	Food for the Hungry International
Switzerland	Interaid International
Switzerland	MEDAIR
Switzerland	RedR International

Switzerland	World Vision International		UK	Post-War Reconstruction and Development Unit (PRDU)
Thailand	ADRA		UK	HedR
UK	Action Against Hunger		UK	Save the Children Fund
UK	Actionaid		UK	Tear Fund
UK	ADRA, Trans-Europe		UK	The Ockenden Venture
UK	CAFOD		UK	The Salvation Army
UK	Children in Crisis		UK	UK Foundation for the Peoples of the South Pacific
UK	Children's Aid Direct		UK	War on Want
UK	Christian Aid		UK	World Association of Girl Guides and Girl Scouts
UK	Christian Children's Fund of Great Britain		USA	American Refugee Committee
UK	European Mental Health Trust		USA	International Medical Corps
UK	FOCUS Humanitarian Assistance Europe Foundation		USA	International Rescue Committee
UK	Helpage International		USA	Lutheran World Relief
UK	Help the Aged		USA	MAP International
UK	Hope and Homes for Children		USA	Operation USA
UK	Human Appeal International		USA	Oxfam
UK	ITACoR International Association for Conflict Resolution		USA	Truck Aid International
UK	International Care and Relief (ICR)		USA	Women's Commission for Refugee Women and Children
UK	International Extension College		Zambia	PIMMPRO International NGO for Relief and Development
UK	Marie Stopes International			
UK	Medical Emergency Relief International (MERLIN)			

Operating in areas of anti-government forces, OLS (southern sector) started a programme in 1994 to tackle these issues by promoting the humanitarian imperative – that the highest priority was to meet human needs – and the importance of protecting and assisting affected civilians. The programme strategy had three elements:

■ dissemination and advocacy to raise awareness of humanitarian principles as the key to promoting their observance;

■ strengthening southern Sudanese capacity to protect humanitarian principles through advocacy, training and capacity building; and

■ using local traditional values as well as international standards as reference points for humanitarian principles, and establishing a capacity to monitor and follow up violations.

The programme's underlying ethical position was based upon two fundamental assumptions:

■ Protecting the safety and dignity of victims of conflict is an integral part of a humanitarian mandate.

■ Access to assistance is a fundamental right and the integrity of humanitarian aid – ensuring its timely, targeted arrival – must be protected. While the concept of humanitarian assistance as a legal right is still debated, OLS chose to promote it as a minimum ethical standard.

The programme was encapsulated in the "Ground Rules" document, signed by the OLS coordinator on behalf of consortium agencies and by the commanders-in-chief of the three anti-government movements. Its joint statement of humanitarian principles provided a common framework of values and standards. The Ground Rules recognized that while the ultimate responsibility for civilians depends on their political authorities, humanitarian agencies are also responsible for accountability to beneficiaries.

The OLS Ground Rules were based on internationally recognized humanitarian principles and two global legal treaties, the Convention on the Rights of the Child and the Geneva Conventions of 1949 and their Additional Protocols of 1977. Its ethical principles included:

■ promotion of humanitarian neutrality;

■ right to receive and offer humanitarian assistance;

■ accountability to beneficiaries and donors;

■ neutrality (refusal to take sides);

■ impartiality (aid provided on the basis of needs alone);

■ transparency; and

■ respect for relief worker safety.

The Convention on the Rights of the Child is perhaps the most underrated humanitarian tool. Signed by 190 governments, it is the world's most ratified human rights treaty, and the most comprehensive, covering political and civil liberties as well as social, economic and cultural rights. More than half of any war-affected group is usually children, so it covers the largest and most vulnerable segment of the population.

Built on the inherent neutrality of children, the Convention has powerful moral weight. OLS gained a vital commitment from the anti-government movements by integrating it into the Ground Rules when they would have rejected any mention of human rights treaties.

An important feature of the Ground Rules was that they attempted to move beyond a statement of principles to definitions of concrete and practical obligations for all those involved, a means of implementation, and a mechanism for responding to violations, though the latter has been the least successful part of the programme so far.

Southern Sudan's most important lesson is that accountability to beneficiaries can best be fostered within a culture of rights and a sense of responsibility to "the people". As well as providing a framework for accountability to beneficiaries, the humanitarian principles programme improved dialogue between humanitarian agencies and warring parties by securing their commitment to a common framework and set of values.

None of the principles were new to south Sudan; what was different was their integration into an agreement with anti-government military forces, in control of territory and populations.

Measuring the programme's impact is almost impossible, given the problems of monitoring and indicators in this vast, conflict-ridden region. There is no quantifiable proof that it has reduced abuses of humanitarian assistance or enhanced affected people's human rights, but anecdotal evidence suggests that this is the case.

Humanitarian agencies need to accept unequivocally that their accountability to victims of conflict includes protection of basic rights under international humanitarian and human rights law. For many, this is not an easy step; compromises between protection and assistance are inevitable. Humanitarian and human rights agencies need to learn to work more effectively together and to recognize their common concerns and commitments.

It is important that the obligations of both humanitarian agencies and warring parties are clearly stated as joint commitments to the beneficiaries of humanitarian action. Attempts – or being perceived as trying – to impose values will have a negative impact. For this reason, the Code of Conduct, which was an important source for the Ground Rules, should evolve from a statement of agency ethical positions to a basis for programmes and relationships.

OLS is still a long way from providing all the answers to issues of principles and accountability, though its approach is still accepted and active. It has yet to deal with issues of enforcement, responses to Ground Rules violations or the difficult

---

Box 5.3 InterAction protocol improves NGO cooperation and coherence

The NGO Field Cooperation Protocol was created by InterAction in an effort to ensure more coherent NGO performance following the flaws highlighted by the Rwandan exodus of 1994.

InterAction has also developed training curricula for NGO staff dealing with health problems in complex emergencies, and with security challenges in both relief and development settings.

The protocol commits signatory agencies to instruct field directors to try and reach consensus with counterparts at disaster sites on a range of potentially divisive issues which can impede service delivery to disaster victims.

The document was shared in draft with Europe-based disaster response agencies and can be signed by any NGO. InterAction is prepared to discuss modifications to make the document of greater interest to NGOs outside its own network. The protocol has been adopted by all but one InterAction agency providing field services to disaster victims.

The protocol is being sent to field staff and incorporated in the training programmes of individual agencies. In some cases, protocol compliance has become an agency performance indicator for rating field directors.

From 1997 to 2000, InterAction is conducting six evaluations of NGO cooperation in international disaster response, including how far the protocol and the health and security training programmes have been adopted and used. The evaluations will emphasize lessons learned from practical experience so that the protocol and other tools can be refined.

As well as collaborating in the Sphere Project to identify standards and best practices to be employed in disaster response, InterAction is working with People in Aid to develop best practices for human resource utilization, and with ALNAP to identify best practices in evaluation of relief and development projects.

question of whether conditions can be imposed for aid delivery, but it has fostered a very positive debate.

Far from operational decisions in Sudan, accountability in the donor world is being tackled from a very different angle. Evaluation is a key tool in efforts to improve accountability and performance in the international humanitarian aid system.

Evaluating excellence

Until recently, humanitarian aid was subjected to less rigorous monitoring and evaluation than development aid. Evaluations of humanitarian aid operations have varied enormously in approach, resources and management. This methodological anarchy of widely varying evaluation quality, scope and depth makes it hard to judge the reliability, relevance and accuracy of individual studies, and severely hampers comparative analysis.

Given the rising share of overseas development assistance allocated to humanitarian aid, and the growing awareness of the complexity of humanitarian assistance, the development of appropriate methodologies for relief aid evaluation is imperative

The Humanitarian Policy Programme of the Overseas Development Institute (ODI), on behalf of the Organisation for Economic Co-operation and

---

Box 5.4 **People in Aid measures agency performance in management**

The inter-agency, People in Aid project is committed to enhancing the effectiveness of development and humanitarian assistance programmes.

As the project focuses on people, the agencies involved consider that a good measure of their performance, and a likely indicator of field programme quality, is how well they manage and support the people who work for them.

Global development agencies are mandated to assist and serve their beneficiaries. People in Aid's members believe that, in addition, their support must extend to aid personnel.

The project has attracted increasing attention from aid workers and agencies. Over 3,000 copies of the *People in Aid Code of Best Practice in the Management and Support of Aid Personnel* have been requested by field staff and humanitarian and development organizations worldwide since it was published in 1997.

The UK government's Department for International Development says the Code, although voluntary, helps indicate that agencies are committed to the quality and effectiveness of aid, good management of aid personnel, and protection and well-being of staff working in difficult and dangerous environments.

The *People in Aid Code* gives agencies a framework within which they can monitor and improve their field staff management and support, by assessing current procedures and drawing up and implementing their own action plan. People in Aid supports them by sharing best practice through workshops, a resource centre and implementation guidelines.

Matching independent financial auditing, the 12 relief and development agencies formally piloting the Code have agreed to independent auditing of field staff management. This emerging process is expected to draw on the growing experience of aid agencies in ethical and non-financial auditing.

The People in Aid Statement of Principles:

1. The people who work for us are integral to our effectiveness and success.
2. Our human resource policies aim for best practice.
3. Our human resource policies aim to be effective, efficient, fair and transparent.
4. We consult our field staff when we develop human resource policy.
5. Plans and budgets reflect our responsibilities towards our field staff.
6. We provide appropriate training and support.
7. We take all reasonable steps to ensure staff security and well-being.

Development's (OECD) Development Assistance Committee (DAC) Expert Group on Aid Evaluation, has completed a study to identify and disseminate best practice in evaluation of humanitarian assistance programmes, with the goal of improving accountability and performance.

The study will result in a report on best practice to be published as a technical paper by the DAC Expert Group on Aid Evaluation and a "good practice review" by ODI's Relief and Rehabilitation Network. The work may also result in the adoption, by the OECD/DAC, of guidelines on the evaluation of humanitarian assistance programmes.

The study involved a literature review, evaluator questionnaire and interviews. It also drew on expertise from the ODI-coordinated Active Learning Network on Accountability and Performance in Humanitarian Aid (ALNAP), which has a peer review process to share best practice.

Recent evaluations have highlighted that their quality is significantly influenced by the monitoring and reporting data available. This initial work on evaluation may be followed by analysis of monitoring and reporting systems to identify best practice in these areas.

National initiatives

In the UK, where many international NGOs are based or represented, accountability self-regulation through an ombudsman is being considered.

"Accountability in International Humanitarian Assistance" was the theme of the 1997 World Disasters Forum in London, attended by staff from the International Red Cross and Red Crescent Movement, NGOs, UN agencies and donors.

Keynote presentations documented the rapid growth in influence and power of humanitarian agencies and stressed the need for greater accountability to beneficiaries and donors. Despite important standards initiatives – from the Code of Conduct to the People in Aid Code of Best Practice and the Sphere Project – present mechanisms to hold agencies to account are weak or non-existent, most notably for the claimants of aid.

Forum participants agreed that some form of self-regulation is needed to strengthen NGO accountability and there was a consensus to examine an ombudsman-style system. The British Red Cross is thus coordinating an inter-agency feasibility project to develop the idea.

In principle, a humanitarian ombudsman would be given a mandate to regulate NGO activities in the field, at international level or on a crisis-by-crisis basis, and also to investigate complaints from beneficiaries of humanitarian assistance. The humanitarian ombudsman would act as an independent, impartial body to monitor NGO misconduct and malpractice, which may include failure to comply with legal obligations or codes of practice.

Research is underway into ombudsmen in international organizations, such as the UN and World Bank, the public sector and business. The project has sought to involve local NGOs in the debate and UK NGOs have been invited to contribute "accountability case studies" on the views and experiences of stakeholders in recipient countries. It is examining who would be the humanitarian ombudsman or be on a watchdog panel; how monitoring and grievances would be handled; who would be able to bring grievances; and how recommendations or sanctions could be imposed.

Initiatives are also being developed to create an international forum for accountability and action, recognizing that agencies need to look beyond the aid community for new ways to affect change. One tentative experiment, named the "International Council", aims to improve how the international community, not just aid agencies, responds to major crises.

Its genesis lies in the Multi-Donor Rwanda Evaluation, which identified many gaps between the aid community and influential politico-economic actors. The evaluation's review showed that while many of its technical and field-oriented recommendations had been adopted, none of the political or policy-oriented proposals had been implemented.

Going global

The evaluation follow-up group identified three shortcomings in how complex emergencies are addressed, and the International Council will attempt to meet these needs:

■ No forum regularly brings together all the critical actors affecting complex emergencies: aid, peacekeeping, the commercial sector, media and the affected countries.

■ No structure tries to provide a digest of current thinking and research on critical issues affecting complex emergencies.

■ No organization systematically evaluates how well the international community responds to major crises.

Initiated by leading international agencies and donors, the International Council offers a forum for dialogue and a mechanism through which public and private sector actors can together champion improvements in how the international community manages the prevention and impact of violent conflicts.

Its objectives will be to:

■ improve understanding of the issues and explore innovative ways to address the causes and effects of complex emergencies through analysis, monitoring, review, reporting and dialogue; and

■ influence the effectiveness of the international community's progress in preventing, mitigating and resolving violent conflict.

The Council's mandate will be broader than humanitarian issues, giving equal attention to long-term conflict prevention, post-conflict transitions and humanitarian assistance. It will bring together a diverse range of perspectives and experience relevant to the prevention and mitigation of complex emergencies and draw its membership from the main actors involved in dealing with conflict, including representation from affected countries.

Council members will be expected to share a commitment to improve the international community's response to complex emergencies and be able to support independent and objective analysis. The Council's multi-disciplinary work will require members to think and act outside their often narrowly defined operational and organizational limits.

Through its programme of work, including research and analysis, the Council will focus on issues, rather than specific countries. In most instances, the Council will monitor and synthesize research and analysis, and focus attention on actions its studies show are required. Original research will not be undertaken unless there is a real gap in present work.

From all these international and national initiatives, it is clear that humanitarian agencies, particularly in the North, are taking a lead in developing structures and standards to create the type of organizations needed in the 21st century.

Importantly, these initiatives are not only looking at aid itself, but drawing in all other actors in the international community, reflecting on the politico-economic context in which humanitarian assistance must operate, and looking for relevant experiences well beyond Northern relief agencies.

The more fundamental challenge to be faced is taking the drive for accountability and standards out of Northern-based agencies and their donors, and moving it into the growing number of Southern agencies getting involved in international humanitarian work, while creating mechanisms to respond effectively to those most in need: the aid claimants.

Ironically, agencies' efforts to become more accountable and aspire to higher standards have suggested to some states that the solution to humanitarian problems lies here, in the work of the agencies. Organizations aspiring to higher standards therefore face the double task of internal improvement and continued pressure on governments to fulfil their obligations to address the political and economic causes of crisis.

Chapter 5 Sources, references and further reading

Levine, Ian. *Promoting humanitarian principles: the Southern Sudan experience. Relief and Rehabilitation Network,* Network Paper No. 21, May 1997.

Web sites

ICRC: http://www.icrc.org

InterAction: http://www.interaction.org/

International Federation: http://www.ifrc.org

International Humanitarian Law Database: http://www.icrc.org/unicc/ihl_eng.nsf/

OECD/DAC: http://www.oecd.org/dac/htm/pubs/p-pdggev.htm

Relief and Rehabilitation Network: http://www.oneworld.org/odi/rrn/index.html

Sphere Project: http://www.ifrc.org/pubs/sphere

As funding for humanitarian assistance falls and major donors toy with the political integration of assistance into more holistic action, aid agencies increasingly need to defend the independence and rationale behind their work. The new disasters arising out of socio-economic depression and endemic poverty mean there is no prospect of a fall in demand for emergency assistance, but is there the political will to maintain the supply?

Christopher Black/International Federation. Democratic Republic of the Congo, 1997.

Chapter

6

Global trends squeeze
international assistance

Falling funds, performance pressures, political integration: three global trends are shaping international assistance – from its structure and systems to priorities and policies – on the eve of the 21st century.

First, aid volume has substantially declined over five years. It is already down 17 per cent in real terms between 1992 and 1996, with further falls to come, although emergency aid – despite falling from its 1994 peak of almost US$ 3.5 billion to $2.7 billion in 1996 – remains almost three times its 1990 level. Aid's decline is happening in the context of expanding economies, trade flows and foreign direct investment in the developing world; aid is being outpaced by the market and risks marginalization unless it can show steadily improving performance.

The result is not just a squeeze on bilateral funding for long-term development, but also puts pressure on aid agencies in the form of new attempts to identify clear and achievable goals to shore up fragile public and political support by showing that aid does make a difference. Donors are looking at links between poverty and instability, and exploring aid's role in promoting human rights, good governance and preventing conflict.

That exploration leads into the third trend, evident since 1990: the gradual integration of aid, development cooperation and foreign policy by many donor countries. Emergency aid and long-term development had been seen as separate, or at best chronologically linked, activities, and competitors for resources. In recent years, a fundamental shift has begun: relief, peacekeeping, prevention, development, participation of civil society and governance are being seen as simultaneous, necessary elements of successful strategies.

The progress of these trends together imply the transformation of international assistance and its agents. Both non-governmental organizations (NGOs) and the

---

Box 6.1 A user's guide to the who, what and why of today's aid

What is aid? Official development assistance (ODA) counts towards the UN target of 0.7 per cent of an industrialized country's GNP being spent on overseas aid to an agreed list of developing countries. Most former Soviet bloc countries are not on the UN developing country list, except for former Yugoslavia and the Central Asian republics. ODA must be given by a government, be concessional – if it is a loan, at least 25 per cent must be as a grant – and have economic development or welfare as its main objective.

Who gives aid? Most "official" aid is given by the 21 members of OECD's DAC: Australia, Austria, Belgium, Canada, Denmark, Finland, France, Germany, Ireland, Italy, Japan, Luxembourg, Netherlands, New Zealand, Norway, Portugal, Spain, Sweden, Switzerland, United Kingdom, United States. Official aid is also given by Arab donors and other countries, including the Republic of Korea, Thailand, Singapore, Malaysia and Taiwan. Unofficial aid includes public donations through NGOs.

What does DAC do? DAC brings OECD donors together and aims to increase the quantity and quality of resources going to developing countries. DAC monitors aid through published Aid Reviews conducted with each donor every two years, an annual report on development cooperation and an analysis of financial flows to aid recipients.

What is the difference between bilateral and multilateral aid? Governments give bilateral aid to a developing country either directly (government to government) or through an institution (such as an NGO). They give multilateral aid through international bodies, such as the EU, World Bank or UN agencies. Some multilateral aid is given voluntarily but other multilateral commitments, for instance member state contributions to the EU budget, are obligatory and based on a pre-agreed formula.

What is humanitarian aid? This usually means emergency relief and rehabilitation in natural disasters or conflicts. More strictly, "humanitarian" describes how aid is given, using principles of neutrality (taking no side in conflict) and impartiality (based solely on need).

How is aid measured? By volume and as a percentage of donor GNP. This follows the principle that states should give according to their wealth and allows easier comparison between nations and against the UN 0.7 per cent target. Aid amounts are often put in "real terms", taking account of inflation and exchange rates to allow like-with-like comparisons over time.

aid administrators of member nations of the Organisation for Economic Co-operation and Development (OECD) are under pressure to make a visible

Box 6.2 Guidelines on conflict, peace and development cooperation

To improve donors' development efforts, the OECD Development Assistance Committee (DAC) issued a policy statement in May 1997 to provide "Guidelines on Conflict, Peace and Development Cooperation on the threshold of the 21st Century".

The key points include basic principles:

■ The basis for sustainable development must be to help a society strengthen its capacity to manage conflict without violence.

■ Humanitarian assistance is not a substitute for sustained political commitment in support of peace. This commitment requires the application of all instruments open to the international community – economic, social, legal, environmental and military. Coordinated coherent responses between governments, inter- and non-governmental bodies are also necessary.

■ Developing countries, even in crisis, are responsible for their own development, and the task of international assistance is to strengthen indigenous capacities.

■ Development cooperation should seek structural stability embracing social peace, human rights, accountable military forces and broadly shared social and economic development, supported by dynamic and representative political structures.

■ Development assistance should seek to address the root causes of conflict.

■ Development cooperation should recognize the important role played by women.

The primary objective of development cooperation is to enhance the rule of law and promote popular participation, but specific roles are assigned for different stages of a conflict:

■ Before conflict flares, the emphasis is on promoting democratic stability, including attention to arms and military expenditure.

■ In open conflict, development agencies should seize opportunities to contribute to conflict resolution, and plan and prepare for post-conflict reconstruction as well as providing short-term emergency relief.

■ In fragile transitional situations, the emphasis should be on saving livelihoods, increasing incentives for peace and promoting reconciliation.

■ After conflict, restoring a sense of security is paramount, including restoring legitimate government institutions, encouraging sound macro-economic stabilization plans and taking advantage of opportunities for reform – for instance for participatory debate about the role of the military.

The ten key actions for development cooperation are:

■ To recognize structural stability as a foundation for sustainable development and advance public understanding of conflict prevention.

■ To strengthen analysis of risks and causes of violent conflict and opportunities for aid to address root causes.

■ To ensure that all policies, including security, political and economic relations, human rights, environment and development cooperation, are fostering structural stability, including support for cease-fires, UN arms embargoes, working to prevent illegal arms supplies and harmonized and responsible behaviour with respect to the supply of military goods, particularly small arms.

■ To strive for greater coherence and transparency by the international community: linking early warning to decision making; coordinating actions; sharing analysis, and agreeing strategic frameworks and responsibility for leadership in coordination.

■ To support regional initiatives for conflict prevention.

■ To reduce budgetary and functional barriers between relief, rehabilitation and development cooperation; reform of the social and economic sectors of the UN system to strengthen synergies in international responses.

■ To work for internationally agreed performance standards and principles to govern operational methods of all implementing agencies.

■ To set up responsive but accountable procedures for resource mobilization, including capacity for crisis management, crisis resolution and ensuring that assistance does not prolong conflict.

■ To promote open and participatory dialogue and strengthened capacity to meet security needs at reduced levels of military expenditure and strengthened capacity for the exercise of civil authority over military forces.

■ To monitor and evaluate performance in peace and conflict prevention and amplification of best practice.

impact on poverty in ways that contribute to broader goals, such as building civil society or promoting stability.

Donors want to achieve more with less. Official aid agencies are expected to pursue the donor's own priorities while ensuring sustainability by taking a participatory approach and stressing recipient responsibility. NGOs are expected to professionalize their work and be more accountable while retaining their flexibility, maintaining traditional values – be they neutrality and impartiality or justice and solidarity – and keeping in close touch with their grassroots supporters and partners in the North and South.

Christopher Black/
International Federation

Falling funds

Having peaked in 1992, global aid has fallen in real terms by 17 per cent in five years. In cash terms, aid in 1996 at $57.7 billion is the same as the 1992 cash figure. However, in real terms at 1995 prices, aid has declined over the period by $11.5 billion, from almost $68 billion to $56.4 billion, according to OECD Development Assistance Committee (DAC) statistics. And $11.5 billion is more than the 1996 spending of either Japan or the USA, the world's largest donors. Excluding bilateral food aid, it is twice as much as all donors spent in 1995 on emergency aid – bilateral and multilateral – and refugee assistance.

Having held steady at under half the United Nations (UN) target of 0.7 per cent of gross national product (GNP) for more than 20 years, aid as a share of donors' wealth fell from 0.33 per cent of GNP in 1992, to 0.30 per cent in 1994, 0.27 per cent in 1995, and 0.25 per cent in 1996, its lowest level ever. Between 1994 and 1995, aid from the world's biggest provider of relief, the USA, fell by a quarter. Italian aid fell over 40 per cent. In 1996 aid from Japan declined by almost a quarter. Australia, Austria, Canada, France and Portugal also registered double-digit declines.

Denmark, Norway and Sweden still exceed the UN target. But in June 1997, Japan announced a 10 per cent cut for fiscal year 1998, with further unspecified cuts in the following two years. This knocks around a billion dollars off global aid for 1998, with little prospect of compensating increases among other major donors. If aid budgets went into free fall (a possibility about which the aid community has preferred not to speculate), it seems likely that what remained would mainly go to an unavoidable minimum of emergency relief.

Globalization is transforming the context of aid. Annual private flows to developing countries have mushroomed over the last decade. At $234 billion they are now four times official development assistance (ODA). But these flows are not a substitute for aid. They are heavily concentrated on a few bright investment prospects in the developing world and private investment is not focused on basic human needs or the countries worst affected by complex emergencies.

However, private sector companies are taking an expanding role in the management and delivery of relief, and there are some signs of increased dialogue between the private sector, NGOs and official aid agencies on the role of the corporate sector in development.

With the growing strength of ethical consumerism at home and the corporate need for a stable environment in which to operate abroad - from mining in Africa to manufacturing in Asia or retail sales in Latin America - the private sector is recognizing the role of aid agencies. Companies are increasingly sympathetic to the idea that actions to reduce poverty, instability and human rights abuses are not beyond their remit, but issues which, in the interests of good corporate citizenship and sustainable profits, cannot be ignored.

An increasing number of multinationals are accepting wider responsibilities for workforce and community welfare. Where once aid agencies worked alone or alongside governments, the private sector has the potential to become an increasingly important and dynamic partner.

In reaction to both unleashed conflicts and new intervention opportunities, bilateral spending by DAC donors on emergency aid increased dramatically following the end of the Cold War, to peak in 1994 at around $3.5 billion dollars or 8.4 per cent of bilateral aid. In 1995, spending was just over $3 billion, at 7.5

Box 6.3 Making sense of millions when the financial figures don't add up

The most useful standardized information on humanitarian aid spending is found in two sources: the database of the OECD's DAC, and the complex emergencies financial tracking database from the ReliefWeb of the UN Department of Humanitarian Affairs (DHA). However, they are not very compatible, and there are major differences between them and donors in the way that they categorize and report aid.

The DAC database is used for international comparisons and its annual *Development Cooperation Report* includes recognized data on development assistance. But the modest data included on humanitarian aid expenditures are difficult to interpret since they rarely match the figures from individual countries. Among the methodological differences are:

■ DAC figures include assistance to refugees in donor countries for their first year of stay. These figures became significant – $1 billion in each of 1992, 1993 and 1994 – as people from former Yugoslavia sought refuge in DAC member countries. These costs are not normally shown in the humanitarian aid budget of the donor country.

■ DAC figures do not include aid to Central and Eastern Europe or the former Soviet Union in the same frame as developing countries. Some donors, such as Belgium, Denmark, Finland, France and Ireland, often report and manage their humanitarian assistance globally; others, like the Netherlands, have a discreet budget line for non-developing countries.

■ DAC reports do not distinguish between emergency food aid and structural food assistance, underestimating the total humanitarian assistance provided.

EU member states have agreed to provide humanitarian aid funding data to both DHA and ECHO in a standard 14-point format. The core objective is to capture all humanitarian contributions regardless of which government department is responsible for them. However, these statistics are not compatible with the DAC reporting.

As well as compatibility, it is difficult to get a clear picture of the volume and distribution of humanitarian aid spending. Responsibility for humanitarian aid is dispersed across government departments – most commonly defence, development cooperation and foreign affairs – and definitions of "humanitarian aid" are increasingly complex and ambiguous:

■ Some states, such as the UK, Netherlands and Denmark, are preparing clearer humanitarian aid policies and creating new departments and budget lines, but classification of activities, from human rights support to genocide-related legal services, remain vague and inconsistent.

■ Mandates for humanitarian assistance and long-term development cooperation overlap.

■ Donors do not always identify how much of their multilateral funds go to humanitarian aid.

■ Donors differ in their classification of peacekeeping activities. Some EU countries have included these expenditures when reporting their humanitarian aid figures; others have not.

There is an evident need both for more coordination and standardization of reporting between DAC and DHA, and for a convention on what should be reported as humanitarian action.

This box is based on research for a comparative study on the humanitarian aid policies of EU countries by the Centre for Research on the Epidemiology of Disasters.

Figure 6.1 Emergency priorities I: Figures for bilateral spending for emergencies 1996 by DAC donors in millions of dollars show that the EU has overtaken the United States as the largest provider of disaster and conflict relief. In this league table, the EU and US together provide almost half of all DAC emergency spending.
Source: OECD/DAC

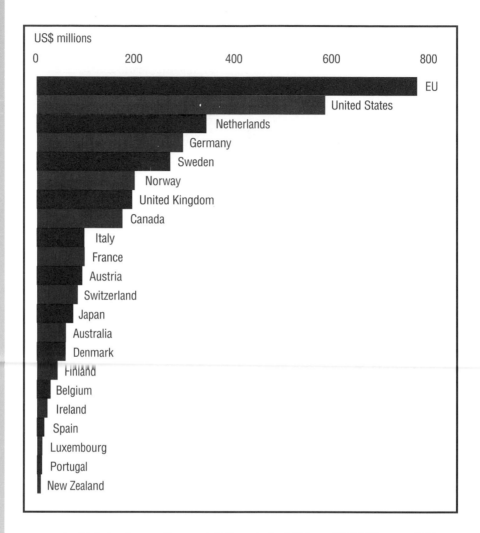

per cent of bilateral spending, and fell again in 1996 to $2.7 billion or 6.94 per cent.

While emergency aid spending – in the narrow sense of food, tents and medicines – may have peaked, there is strong donor interest in funding activities which they believe will reinforce civil society and prevent instability, such as governance and promoting human rights.

In volume, the United States and the European Union (EU) are the largest emergency aid providers. As a percentage of bilateral assistance, Sweden, Norway and Austria head the table, spending over one-fifth of bilateral aid on relief. In 1996, Japan spent just 0.88 per cent of bilateral aid to emergencies, while France, another big donor, devoted only 1.67 per cent.

Distribution of humanitarian assistance is heavily skewed. Three emergencies in the northern hemisphere – former Yugoslavia, Haiti, Iraq – took almost 60 per cent of 1995 bilateral emergency spending, while the rest went to 17 countries, principally in Africa. Bilateral spending on each affected person in Haiti and the

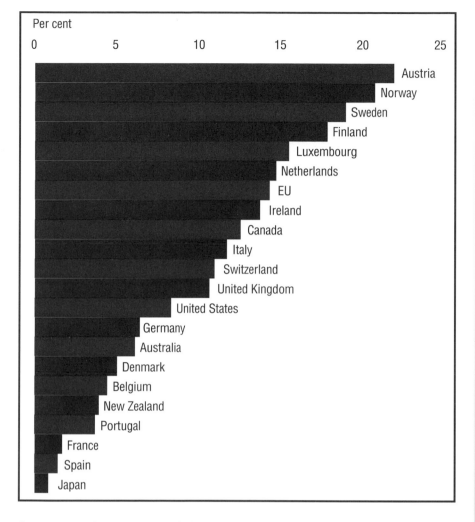

Figure 6.2
*Emergency
priorities II: The
percentage of
bilateral
assistance
allocated to
emergencies
among DAC
members in 1996
varies from
Japan, the
world's largest
aid donor, which
gives less than 1
per cent to relief,
and countries
such as Austria,
Sweden and
Norway, which
devote around
one-fifth to
disasters.*
Source: OECD/DAC

former Yugoslavia, at around $200, was roughly twice that in other affected countries.

The aid squeeze adds impetus to the search for new sources of assistance. In 1997 the DAC and non-OECD-donors met to exchange development cooperation ideas. In a later UK parliamentary debate, the chair of its new International Development Committee noted that emergencies had cut into development aid and suggested Gulf states could contribute more emergency assistance.

Other factors can affect budgets. The DAC, for example, agreed that initial support costs for would-be refugees in donor countries could be met from aid budgets. This has made it possible to save almost 3 billion dollars over three years from home affairs budgets.

Most countries only charge the incremental costs of military resources used in relief to the aid budget, but a lack of transparency in these and other transactions does not help the already poor information on emergency aid spending, which matches the inadequate knowledge of disaster costs. A lack of data undermines the case of those urging greater investment in disaster prevention.

*Figure 6.3
Peak passed I:
Emergency
spending by DAC
donors in billions
of dollars in the
1980s and 1990s
showed a steep
rise, reflecting the
instability
following the end
of the Cold War
and an appetite for
intervention in
crises
increasingly
brought to the
notice of Northern
publics by
globalized
communications.
The peak of
spending appears
to have passed.*

Source: OECD/DAC

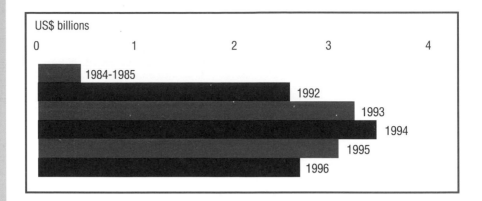

Measuring impact

Concern over ODA's decline has been an important factor behind DAC attempts to refocus aid and demonstrate its effectiveness. In 1996 OECD ministers endorsed a new strategy, *Shaping the 21st Century: the Contribution of Development Cooperation.* This new vision for aid outlines development's role in avoiding a future of conflict, chaos and poverty by aiming to create a stable global order in which people have secure, productive lives.

In summary, its targets – most for 2015, some earlier – are:

■ at least halving the proportion of people living in extreme poverty;

■ universal primary education in all countries;

■ eliminating primary and secondary education gender disparity;

■ reducing under-five death rate by two-thirds of 1990 levels;

■ cutting maternal mortality by three-quarters;

■ access for all to safe and reliable family planning;

■ national sustainable development strategies; and

■ reversing current trends of environmental resource losses.

Shaping the 21st Century features prominently in many donors' aid policy documents, from Japan's 1996 Ministry of Foreign Affairs aid report to the 1997 UK International Development White Paper, and its targets reflect donor concerns. One is that too much has been expected from aid resources, which are modest in relation to the scale of absolute poverty. Politicians and the media sometimes seem to suggest that aid has failed because more than a billion people remain in poverty and many states need emergency relief.

Identifying ambitious but specific targets to which aid is expected to contribute – but not tackle alone – may scale down unrealistic expectations and help galvanize support by offering precise and achievable aims. The idea that backing for aid will be enhanced if targets are clear and address basic human needs highlights an important point about the limits of Northern public support for aid. Opinion polls show that most support is altruistic not self-interested but is restricted in scope, responding best to short-term, basic human needs, such as food, water and medical care.

Official aid's origins can be traced back to international relief efforts after this century's major conflicts. Many aid agencies were inspired by crisis, such as the International Red Cross and Red Crescent Movement at the 19th century battle of Solferino, Save the Children Fund after World War I, and Oxfam and Care during and after World War II.

In the public mind, aid is still about acute human needs. This may be cause or effect, since most public exposure to aid is through television coverage of emergency response and disaster-related charity advertising. Aid agencies have always tapped a public impulse to do something immediate about human suffering, though this may hamper efforts to build constituencies to support long-term development work.

Aid's higher profile in the 1990s, principally because of the series of human emergencies, has offered new opportunities to engage the public. As Live Aid

---

Box 6.4 New coalitions for disaster recovery

It is hopefully not too optimistic to believe that there is a growing understanding that disaster hazards have a significant effect on the conduct of business as well as the well-being of societies. Whether the concern is designated as business continuity or risk management practice, it has become a more evident management responsibility being practised by the chief executives of both corporate and public sector enterprises.

This is partly based on the fact that there has been an increase in the frequency of emergency conditions and the severity of resulting disasters which adversely affect the environments on which modern societies must depend. Costs and consequences have soared. In its annual summary of events for 1997, Munich Re-insurance noted that the number of natural disasters was three times higher worldwide in the past ten years than in the 1960s. Economic losses are eight times greater, generally exceeding $60 billion a year. With this amount of money involved, there is a growing global recognition of the possibility, indeed the necessity, to move disaster perceptions beyond urgent responses to an event. Prevention becomes possible.

The costs, and the complexities of the tasks involved, in mitigating the effects of disasters also limit what any single entity can do. There has thus been an increase in public-private partnerships to share the burden of greater levels of protection and to provide resources necessary to ensure a safer society.

One such affiliation of leading executives dedicated to increase public hazard awareness, and risk management practice for greater disaster reduction is the Leadership Coalition for Global Business Protection. This effort, first spearheaded by IBM Business Recovery Services and the UN International Decade for Natural Disaster Reduction secretariat, has brought together leaders drawn from industry, public policy administration, the insurance sector, international organizations including the International Federation, and other professional interests committed to joint efforts for the protection of economic assets and social resources. This coalition is a global task force founded in 1996 to secure public and private sector assistance with the preparation for, prevention of, and recovery from human, economic and physical losses associated with unavoidable natural and man-made disasters worldwide.

By outlining requirements for responsible, comprehensive disaster planning and management for leaders, the coalition hopes to make these issues more evident among decision makers around the world. Through collaborative efforts unified standards for risk management, response and recovery initiatives, and management processes for protection may become more readily adopted by the leaders in business and government. The Leadership Coalition is striving to develop global guidelines, management standards and best practices for disaster recovery, and to encourage public and private sector cooperation and strengthened partnerships in disaster planning and management.

In the public as well as the commercial sector, disasters are clearly moving beyond a focus of responding to singular events, and are becoming integrated into the realm of expected leadership responsibilities, essential for the well-being of our societies. As economic assets grow, and social resources are nurtured, there must be an equal responsibility for our societies to protect them.

Figure 6.4
Peak passed II:
The rising
percentage of
bilateral aid
allocated to
emergencies by
DAC donors in the
1980s and 1990s –
up four-fold from
around 2 per cent
– squeezed
spending on long
term development.
The percentage
has now fallen
back from its peak.
Source: OECD/DAC

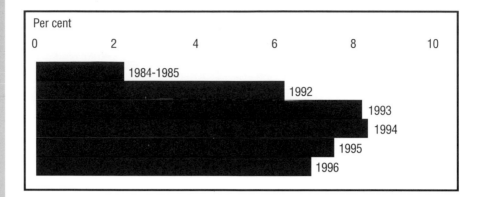

showed, emergency response can be a catalyst if used to create a greater commitment to development cooperation and poverty reduction. But as emergency response becomes ever more complex and political, the challenge to relief agencies is to explain new uses of aid in a way that retains public support. As NGOs found in the Great Lakes crisis in late 1996, this is a difficult task.

The empathetic response to emergencies has led to an interesting trend involving the practical engagement of Northern citizens. Many countries have seen "direct aid" initiatives to former Yugoslavia, in which communities take food, clothes and equipment directly to the country concerned. Sometimes this has been linked to community support for refugees.

In Italy this has developed beyond individual initiatives into a programme known as *"Tavolo de Coordinamento",* with contacts between towns, schools, companies and sporting groups. A significant amount of Italian aid is now given through municipalities, many of which have been twinned with Bosnian cities.

The DAC's 1996 *Development Cooperation Review* reported that Italian assistance to Bosnia "emphasised people, social relations and local institutions, not simply the logistics of delivering supplies.... It draws deeply on the moral resources and organizational talents of Italian regions and cities, voluntary organizations and NGOs.... The Italian approach to emergency and reconstruction efforts in conflict zones demonstrates the importance of going beyond material assistance to the 'reconnection of the social tissue'."

One agenda

Ironically, as aid becomes less important economically – in volume and in comparison with GNP, trade and foreign direct investment – a major trend of this decade has been the integration of aid and development cooperation policy into the mainstream of international political relations. While in the 1970s the Brandt Report's interdependence message created little interest outside the aid lobby, the impact of globalization is today a key government preoccupation.

Since 1990, UN summits have highlighted a range of global challenges, from environment to population. Aid is now expected to have a significant role to play in responding to the diverse challenges of globalization, from helping poor countries to integrate in a globalized economy to reducing the threat to the global environment.

A decade ago, most politicians did not see links between security – at that time a military concept – and aid. Somalia and Haiti demonstrated the connections between poverty, fragile civil society and instability. Using aid to address acute need and prevent conflict by promoting participation in society has become a key theme in the foreign policy reviews by OECD countries, such as Canada and the Netherlands.

Humanitarian assistance, peacekeeping, conflict resolution, preventive diplomacy and other efforts to bring stability and security cut across different government departments. Diplomats, soldiers and aid staff work side by side in the field. Donors' foreign affairs, defence and development cooperation departments increasingly share agendas.

Emergency roles today involve many ministries, some with few past links with developing countries. US sources of assistance, for example, include the Agency for International Development's (USAID) Office of Foreign Disaster Assistance; the State Department's Bureau of Population, Refugees and Migration; and the agriculture and defence departments.

Within aid administrations, distinctions between relief and development have blurred. Ideas of timelines spanning relief to sustainable development do not stand up, and donors find themselves taking actions which can simultaneously be concerned with relief, prevention, rehabilitation, development, civil society and democratization. Classifying aid spending, procedures and activity into either relief or development is crude.

The relief agenda is also widening, taking in social development issues. USAID's report *Providing Humanitarian Assistance and Aid Post Crisis Transition* lists the "main challenges" as prevention, building local capacity, and institutions of civil governance and democracy. The US focuses on partnership programmes with Southern NGOs and civil society to empower local communities to contribute to rehabilitation and recovery.

Many donors, such as Belgium, are placing increased emphasis on conflict prevention, strengthening democratic institutions and restoring confidence in civil society. There are also widespread new initiatives on human rights and democracy, including a new Irish budget line, new specialized departments in the Norwegian and Dutch aid administrations and a Conflict Policy Unit in the UK providing advice on conflict reduction.

Gender is a very visible "social development" issue on the emergency agenda. In 1996, the EU Development Council passed a resolution on "Gender and crisis prevention, emergency operations and rehabilitation"; Italy has a special focus on displaced women; and there have been Dutch initiatives on gender, conflict, war victim rehabilitation and women in peacebuilding. The DAC *Guidelines on Conflict, Peace and Development Cooperation* stress the special needs of women and the importance of women's empowerment in conflict resolution.

Even as the agenda widens, policy integration brings a focus on coherence, which in turn reinforces the pressures for performance. Operational procedures and management structures are starting to recognize that integrated disaster response is more effective. Japan began a rehabilitation and development programme in 1996, Germany has an extra budget line integrating emergency aid, food aid and refugee support, and new EU task forces enable crisis interventions to flow into rehabilitation and development.

At the broader policy level, incoherence still reduces the impact and credibility of aid and may even prolong complex emergencies. Belgian NGOs reported that conflict prevention has been frustrated by the actions of other ministries, including export credit guarantees for weapons and construction of an arms plant in Kenya.

In *Shaping the 21st Century,* donors explicitly accepted responsibility for "supporting coherent policies...including consistency in policies affecting human rights and the risks of violent conflicts". Easier said than done. Sweden is a major provider of emergency aid, both in absolute terms – $269 million in 1996 – and as a proportion of its bilateral aid – 19.28 per cent. It is also the twelfth largest arms exporter with the world's seventh largest military industry. NGOs report that "exceptions" occur despite adoption of strict legal rules.

The 1997 DAC policy statement on conflict, peace and development refers explicitly to arms exports, noting the need for "harmonised and responsible behaviour with respect to the supply of military goods" to "prevent illegal arms supplies from fuelling conflicts".

Aid and trade

In a globalized world, donors who want to make an impact on sustainable development have recognized the need for coherence between aid and trade policies. In the same way, relief interventions and political engagement are seen as inextricably linked. Experience in complex emergencies has helped to reinforce the donor trend towards post-Cold War integration of foreign policy and development cooperation. Aid strategies have to incorporate political response, diplomacy, emergency relief and development.

Belgium saw field diplomacy opportunities held back because they were outside the development cooperation ministry's mandate. Now there are proposals for a single ministry integrating foreign policy and development to allow a more coherent approach to conflict resolution. In the Netherlands, the "de-partitioning" principle governs foreign policy, defence and development cooperation.

In the UK, while development cooperation has been given its own ministry, foreign policy must take ethical considerations into account. Canada is pursuing an activist and values-based foreign policy, which includes efforts to ban anti-personnel landmines, supporting human rights and peacekeeping.

These changes reflect increasing donor preoccupation with the search for political solutions to complex emergencies. It is less clear how much aid management is affected. The European Community Humanitarian Office (ECHO) – the second largest donor of emergency assistance in the world – takes a strongly apolitical line and emphasizes management, efficiency and procedure, not broader political engagement.

For many countries, the Red Cross and Red Crescent and NGOs have become the major channels for emergency assistance. They are engaged not only in spending emergency funds, but in policy dialogue, public awareness and conflict resolution. NGOs have been seen as offering a positive advantage over states, able to bypass government structures and work directly with affected populations. Within Southern countries there has been a massive growth in NGO numbers, sometimes directly as a result of aid flows during emergencies and the need for local agents for long-term change.

But as concern over the political dimension grows, the role of NGOs becomes more problematic. Not only do NGOs worry about their independence, but integrating aid into political or military strategies destroys any humanitarian –

neutral and impartial – character, and may well undermine the credibility of agencies motivated by solidarity or justice.

From a government perspective, there is a dilemma over how far non-state actors, who are nonetheless often substantially state-funded, will be allowed to go. Humanitarian assistance by national NGOs in the politically charged context of a complex humanitarian emergency can prompt or shape government foreign policy.

A study of Norwegian aid in the Horn of Africa examined the country's role in the two main regional issues: Eritrea's secession from Ethiopia and Sudan's conflict. The study concluded: "The main reason why Norway became politically involved in these conflict areas was not basic policy considerations or an assessment of the importance of the issues, but mainly because of the fact that Norwegian NGOs were working there."

Having got involved, almost by chance, governments may find themselves influencing political outcomes: "The map had been changed with Norwegian support, but not as a result of deliberate long-term policies and without being followed up with either business investment or aid." One implication is that NGOs risk breaking their *Code of Conduct,* which demands that "NGOs shall endeavour not to act as instruments of government foreign policy".

Often partisan in the focus of their knowledge and engagement on particular groups or geographical areas, NGO ideologies and values differ. In these circumstances how much can governments prioritizing political solutions help NGOs deliver humanitarian aid? These problems would suggest that the levels of aid going through NGO channels may decline.

Performance pressures

Governments looking for maximum political impact may seek other partners who offer increased understanding of the context, but from a more neutral – or flexible – perspective, such as companies, or could begin to offer greater support to those NGOs willing to be service providers, such as new institutions in the South.

The three trends identified – falling funds, performance pressures, political integration – are already well established and the most recent evidence suggests they are gathering pace. It might have been possible for the aid community to resist or adapt to any one of these factors without fundamental change, but together they pose a substantial challenge to the structure and systems of those working at the front line of both relief and development.

As those trends combine into a demand from donors for low-cost, high-quality, integrated assistance with multiplier impact, many agencies are looking to secure at least a measure of independence – to preserve their neutrality and impartiality, or to ensure they can still act with solidarity to pursue justice – by reaffirming their fundamental responsibility to beneficiaries.

Whether this is successful or not, the trends identified still leave at least three questions to be explored as aid is transformed: What can aid do best, such as enhancing human and institutional capacities to avert future catastrophes; how can it do it better, by working catalytically within the new economic and political context; and who will do it in the future?

Are the rapidly growing numbers of Southern NGOs, for example, able to meet the developmental and emergency needs on their doorsteps if given sufficient funding, and if so, what role is left for Northern NGOs? There is, as yet, no consensus on how best to mix the respective capacities of donors, recipient countries, the private sector, NGOs in the North and in the South, and multilateral agencies to assist states affected by complex emergencies.

Chapter 6 Sources, references and further information

ICVA/EUROSTEP. *The Reality of Aid.* London: Earthscan (published annually).

ODI. *Disasters.* Quarterly journal. London: Blackwells.

OECD/DAC *Shaping the 21st Century, The Contribution of Development Cooperation.* Paris: OECD, May 1996.

OECD/DAC. *Guidelines on Conflict, Peace and Development Cooperation on the Threshold of the 21st Century.* Paris: OECD, 1997.

OECD/DAC. *Development Cooperation Review Series.* No 16, Italy. Paris: OECD, 1996.

OECD/DAC. *Geographical Distribution of Financial Flows to Aid Recipients 1991-1995.* Paris: OECD/DAC, 1996.

OECD/DAC. *Development Cooperation.* Annual report. Paris: OECD/DAC.

Overseas Development Institute (ODI). *The Relief and Rehabilitation Network produces three different series of publications: Good Practice Reviews, Network Papers and Newsletters.* Contact: Portland House, Stag Place, London SWIE 5DP, UK.

USAID. *Providing Humanitarian Assistance and Aid Post Crisis Transition.* Washington: USAID.

Web sites

ECHO: http://europa.eu.int/en/comm/echo/stats/home.htm

Humanitarianism and War Project,: http://www.brown.edu/Departments/Watson_Institute/H_W/H_W_ms.shtml

ODI: http://www.oneworld.org/odi/rrn/

OECD/DAC: http://www.oecd.org/dac

Refugee Participation Network, Refugee Studies Programme: http://www.qeh.ox.ac.uk/rsp/

UNDHA   ReliefWeb: http://www.reliefweb.int/fts/index.html

Chapter

7 Rebuilding Sarajevo with more than bricks

War-time graffiti on one building offers the greeting, "Welcome to Hell". Another echoes: "Paradise Lost". The paint may be peeling, but Sarajevo is a city still in shock, struggling to recover from a war which devastated its economy, brought

*Figure 7.1
Employment –
percentage of
workforce.
While many
more people
have jobs, and
that proportion
is expected to
rise, the levels
of
unemployment
still mean great
poverty,
deprivation and
vulnerability; all
factors for
anger and
resentment to
continue.*
Source: Donor
community
estimates.

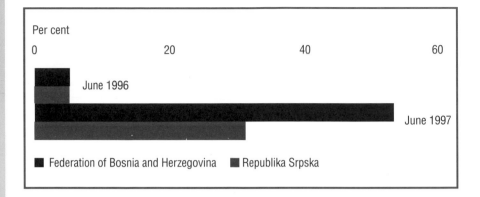

mass populations shifts, and destroyed homes, schools, factories and much more.

It was a city under siege for nearly four years – from April 1992 until December 1995's Dayton agreement – when every foray for food, water or firewood risked a sniper bullet or exploding shell. Public transport was destroyed, telecommunications were cut and homes became heaps of rubble.

In Sarajevo today it is easier to ask "What survived?" than "What was destroyed?". Rebuilding the city has thrown up issues of assistance well beyond bricks and mortar, and presents a massive challenge for international agencies. Among the problems facing the city and humanitarian organizations are.

■ Welfare social services may be unaffordable for years, leaving thousands vulnerable. Tackling that, however, will be hard, since international aid agencies have their limits, both in principle – how far and for how long should they replace the state? – and in practice, as aid funding is falling fast.

■ Dayton integrated aid, its agencies and its staff as the tools of politics, undermining their neutrality and risking their security if conflict resumes. Meanwhile, inter-agency competition has damaged effectiveness and local confidence.

■ Agencies have two problems with unsustainable aid. Their operations must be systematically handed over to local staff and organizations, not abandoned when money runs out or fighting resumes, and an exit strategy is needed to avoid a shock for the aid-fuelled economic boom.

■ Pressure on refugees to return will squeeze city jobs, housing and more, while prompting resentment from those who stayed. New business-linked strategies are needed, as are sensitivities to help a city of old hatreds and new divisions.

■ Legal issues regarding house ownership have seriously delayed post-war rehabilitation and refugee return. This reflects the problem of not only recovering from war, but at the same time converting from a socialist command economy to a market economy.

The war certainly caused massive dislocation. Most of Sarajevo's substantial pre-war Serb minority has left and the population of the city, once famous for its multi-ethnic mix, is now predominantly Bosniak (Bosnian Muslim), a community with its own divisions. Even the language has changed, replacing Serbo-Croat with the trio of Bosnian, Croatian and Serbian.

In some respects, however, Sarajevo has emerged from war a far more powerful and unified city. It is the seat of many administrative centres in the complex layers of government established under the Dayton agreement, which created one country comprised of two entities: the Federation of Bosnia and Herzegovina, and Republika Srpska. Sarajevo is both the capital of the Bosnian Federation and of the state of Bosnia and Herzegovina, as well as being one of the Federation's ten cantons.

Sarajevo canton has largely escaped inter-ethnic violence seen elsewhere since the end of the war. Sarajevo is ethnically homogeneous in comparison with other areas, and the police force is unified and subordinated to cantonal authorities.

Despite this, many Sarajevans are nostalgic for their ethnically-open pre-war city. Hatred has poisoned ethnic relations, while many Bosniaks from war-ravaged villages have moved into houses and apartments abandoned by those who left during the conflict. The city planning institute estimates that about one-third of the population are people displaced by fighting, and there is tension between "old Sarajevans" and "new Sarajevans".

The former typically perceive the latter as uncultured country people. A young student sums up the attitude: "These are people who are seeing trams for the first time. How do you explain to them that the first door is for entering and that the second is for exiting? It would be like trying to teach me how to use a horse and plough. It's not their fault; it's just that we don't want to mix with them. Perhaps that's our mistake."

Both sides are fearful; one that the city's culture will change, the other of discrimination. The divide between old and new Sarajevans is like two cities living in one space.

Having begun work at different stages of the war and peace, the International Federation of Red Cross and Red Crescent Societies and the International Committee of the Red Cross (ICRC) today have headquarters in Sarajevo for

---

Box 7.1 Patchy support for moves to remove the menace of mines

Like the ring of troops at the height of fighting, some maps show Sarajevo encircled with red dots – guidance for de-miners tackling one of the war's worst legacies.

The United Nations Mine Action Centre (UNMAC) estimates that one million landmines litter the countryside, and the ICRC says landmines injure or kill 50 to 80 people a month in Bosnia and Herzegovina. Many are children or farm workers.

UNMAC's David Bax says: "Kabul has a mines problem ten times worse than Sarajevo, but Sarajevo is an unusual situation for a first world city. You have mines planted in urban high-rise areas, in grassy patches among the concrete paving stones. Refugees are moving into buildings before they have been de-mined. They throw piles of garbage out of the windows which makes it hard to detect the mines.

"Many humanitarian organizations don't think about de-mining, but it's what they should think about

first. They come to us at the last minute and ask for help but no one has even thought about setting money aside."

Mine clearing is expensive but international support has been patchy. In Bosnia and Herzegovina, 500 sq km may be mined. UNMAC alone wants $40 million but donors have pledged only $8 million.

Tasks are divided. UNMAC handles what is seen as the humanitarian mine clearance; the military clear full-scale minefields. Politics slow the process. Ethnically-based mine teams work where their armies once controlled. Negotiating access to mined areas takes time and post-war profiteering has driven up costs.

An International Crisis Group report says that disorganized mine-laying and unreliable records mean that as of July 1997 less than 1 per cent of Bosnia could confidently be called cleared.

---

countrywide operations. Both work in cooperation with Red Cross branches, which continued relief efforts throughout the conflict, despite the destruction of their National Society.

© Christopher Black

During the war, humanitarian rules were flouted and the Red Cross and Red Crescent symbols misused. The ICRC is promoting international humanitarian law among soldiers and disseminating humanitarian principles through a programme called "Human Values". It is also warning of the dangers of the estimated one million landmines and unexploded ordnance littering the country, monitoring the release of people detained in connection with the conflict and tracing the missing.

The ICRC worked with the local Red Cross during the war to establish soup kitchens and provide the city with clothes, blankets and medical supplies. At the height of the fighting, Sarajevo Red Cross kitchens fed up to 20,000 people. In post-war Sarajevo feeding continues for 9,000 of the most needy, a figure unlikely to fall as chronic poverty – especially among the elderly, disabled people and orphans – becomes a feature of the city.

The International Federation is supporting local Red Cross home care and mobile technical teams throughout the country. These visit elderly and disabled people living alone to help with chores and repairs – from chopping wood to patching roofs – and refer them to medical clinics for glasses, walking sticks or dentures. The isolated are offered social activities.

The Red Cross dramatically increased its public profile during the war. Thousands queued to give blood or become volunteers. Just as local Red Cross branches faced the immense challenge of working in war, however, the National Society came under intense pressure. Vehicles and supplies were stolen, its main building was destroyed, and some Red Cross structures began to organize themselves along ethnic lines.

As well as practical help to resume work with vehicles and equipment, since the end of the war the International Federation has helped Red Cross organizations tackle this disunity. Structures now exist for both the Red Cross of Republika Srpska and the Red Cross of the Federation of Bosnia and Herzegovina. Ultimately, it is hoped that these will unite in one National Society for Bosnia and Herzegovina.

Competitive aid

The international community says more than US$ 5 billion in foreign aid is needed for reconstruction efforts in Bosnia and Herzegovina; just over $3 billion has been pledged since the Dayton peace deal.

Dayton ensured that politics and aid are intertwined. Most international organizations have a link, direct or indirect, to the agreement, which assigned lead role in coordinating its civilian aspects to the Office of the High Representative (OHR). Although the International Federation operates under its own, independent principles, the donors' conference tied pledges to Dayton's fulfilment. In 1996, Republika Srpska received only two per cent of the $1 billion pledged for the country because it failed to comply with the agreement.

Sarajevo and the Federation entity as a whole have been aid's chief beneficiaries, but even here the political ties have bred an uneasy relationship between international agencies and the people they are trying to help. There is a lack of trust, linked to local negative perceptions of Dayton as an internationally dictated and enforced peace, and thus that aid workers are not neutral. If security deteriorates, this could make agency staff targets for violence.

Peacekeeping troops put an end to fighting, giving aid staff a secure environment and encouraging the usual flood of agencies seen after major disasters. The International Council of Voluntary Agencies found that by August 1997 there were 200 international non-governmental organizations (NGOs), 62 UN, government and international organizations, and 130 national NGOs registered in Bosnia and Herzegovina. Most of them are located in Sarajevo, and it shows. In the city, thousands of people – one in eight residents – are foreigners, usually working for international organizations.

Reconstruction has focused on rebuilding infrastructure and emergency repairs. Though the destruction astonishes some visitors, residents comment on the city's remarkable face-lift. Some of the most successful reconstruction projects in Sarajevo have been carried out by the local authorities, with money from international organizations but without the direct involvement of those organizations in the actual repair work. Today, public transport runs, traffic lights work, window glass has replaced plastic sheeting, electricity is restored and the telephones ring. Water, though rationed as repairs continue, is available throughout the city.

Sarajevo is likely to emerge with a better water system than before the war. The same may be true of housing, one of the most politically volatile reconstruction sectors. When Dayton was agreed, the local parliament allowed people who had fled the war only a few weeks to return to reclaim property. Condemned as illegal by the international community, that legislation has spawned competing claims, pitting Sarajevans against their government and one another.

The situation has been complicated by communist-era laws allowing some who remained in Sarajevo during the war to occupy additional flats. The government and large businesses have also established control over a number of units. Returning Bosniaks report a reasonable success rate in securing housing, even if they fail to reclaim their pre-war apartment. Ethnic Serbs, Croats and other minorities still suffer discrimination.

Difficult transition

For political reasons, most post-war reconstruction has taken place in Sarajevo and other urban centres, which has led to increased population transfers from rural areas to towns and cities. Relief and social benefits are also probably biased to the urban centres thus encouraging further movements. Many people moved to towns and cities during the war for security reasons, and this will not be reversed with present policies.

Reconstruction means more than restoring basic infrastructure. A report by the European Commission and World Bank set more comprehensive goals: "1996 was a year for implementing quick impact emergency projects. In 1997 donors' assistance must move toward supporting sustainable investments and reforms." That transition is proving difficult.

Donor delays and claims of fraud slowed progress. More fundamentally, there is the economic legacy of communism. During the war, Sarajevo's once-thriving –

if somewhat outdated – industries ground to a halt as staff fled and machinery was stolen. OHR economists say Sarajevo's eager, well-educated and relatively cheap labour force is its current greatest asset, but suggest a serious lack of management expertise in the city. George Milder, of the OHR, said: "The problem lies in the old command economy mentality. In the old system you did not have to fight for working capital. Managers never before had to think about securing supplies and markets. Many of the factories have been repaired but they are sitting still."

Sarajevo's chamber of commerce and planning institute both want the city to shift from manufacturing to a service-based economy with foreign investment. Despite international guarantees for investors worried about a resumed war, the OHR estimates that less than $10 million in private investment funds has flowed into Bosnia. The chamber of commerce's Branka Tankovic reports few results from her organization's discussions with 2,500 potential foreign partners: "The political situation is not good for foreign investment."

Meanwhile, with much aid focused on economic and political reforms, less attention is paid to social support programmes. Aid programmes – for the isolated old, disabled people, traumatized children – cover a fraction of the need. Jobs created by an expanded economy won't reach them, while there will be many other pressures on state spending priorities, and aid agencies will be reluctant

---

Box 7.2 Migration, multi-ethnicity and protecting minorities

The offices of the Catholic Croat cardinal, Vinko Puljic, and the Muslim deputy reis, Ismet Efedjia Spahic, are divided by more than the river which splits the once multi-ethnic city of Sarajevo.

The deputy reis, the country's second highest Islamic religious leader, is a man who paid personally for the war. Shelling killed his wife and other family members. Yet he is determined to preach for forgiveness and reconciliation.

"There is enough room for all people; Bosniaks will extend their hands to help those here. We want to build a new home jointly. That home is Bosnia. I won't say that there aren't cases against Croat people and other ethnic minorities, but Islam does not allow this: we have managed to preserve the soul of the city."

Reconciliation is hard: Bosniaks and Croats are faced with a crisis which they have to overcome. War memories are fresh and the grass has yet to grow over the camps.

In his office close to the main Catholic cathedral, Cardinal Puljic says the city's Catholic, predominantly Croat, minority – down from 70,000 pre-war to fewer than 30,000, he believes – faces discrimination. "All of them have lost their apartments because they left. There are no jobs; those with jobs have been fired.

"During the communist period we were fighting for survival. Now I cannot tell you what I am fighting for. I always said that Bosnia and Herzegovina should be multi-ethnic. I'm a betrayed man. My Catholic people who believed in me said they would stay here because of me. What now? I cannot protect them."

He says minority rights must be guaranteed: "In the international community, it is possible to see that political interests, not human rights, dictate policies. They are making an ethnic cleansing. People who do not have rights will simply run away."

It is a crucial issue for the Office of the High Representative (OHR), which coordinates civilian aspects of the Dayton peace deal. OHR spokesman Simon Haselock says: "The whole business of Dayton is multi-ethnicity and reintegration in the country."

OHR-drafted rules for the future city government should guarantee protection of minorities. A painful memory for international agencies was the Serbian exodus from previously Serb-controlled municipalities of Grbavica and Ilidza, following their 1996 handover to the Federation of Bosnia and Herzegovina.

Sarajevo has a generally good record for reintegrating minority groups in comparison with other areas, according to UNHCR, which has criticized some cantonal ministries for blocking ethnic groups through housing discrimination, but says others encourage minorities to return.

Deaths	11,000 people
Wounded	61,000 people
Destruction and damage to total housing stock	63%
Severe damage to public transport (trams, buses, trolleys)	75%
Losses of total water distribution network	70%
Destruction of trees in city parks and streets	95%
Destruction and theft of communal hygiene equipment (street-washing machines, snow ploughs, etc.)	40%
Total estimated war damage	CHF 17.7 billion

Figure 7.2 Starting again: The level of damage from conflict means that reconstruction and rehabilitation will take years and cost billions of dollars. Some of the finance will come from international donors; the rest will have to come from the city's own efforts, limiting spending on other vital tasks, from health to education.
Source: Sarajevo City Planning Institute.

to make the long-term political and financial commitments. The young, struggling to catch up on disrupted schooling, face a future of high unemployment. Jobless demobilized soldiers cannot get retraining and are unable to support their families.

Other problems are posed by collective centres for the internally displaced – and there are still about 120 in Bosnia and Herzegovina. The more able may find durable solutions outside these centres, but many – the extremely vulnerable – will not. The centres will shelter only the most vulnerable of the displaced, and may indeed eventually replace institutional care, such as homes for the elderly or psychiatric centres. There are few indications these centres will close in the coming decade. As they house those who have little political voice, the post-war reconstruction effort may well pass these centres by, as the politically powerful concentrate on alternative projects for the resources available.

Many former fighters are bitter that the international peace was negotiated at a time when they felt they were winning. That anger and their dire economic circumstances are fuelling a desire among some to return to war. Peacebuilding may require more funding for social support programmes which the Bosnian government cannot itself afford.

Many NGOs were founded in Bosnia to meet these needs. But they and some international NGOs now face shifting priorities and delayed donor funding. Documenting such difficulties, Ian Smillie from Care Canada wrote: "Because of a donor shift away from emergency and psychosocial work, many NGOs are currently in despair for the people with whom they work. And because many NGOs and their workers have a social welfare orientation, they are unequipped for reconstruction and micro-enterprise development."

Smillie also accuses donors and international NGOs of opportunism, saying they have used national NGOs as a "cheap delivery service". Smillie describes a "building fund" established as an endowment to "contribute to the long-term financial sustainability of the NGO sector".

Sarajevo perceptions

Competition has had a negative effect on the perception of international NGOs among Bosnians, who increasingly view them as self-serving institutions. Nedeljko Despotovic, the Federation minister without portfolio, in overall charge of the economy, says: "There are rumours here in Bosnia that the NGOs exist for themselves. Certain reports indicate that more than 50 per cent of the funds provided are used for the NGOs' own needs."

Bosnia and Herzegovina 1997: the interface of politics and geography.

Despite weekly inter-agency meetings, Bosnian officials complain of poor coordination or even competition for the right to carry out a particular reconstruction project. Despotovic adds: "We find ourselves in the situation where we are having to deal with six or seven international organizations, all of whom have different approaches. Sometimes we find ourselves in the position of having to take on the role of mediator." Often they neglect to inform ministries of their activities, so the Federation government has considered legislation to oblige foreign organizations to register projects to help coordination and planning.

Reconstruction has been lucrative for some Bosnians. Cafes for a wealthy and predominantly international clientele are opening all over the city. Those with accommodation to let find foreigners driving up the prices, while there are good jobs going as drivers, interpreters, secretaries and accountants.

But the boom raises questions of sustainability. Peter Hanney, an OHR economist, says: "Without major economic reforms that will lead to an inflow of foreign investment, the economy of Bosnia and Herzegovina will not be viable." Is aid's artificial stimulus masking economic weaknesses that will mean sharp recession when the foreigners leave, and if this is the case, does the international community have an exit strategy?

Other questions are being asked, about whether the foreign aid workers roaming the city in sleek vehicles have overstayed their welcome, and why more is not being done about arresting indicted war criminals. Many Sarajevans say they

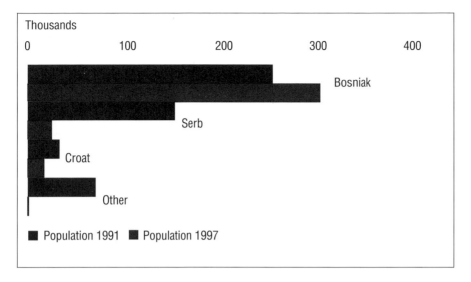

**Figure 7.3
Changed city:
Even allowing
for the city's
shifted
boundaries and
still-evolving
housing
policies and
practices, the
war has
transformed the
once
multi-ethnic
composition of
Sarajevo.**
Source: Sarajevo
City Planning
Institute.

cannot move forward without the capture of those who have been indicted. For some it is a quesåst feel unsafe knowing that such men live nearby.

These sentiments are a reminder that aid and reconstruction activities in Sarajevo are not being carried out in peacetime but in the "absence of war", and that the role of aid is – as so often in conflict – being confused with other functions. In the attempt to create peace, something fundamentally a political process, aid is being used as a tool and is performing routine tasks perhaps better suited to companies. The role of the military is also less than clear. Peacekeeping troops have being rebuilding bridges and repairing houses.

Bosnians themselves hope that renewing old trade ties with Serbs will revive the economy and heal the wounds of war. Enver Backovic, deputy head of the Central Bank of Bosnia and Herzegovina, said: "It's economics that will push us forward despite politics. Trading was going on between us even during the war. As in Germany, economics will force change. Politics didn't bring down the Berlin Wall, economics did; politics just provided the final hit."

In Sarajevo, usually relief-focused humanitarian organizations are examining forms of business-focused small-scale economic aid. World Vision International has conducted a successful micro-credit pilot in Tuzla and is introducing it in Sarajevo. Elizabeth Hughes, a World Vision programme officer, says: "Micro-enterprise development is the single greatest impact you can have on the economy. You target people with skills and a business aptitude. We will be dealing with business people who lost everything. The missing link for rebuilding is capital. These people are not the most vulnerable but they will help other groups by creating jobs."

Micro-credit schemes also appear to be attracting the interest of some Bosnian refugees who would like to return home but are anxious about finding work. Nearly a million refugees are still living in countries which accepted them during the war but which have not granted them permanent status. Pressure to return is rising.

In 1997, Bosnian refugees from Denmark returned for two-week visits to assess the prospects. In one group, none believed conditions were right for return, citing unemployment and the lack of housing. They suggested funds allocated for refugee return should be given instead to the internally displaced trying to salvage a life among the ruins.

Local communities can be openly hostile to returning refugees, especially those from wealthy Western countries perceived as pampered individuals who ran away. Whether refugees will be able to return without destabilizing communities will hinge on the success of reconstruction in its broadest sense, from housing and physical infrastructure to social services and progress in security.

Sarajevo is a city struggling through multiple transformations – political, economic, social – at one time. In 1990, Sarajevo held the first elections which ushered non-communist parties into power. War broke out as Sarajevo was beginning the difficult shift from communism to a pluralist political system and market economy. The siege economy and its warlords may have gone but, amid the city's reconstruction, those transformations have still to be finished.

Despite all these concerns, staff at the Sarajevo Planning Institute are drafting guidelines for development well into the 21st century, confident that their city will make a strong recovery. They say the war's destruction accelerated changes inevitable with the collapse of communism and the revolution in computing and communications.

The question is whether Sarajevo, with the help of the international community, will be able to avoid renewed conflict and become part of the free market without neglecting its most vulnerable. Some have their eyes firmly on a high-profile horizon. Sarajevo hosted the Winter Olympics in 1984; the planners believe the bench mark for success will be if the city is fit to bid again for the Games by 2015.

Chapter 7 Sources, reference and further information

Badal, Yvonne. "Rethinking Home in Postwar Sarajevo". Transition. 12 July 1996.

Chamber of Economy of the Sarajevo Region. Export Possibilities of Sarajevo Canton Economy 97/98. Sarajevo: Chamber of Economy of the Sarajevo Region, 1997.

City Planning Institute, City of Sarajevo. Guide for the Sarajevo Canton Investments. Sarajevo: Muller, 1997.

City Planning Institute, City of Sarajevo. Priority Projects of the Sarajevo Canton Reconstruction in 1997. Sarajevo: Muller, 1997.

City Planning Institute, City of Sarajevo. Sarajevo Reconstruction Projects. Summary no. 3. Sarajevo: Muller, February 1997.

European Commission and Central Europe Department of the World Bank. The Priority Reconstruction Program: 1996 Achievements and 1997 Objectives. European Commission and World Bank, March 1997.

International Council of Voluntary Agencies (ICVA). The ICVA Directory of Humanitarian and Development Agencies Operating in Bosnia and Herzegovina. Geneva: ICVA, August 1997.

International Crisis Group. Ridding Bosnia and Herzegovina of Landmines: The Urgent Need for a Sustainable Policy. 18 July 1997.

International Federation of Red Cross and Red Crescent Societies. Going Home: A Guidebook for Refugees. Sarajevo: Sahinpasic, 1997.

Smillie, Ian, Service Delivery or Civil Society? Non-Governmental Organizations in Bosnia & Herzegovina. Care Canada, December 1996.

UN. Protocol on the Organization of Sarajevo. Office of the High Representative.

USIA. The Dayton Peace Accords. Vienna: USIA Regional Program Office, 1995.

World Bank, Bosnia and Herzegovina. Priority Reconstruction Projects. World Bank, July 1997.

Web sites

ICRC: http://www.icrc.orgl

International   Federation: http://www.ifrc.org

Repatriation   Information   Centre: http://www.ric.com.ba

Iraq is in its eighth year of sanctions and economic stagnation. People survive, famine does not stalk the land, but growing chronic malnutrition is building up dire consequences for the young of Iraq.

© Jean-Pierre Revel.
Iraq, 1997.

Chapter

8 Iraq sanctions create their own disaster

Sanctions, as the former United States President Woodrow Wilson put it, "provide a peaceful, silent and deadly remedy," a form of unarmed warfare. Full economic sanctions have been applied to Iraq for over seven years now in an attempt by the international community to persuade its government to abide by United Nations (UN) resolutions and renounce all association with weapons of mass destruction.

But today, with the weapons issue still not resolved, many – humanitarian agencies and governments alike – are questioning both the effectiveness and efficiency of economic sanctions.

One of the basic tenets of the laws of war makes the distinction between the combatant and the civilian. The civilian should not be a target. Weapons should be designed and used so that they can be targeted at the combatants and avoid unduly harming civilians. But economic sanctions are proving to be no Cruise missile. Practice has shown that they are not surgical strikes but extraordinarily messy weapons, the economic equivalent of blanket bombing.

In Iraq, the welfare of the most vulnerable is inextricably linked to the political and economic decisions that surround the imposition, or relaxing, of UN sanctions. To address the growing malnutrition and public health crisis, to assist those in need, humanitarian agencies have to tread a wary path through this minefield, addressing the effects of crisis whilst steering clear of being drawn into, or implicated in, the political debate over root causes.

Sanctions and malnutrition

In the back room of a Baghdad hospital, the Iraqi Red Crescent runs one of its special feeding posts targeted at the most vulnerable children in the capital. The mothers who leave the hospital with bags of rice and bottles of oil may themselves be hungry: many live on far less than US$ 1-a-day World Bank-defined world poverty level. As they leave the hospital, the women pass by as the young rich from a nearby private college gather at a cafe; begging is unthinkable as each

---

Box 8.1 Eight years under embargo, from 661 to the oil-for-food 986

Sanctions began in August 1990 with UN Security Council resolution 661 barring all imports and exports except essential food and medicines as part of international pressure for Iraqi troops to leave Kuwait.

Eight further Security Council resolutions were passed from 1990 to 1992, covering sea and air blockades, the ceasefire, Iraqi assets overseas and two on the sale of oil for food.

In April 1995, with the situation of ordinary Iraqis worsening and surveys by UN agencies revealing increasing hunger and illness, the Security Council passed resolution 986 allowing the sale of $2 billion of Iraqi oil every six months and the purchase of food and medicines, as well as spare parts and supplies for the electricity, water, sanitation, agriculture and education sectors.

A memorandum of understanding on resolution 986 signed by the UN and Iraq in May 1996 set out how each $2 billion should be divided: $1.32 billion for "humanitarian" supplies; $600 million into a compensation fund for those affected by the Kuwait occupation; $44 million for the administrative costs of UN aid operations; and $15 million for UN arms inspectors.

A range of geographical and multi-disciplinary UN observers across the country assess supplies, monitor transportation, interview beneficiaries, and check the records of hospitals, warehouses and the tens of thousands of distribution agents.

UN agencies have a sectoral role, tracking supplies and gathering data, such as WHO for medical supplies; WFP in food distribution; UNICEF on nutrition and immunization; FAO for agriculture and markets; Habitat in shelter; the UN Development Programme with electricity generation and transmission.

The first supplies paid for through resolution 986 arrived in March 1997, and the first full enhanced food ration was distributed in August 1997.

---

group passes the other. Such contrasts are common currency in Iraq today, giving a hint of the complexity of the relationship between the political effectiveness and the humanitarian efficiency of sanctions.

Although vital to restore a malnourished child to its full weight, extra rations are not a solution to Iraq's crisis, but a temporary treatment of the symptoms of this

---

Box 8.2 Scenes from a sanctions siege

The combination of sanctions and "no-fly" zones in both north and south mean that while UN staff arrive on special flights, the road from Amman in Jordan is the main route into Baghdad for all other aid workers. It's a journey that gives the first indications of the unique blend of challenges, opportunities and contradictions in a country under siege.

Even on the fast highway, it takes a long hot day to drive the 850 km across the stony desert, past the occasional wreck and mangled barriers that are evidence of local driving risks. To the road dangers and distances of a big country can be added long delays and paperwork: the inevitable hour of queues and forms – not forgetting a mandatory blood test if you lack a letter certifying your HIV status – at the border crossing.

Sanctions have added their sometimes surprising twist to the situation of aid staff living and working in a divided nation which is emerging all too slowly from two wars, where conflict continues and millions are malnourished, sick or displaced.

This is an oil-producer under embargo, whose economy continues to contract under sanctions and where electricity is limited. Hunger, impoverishment and malnutrition abound. Millions have become steadily poorer trying to survive on inadequate daily rations by selling their jewellery, TV sets, furniture and spare clothes. All true, but no disaster impoverishes everyone.

At the border, anything on four wheels that can be stuffed with trade goods fills up in Iraq with petrol so cheap a tankful costs a few cents. Baghdad can be well-lit, jammed with traffic and noisily busy 24 hours a day, with extensive repairs leaving few signs of air-raid damage. Crowded street markets are full of consumer items, food stalls are piled high with vegetables, and among the growing number of newly refurbished shops are plenty of hamburger bars and ice-cream parlours.

Since the imposition of sanctions in 1990, the 1991 Gulf war and introduction of the mainly Kurdish "safe havens" in three northern governorates, Iraq has experienced an ebb and flow of aid agencies assisting its 22 million people.

Many arrived to work in the safe havens, but years of factional fighting and international conflict have prompted some to leave, while more recently the small number of agencies arriving to work in the 15 central and southern governorates has begun to rise.

From Baghdad, most agencies – from the International Federation of Red Cross and Red Crescent Societies to the Middle East Council of Churches – work in partnership with the Iraqi Red Crescent Society, which was founded in the 1930s and has a nationwide network of offices and staff.

As sanctions manager and monitor, the UN in Iraq has the world's only self-sustaining UN operation. Many of its bills are the first deductions from the multi-billion dollar oil-for-food deal allowing Iraq to buy so-called "humanitarian" goods under tight controls.

With so many roles within one set of initials – investigation, diplomatic, humanitarian, negotiation – UN aid staff live at the centre of the Iraq contradiction: sanctions as war by another means are clearly doing significant damage to civilians, but the response is a less than adequate supply of food and drugs, often delivered late.

Working conditions are not easy. Unexplained delays, cumbersome paperwork and poor communications slow down operations. In the north, the on-off conflicts mean curfews and insecurity are common, with occasional attacks on aid convoys.

Inevitably in Iraq, security of all sorts is tight. Foreigners need formal permission for many actions – travel beyond the capital, importing communications equipment, living outside the few designated hotels – that would usually present fewer problems elsewhere.

Most foreigners are on short contracts – one year is a long time in Iraq – which has its own impact on the continuity of operations. But there are also some positive elements to Iraq's grinding problems.

Few countries could have organized such a fair rationing system. The road network and cheap fuel make travelling easier than in many other disaster zones, and the high level of education and skills available within the Iraqi population makes local staff a key resource in the aid effort.

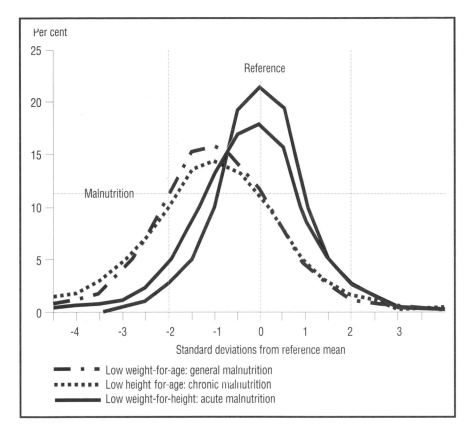

Figure 8.1
Malnutrition impact of sanctions among children. Using statistics of 15,000 children in central and southern regions, this figure shows the distribution of nutritional status. It covers chronic malnutrition (low height-for-age); general malnutrition (low weight-for-age); and acute malnutrition (low weight-for-height)

.

Source: Iraq Ministry of Health, UNICEF, World Food Programme

form of "man-made" disaster: an embargo that may well have killed hundreds of thousands of children – 5,500 per month by Iraqi government estimates – and has been slowly pushing almost an entire country into impoverishment since the first UN Security Council resolution was passed in August 1990.

A survey by UNICEF and the Iraqi government in 1997 suggested that 31 per cent – equivalent to 960,000 children – were suffering from either mild, moderate or acute chronic malnutrition, up from 18 per cent in the already worsening situation of 1991. Eleven per cent – around 340,000 children – had acute malnutrition, up from 3 per cent; and 26 per cent were underweight, against 9 per cent in 1991.

Iraq's eighth year of sanctions ushered in months of controversy over UN weapons inspectors, threats of renewed international conflict, and the negotiation mission to Baghdad by UN Secretary-General Kofi Annan. Meanwhile, despite the stop-start nature of the multi-billion dollar oil-for-food deal, millions remained poor, hungry or displaced, with large numbers of additional deaths through disease, and high levels of child malnutrition.

Oil-for-food

The oil-for-food operation delivered its first food in April 1997. This was six years after it was first mooted, two years after the Security Council approved resolution 986, allowing Iraq to sell $2 billion of oil every six months and use the money to buy food, medicines and other goods under the tight control of a UN Sanctions

Committee, and almost a year after the details had finally been agreed with Baghdad in June 1996.

Despite the years of discussion and planning, it was not until August 1997 that the first full monthly ration under resolution 986 was actually delivered. By early in 1998, a complete ration had been achieved only twice more, in September 1997 and March 1998, while the extent of the emergency in nutrition and health had been highlighted in new UN studies.

On paper, the new food basket of 2,030 kcal and 47 grams of protein per person per day appeared a big improvement over the monthly government ration introduced under sanctions, which had varied from a high of 1,705 kcal to a low of 1,093 kcal. But the new ration was still below minimum Iraqi needs, estimated at 2,600 kcal per person per day by a UN Food and Agriculture Organization (FAO)/World Food Programme (WFP) mission to Iraq in 1997.

There was swift criticism of the ration as too low in energy, vitamins, minerals and protein, and insufficient to prevent continued malnutrition, even if all the food arrived and was distributed efficiently. The FAO/WFP mission called it "inadequate and unbalanced". Other food sources, from aid agency feeding programmes to black-market purchases, would be needed to sustain a healthy population.

UN Secretary-General Kofi Annan recognized these shortcomings. Before heading for Baghdad in early 1998, he proposed raising the value of the oil-for-food deal to $5.2 billion every six months – allowing, after UN and reparation deductions,

---

Box 8.3 Northern needs in the conflict-hit havens with 500,000 displaced

The northern three of Iraq's 18 governorates are still under UN sanctions yet have separate systems of administration as a result of the exodus of Kurds following the Gulf war and the creation of "safe havens" under a no-fly zone to assist their return.

Extensive fighting in the Kurdish-controlled governorates of Erbil, Dohuk and Sulaimaniyah have left these havens rather less than safe, with around 500,000 displaced people in early 1998.

Many of the displaced cannot return to their villages because their homes have been destroyed or political changes have made going back impossible. Living in abandoned military camps, damaged public buildings, pre-fabricated houses or tents, the displaced are left even more vulnerable because they lack land.

Even for the settled, conditions in the mountainous north can be hard, with tough winters, inadequate housing and sanitation, poor electricity supplies, lack of fuel, limited communications, and high unemployment. Agriculture has suffered from the lack of fertilizers and pesticides.

Despite frequent ceasefires in this volatile situation, the conflicts have increased the needs while disrupting humanitarian operations. Aid agency convoys have been fired on, or had vehicles seized, forcing the use of guards.

As well as the same ration as the central and southern regions – delivered by the UN – the north has a supplementary feeding programme for around 250,000 vulnerable people, including pregnant women and malnourished children, supported by WFP.

Although cut off from traditional markets in the rest of Iraq, the north probably benefits from greater trade through porous international borders. It also has significantly higher per capita aid spending from the 986 oil-for-food funds, according to UNOHCI.

Perhaps linked to this, the nutritional status of children in the three northern governorates has been a little better than those in the central and southern region.

There are an estimated 10 to 20 million mines in the north, especially along the border with Iran. In early 1998, the UN began a $4.5 million mine clearance programme in the three northern governorates, financed from the oil-for-food agreement, which will train 120 supervisors, team-leaders, medics and de-miners.

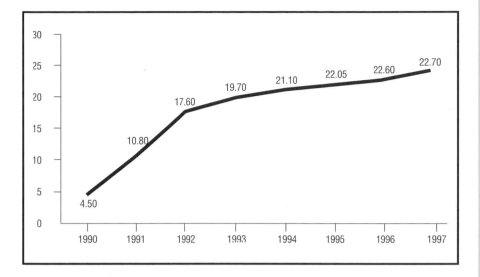

Figure 8.2
Starting life with
low weight.
The percentage
of children
reported with
birth weight
below 2.5 kg –
suggesting
poor maternal
health or
nutrition – has
risen steadily
since 1990 to
almost
one-quarter of
total registered
births. (Note:
from 1991,
excludes three
northern
governorates,
1997 estimates
as of July.)
Source: Iraq
Ministry of Health.

$3.4 billion for humanitarian needs – and overhauling much of the Sanctions Committee's structure and systems.

In part, the extra money was needed to raise the ration to 2,463 kcal and 63.6 grams of vegetable and animal protein, including the addition of cheese and full-cream powdered milk. Over six months, this would mean increasing food spending by $23 to $60 per capita; overall food spending would increase by $619 million to $1.5 billion. Pilot projects would also encourage egg and chicken production for a market low in animal protein.

In addition to extra food, the proposal acknowledged the complexity and depth of the wider crisis, since it would bring significant increases in the money available for many other sectors needing support, from restoring power supplies and repairing water and sanitation systems to improving agriculture, rebuilding schools, assisting resettlement, expanding de-mining and boosting spending on drugs and hospitals.

But that would depend on Iraq pumping far more oil. Baghdad immediately suggested that $4 billion was the limit if oil prices remained low. At 1997 prices, the $55-a-barrel rates of the early 1980s sank to $20 in January 1997 and hit $11.27 in early 1998. Oil producer countries feared greater Iraqi output would depress prices still further.

The oil-for-food deal brought complex new systems for contracts and sanctions approval. In late 1997, the UN Office of the Humanitarian Coordinator for Iraq (UNOHCI) estimated that, on average, in the first phase of the oil-for-food deal, it was taking 66 days to have a food contract approved by the Sanctions Committee system, 59 days for the food to be delivered, and seven to make it available for distribution to Iraqi beneficiaries.

The food and other supplies have arrived through four entry points: Al-Walid opposite Al-Tenf in Syria; the Iraqi Gulf port Umm Qasr; Treibil on the Jordanian border; and Khabour on Turkish border. By 2 April 1998, 5 million metric tons of foodstuffs had been delivered to Iraq. Through government warehouses, silos and distribution points, supplies are delivered to more than 50,000 retail agents.

Each agent distributes rations every month to hundreds of families, with a nominal fee imposed on each recipient to cover transportation and administrative costs. The food basket includes wheat flour, rice, sugar, oil, pulses, tea, salt, soap, detergent and – for families with children under one – infant formula. Food rations typically last for an average of 20 days in the month, and so require significant supplementing from wages, trading, selling possessions, or community and family networks.

Siege economy

Be it $4 billion or $5.2 billion, Iraq could easily absorb additional funds, for the same reasons that made it look so vulnerable to economic sanctions back in 1990. It is not a low-income rural country of small farmers able to eke out an existence from the land if necessary. It is an urban country and had an economically buoyant economy. Iraq claims that sanctions have denied its growing oil-based economy some $120 billion in revenues since 1990.

In the past, that income paid for $2 to $3 billion of annual food imports to meet two-thirds of its needs, thousands of foreign workers, $30 per person a year drug supplies, cheap or free health care, an effective education system, and plenty of jobs in ministries, military forces and state-backed enterprises. In this urbanized society, three-quarters of the 22 million population were dependent on the complex lifelines of towns and cities, from electrical power to piped water.

Since 1990, sanctions have had a profound impact, creating for many a siege economy of price inflation, currency devaluation, soaring unemployment and a widening income gap. Most Iraqis have been gradually selling off all their possessions – from jewellery to furniture and television sets – to survive. By 1995, falling incomes and rising prices were estimated to have reduced earnings to only 5 per cent of their pre-sanctions value in food purchasing terms.

Sanctions have been particularly tough on Iraq's many state employees and others on fixed incomes, and the middle class have seen both income and capital disappear.

While state staff, from civil servants to teachers, have found extra work elsewhere, if only becoming street vendors, wider changes initiated by the Iraqi government have been encouraging a larger role for the private sector in a state-led economy. Iraq has been selling state assets, offering shares in state enterprises to staff, and allowing new private businesses, from hospitals to banks, to emerge.

For Iraqis, some forms of private enterprise may be more welcome (smuggling of all kinds for example, including oil) than others (begging, prostitution, robbery), but all have grown despite often tough punishments for offenders. A worrying side effect of this trend has been that traditional community leaders now play a lesser role. The black-market aristocracy that has emerged will inevitably have repercussions on the form of civic society that eventually emerges in Iraq.

If millions are not to be forced into endemic poverty or to become refugees, rising food prices and limited stocks make rationing vital. Aid agencies have praised the Iraqi government's achievements in creating a well-run national rationing system, which has helped to ensure that, despite delays and shortfalls, the vast majority of the Iraqi population has had access to at least a portion of the minimal food basket since sanctions were imposed.

Establishing and managing the ration system has also had the effect of reinforcing the government's authority, as it registered families across the

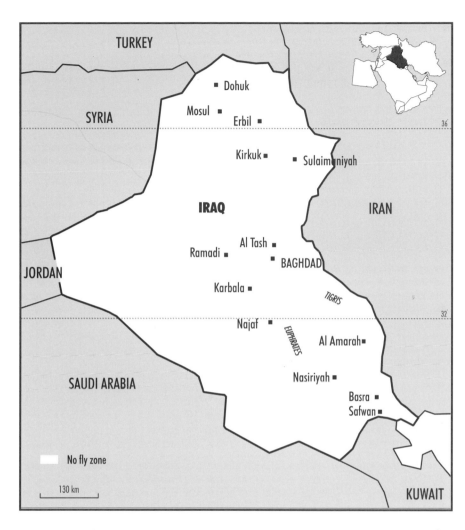

Iraq, 1997.

country, and fostering its legitimacy when it managed to deliver a small but equitable food package every month for more than five years to millions of people without large-scale international support.

Coping with sanctions

Rations have kept the majority of people alive as they gradually converted their assets into cash, but a series of studies involving UN agencies and Iraqi government departments since the start of sanctions have all showed serious health problems that are far worse than regional averages. By 1997, the Iraqi government was claiming that up to 5,500 under-five deaths a month were the result of sanctions. There was a clear rising trend of malnutrition among children under five, although specific figures have varied widely.

In part, that is because of the three rather different forms of malnutrition being measured:

- chronic malnutrition or stunting involves low height-for-age and comes from long-term poor conditions, health and feeding;

- acute malnutrition or wasting is low weight-for-height and shows more immediate problems, such as diarrhoea or other disease, or sudden reduction in feeding; and

- general malnutrition or underweight is low weight-for-age and can result from either or both other conditions.

In 1997, the FAO/WFP mission to Iraq conducted two rapid nutrition surveys in and around Baghdad. They arrived at rather lower ranges of figures, with chronic malnutrition put at 16 to 27 per cent, acute at 3 to 5 per cent (or 93,000 to 155,000) and underweight at 11 to 18 per cent. However, they felt the higher figures were probably more representative of Iraq as a whole since capital cities, for both political and logistical reasons, usually have preferential access to food. They also found that among those under 26 years of age, 25 per cent of men and 16 per cent women were undernourished.

The mission, led by Professor Peter Pellett of the Department of Nutrition at the University of Massachusetts, confirmed the known correlations between the education levels of mothers and the condition of children, with a far lower prevalence of malnutrition among the children of women with college or university degrees. It also showed the connection between bouts of diarrhoea and both chronic and general malnutrition, and highlighted the need to fortify food supplies with additional nutrients, a cost-effective process for bulk supplies.

This confirmed the views of many aid observers that food availability is but one factor in determining the overall nutritional status of children. Illustrative of this is the degenerated state of Iraq's water supply and sanitation systems, particularly in urban areas, which has lead to an increase in water-borne diseases and the incidence of diarrhoea, both of which directly effect nutritional levels.

Another illustration of the complexity of linking cause and effect in malnutrition has been the rising government figures for the proportion of low birthweight babies. From 4 per cent in 1990, the figure for babies born under 2.5 kg has reached around a quarter of registered births today. This may be due to maternal malnutrition or more attributable to the 70 per cent of Iraqi women who suffer from anaemia. Malnutrition and anaemia are closely linked and, although anaemia has traditionally been a concern in Iraq, the figure of 70 per cent is exceptionally high.

The World Health Organization (WHO) has warned that many of these Iraqi children will not catch up in their physical or mental development, laying the foundation for continued long-term health problems in the country.

Although reliable figures are scarce, both infant and under-five mortality rates seem to have risen sharply. One factor may be the way the many positive aspects of breastfeeding – from nutrition to birth spacing and even cost – are not being adequately promoted. This is particularly crucial in Iraq – an urbanized, developed economy where breastfeeding was in decline. Now, with much of its public health infrastructure fallen into decay, old pre-war, pre-sanctions practices need to be changed. The encouragement of, and education on, breastfeeding is a priority for child health programmes.

The standard ration – including that being brought in under UN Security Council resolution 986 – has offered infant formula to all families with children under one year. In the past, three-quarters preferred to take an extra adult ration instead, but that option was removed in May 1997. The FAO/WFP mission in 1997 commented on the lack of breastfeeding seen among the mothers of the malnourished, and urged that the ration choice be reinstated.

Health systems failure

Sanctions, following on the effects of war, have seriously hampered the Iraqi health care system in many ways: cutting imports of drugs and equipment; slowing resumption of local drugs production; causing an exit of foreign medical and nursing staff; and restricting contacts between Iraqi doctors and outside experts. Iraqi spending on medicines fell to about $3 per capita in 1995/1996 but recovered to $16 in 1997, about half of the pre-sanctions level of local production and $500 million in imports.

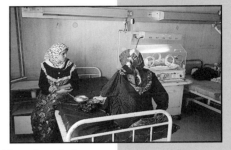

© Jean-Pierre Revel

The 986 deal was due to bring in $210 million of medical supplies every six months, but serious delays allowed widespread shortages of antibiotics, analgesics, anaesthetics and laboratory test materials to continue. Many diseases re-emerged during the embargo, especially those linked to the damaged water and sanitation systems, from cholera to typhoid and malaria.

There were UN proposals to more than triple health spending to $770 million every six months from an expanded oil-for-food deal, plus a one-off $449 million to re-establish systems and facilities, such as the vaccines cold chain. But even if supplies of drugs and equipment improve, problems will remain in staffing health facilities. Many of Iraq's former health care professionals were expatriates; almost all of whom have now left the country. Many Iraqi doctors are now working overseas, while Iraqi women have always shunned nursing as a career. The focus on physical disease also means that not enough attention has been paid to very real needs in mental health. An increasing number of psychological problems have been seen in war widows, orphans and those forced into poverty by sanctions.

There are plenty of other sectors needing money, from education – where once-high primary school enrolment rates have fallen to 75 per cent or less – to de-mining, resettlement, and agriculture, where output has continued to fall, because of problems over the supply of seeds, equipment, fertilizer, pesticides and water from irrigation systems.

Crises loom for Iraq's power, water and sanitation systems. They are linked together in the country's flat landscape, where pumping is essential and the restoration of water treatment desperately required. For many millions, contaminated water – from broken mains or a local river – is the only option. The UN has advocated for an eight-fold increase in the spending on water and sanitation, from $44 million to $321 million. It has suggested an entirely new multi-billion dollar strategy to deal with the bulk of Iraq's power restoration.

The scale of Iraq's needs from both the impact of war and the effects of sanctions has been put in the hundreds of billions of dollars, suggesting that even when the embargo is lifted, it will take the country and its people years to fully recover. Much of the infrastructure for the health system will need to be completely overhauled or replaced. Many health care facilities were built in the early 1980s before the war with Iran, the Gulf war and the imposition of sanctions. They are now out of date and virtually obsolete.

It seems unlikely that anyone expected such a costly and slow scenario in 1990, when sanctions started and war was being prepared. Perhaps it was the ambitious optimism of a time of great change, when many thought far more would be possible in diplomacy, backed up by forces freed from stalemate.

Sanctions have expanded as a tool of both national foreign policy and international coercion since the end of the Cold War, during which such measures could expect superpower veto or evasion. The other international tool that grew after the Cold War – military intervention – has lost a lot of its attraction as casualty figures and the complexity and open-ended nature of peacekeeping operations deter military commitment. Sanctions had been seen as a useful non-violent alternative, but Iraq and other experiences may also be forcing a rethink here.

Whatever its political effectiveness, the success or failure of which is for others to judge, the sanctions regime has clearly had serious consequences for the ordinary Iraqi population: forcing many into poverty, destroying human dignity and taking lives.

The long-awaited oil-for-food response to the crisis that sanctions created has not has the necessary impact either, especially for the most vulnerable. As Kofi Annan concluded in December 1997, it was insufficient "to address, even as a temporary measure, all the humanitarian needs of the Iraqi people", which led to his plans for a "systematic review of the whole process of contracting, processing of applications, approvals, procurement and shipment and distribution"

Aid lessons

The unprecedented nature of the experiments of oil-for-food and comprehensive embargo being carried out in Iraq are offering important lessons for the future. Some are fairly direct. There is the challenge of understanding the real consequences of sanctions through baseline statistics, detailed surveys and regional knowledge so they can be managed as effectively as possible within very limited resources.

There is also the need to go beyond the obvious – lack of food as a cause of malnutrition – to deeper factors – sanitation in one situation, for example, education in another – that might suggest the solution is not only better rations but also a new water main or effective use of radio to promote breastfeeding.

Equally important is the ever-present risk to agency independence and impartiality when operating in a highly political environment, where one side in the political confrontation also controls the majority of the resources available for supplying humanitarian assistance. Aid agencies operating in Iraq need to apply the same clear and uncompromising ground-rules to their work as they would in any other situation where humanitarian aid is provided.

Finally, there is the crucial recognition by the very same governments that have agreed on the imposition of sanctions through the appropriate international systems, that humanitarian organizations have a right to take action to assist the most vulnerable individuals – the unintended victims of the sanctions. Aid agencies have learnt that they need to lobby governments hard to get the message across that humanitarian organizations such as the Red Cross/Red Crescent offer a neutral and impartial channel for well-targeted humanitarian assistance. Governments can choose to support these agencies without compromising their political objectives. Through this crucial recognition and principled support for the right to humanitarian aid, many hundreds of thousands of young children, women and old people have been assisted in Iraq, and in other countries under sanctions.

Chapter 8 Sources, references and further reading

Dario, Bernard. *A Preliminary Evaluation of Children's Nutritional Conditions in the Central Region of Iraq.* Nutrition Research Programme, UN Development Programme, November 1989.

Graham-Brown, Sarah. "The Iraq Sanctions Dilemma; Intervention, Sovereignty and Responsibility" in *Middle East Report,* March-April 1995, London.

Haass, Richard N. "Sanctioning Madness" in *Foreign Affairs.* November/December 1997, Washington DC.

Hoskins, Eric. The Impact of Sanctions; *A Study of Unicef's Perspective.* New York: United Nations Children's Fund, 1998.

Hoskins, Eric. "The Humanitarian Impact of Economic Sanctions and War" in *Political Gain and Civilian Pain.* Lanham: Rowman & Littlefield, 1997.

International Committee of the Red Cross. *Water in Iraq.* Geneva: ICRC, 1996.

International Federation of Red Cross and Red Crescent Societies. I*raq Relief Operation.* Situation Reports. Geneva, 1997.

Iraqi Economists Association. *Human Development Report 1995.* Baghdad.

Office of the UN Humanitarian Coordinator for Iraq. *The Oil-for-Food Operation.* Baghdad, 1997.

Royal Institute of International Affairs. "Saddam's Bazaar" in *The World Today,* March 1998, London.

UN Department of Humanitarian Affairs. *Humanitarian Report 1997.* New York: UNDHA, 1997.

UNICEF. *The 1996 Multiple Indicator Cluster Survey; A Survey to Assess the Situation of Children and Women in Iraq.* Baghdad: UNICEF, October 1997.

UNICEF. *Nutritional Status Survey at Primary Health Centres During Polio National Immunization Days in Iraq, April 1997.* Baghdad: UNICEF, 1997.

UNICEF. *Monthly Situation Reports.* Baghdad.

Web sites

ArabNet: http://www.arab.net/iraq/iraq_contents.html

CIA World Factbook: http://www.odci.gov/cia/publications/factbook/country-frame.html

Columbia University Middle East Studies: http://www.columbia.edu/cu/libraries/indiv/area/MiddleEast

FAO/WFP Food Supply and Nutrition Assessment Mission to Iraq: http://www.fao.org/GIEWS/english/alertes/srirq997.htm

ICRC: http://www.icrc.org

International Federation: http://www.ifrc.org

Iraqnet: http://www.iraq.net/

OneWorld. Iraq articles: http://www.oneworld.org/news/countries/IQ.html

UN Secretary-General's 1998 mission to Iraq: http://www.un.org/NewLinks/mission.htm

UN on Iraq: http://www.un.org/Depts/oip

University of Durham Middle East Studies: http://www.dur.ac.uk/Library/lib/medu.html

USIA. US policy on Iraq: http://www.usia.gov/regional/nea/iraq/iraq.htm

Family life carries on in refugee camps, but the tent becomes the home, the playground, the laundry and the work place. Refugee cities lack almost all of the structures which sustain modern conurbations. Are there alternative ways of helping? Information centres and services for tracing lost relatives provide vital links for refugees often cut off from many of those activities and relationships which define normality.

Christopher Black/International Federation. Democratic Republic of the Congo, 1997.

Chapter

9
Inside the camps that are now refugee cities

Swedish engineer Erik Pleijel frowned as he assessed the falling level of the Malagarasi river in western Tanzania. Pumps near the water surface would soon suck air into the seven-kilometre pipeline to the region's largest town and deprive 35,000 people of their 17-litre daily allowance.

The engineer's contingency plan was to move the pumps downstream to a river bed depression. "All I need is a goat," he muttered. Seeing his companions' glances, he explained: "Bait. There are crocodiles down there. Before our pumps can go in, they must come out."

Christopher Black/ International Federation

The town needing water was Lugufu, a remote Congolese refugee camp 90 kilometres east of the Lake Tanganyika port of Kigoma. Sited in a mosquito-infested swamp, often short of supplies when rains made dirt roads to it impassable, Lugufu depended on resourcefulness.

Pleijel, a delegate with the International Federation of Red Cross and Red Crescent Societies, and Tanzania Red Cross colleagues pumped the river water 137 metres up a cliff to 1,200 metres above sea level. After chlorination, water was piped kilometres to a ring of taps around the refugee camp.

A source of wonder for local villagers, carrying water from the river was an urban necessity for Lugufu, a sprawling community of stick and mud shelters with plastic-sheet roofs. Trucking water was impossible in the rains. In public health terms, the pipeline was a life saver.

Refugee City

With at least 10,000 more inhabitants than Kigoma – administrative centre of the region – Lugufu is a community of urban needs, poverty and problems, urban dangers and social structures. It belongs to a phenomenon increasingly familiar in Africa: Refugee City.

It can sprawl suddenly in a flood-prone valley, malarial swamp, burning desert or by an active volcano. It's rarely planned; villages succumb to urban creep, farm land turns to squalor and the health consequences can be terrible for cross-border refugees or people displaced in-country. Crime and hunger, poverty and politics are all part of this home for thousands without one.

The reality of Refugee City was revealed when refugees fled from Rwanda in 1994, and the population of Nyiragongo region in what was then eastern Zaire rose from 29,000 to 800,000 in days. Tanzania's Ngara district population was tripled by Rwandan and Burundian outpourings. One camp with almost 250,000 inhabitants became Tanzania's second largest city.

The urban nature of these camps may not always be appreciated. If it was, why would anyone have placed the Congolese in Lugufu? Its low-lying land between hills is shunned by local people as flood-prone and malarial. The poor soil's low yields sent a state farm into bankruptcy.

The Tanzania Red Cross and the International Federation, which manage Lugufu, objected to its location but the regional authorities probably had other considerations. Kigoma was overwhelmed as Congolese, fleeing their civil war in late 1996, doubled its population, so Lugufu is a safe distance from Tanzania's regional centres, and far enough from the Congolese border to avoid international complications from neighbours worried about returning insurgents.

The location exacted a hard toll. Opened in February, long rains soon left it awash. Some refugees lost everything in floods, and malaria meant sickness and death. Aid staff were not immune. Three German delegates died: one from malaria and two, with a Tanzanian colleague, in a road crash. The International Federation team leader reported: "This place is unfit for human habitation."

The people who endured Lugufu were mostly from what had been eastern Zaire, predominantly Bembe from the Fizi region, north-east across Lake Tanganyika. By the end of September 1997, the civil war was long over. The UN High Commissioner for Refugees (UNHCR) had repatriated more than 1,100 Lugufu Congolese and 7,000 were registered to follow, but many became wary.

Laurent Kabila consolidated power in the renamed Democratic Republic of the Congo. Warriors from the mainly Bembe "Mai Mai" – Swahili for water, from their sprinkled immortality potions – had at first assisted Kabila. They turned against him when he tried to impose authority in their region. Ex-Mobutu soldiers and Rwandan Hutu fighters joined in. A Democratic Resistance Alliance declared in Tanzania that it would "liberate" the east.

Amid security, monitoring and access problems in the Democratic Republic of the Congo, UNHCR suspended repatriation. One leading refugee said: "Repatriation is not for everyone. It is not yet safe. I hear there are still night attacks." Lugufu prepared for another rainy season.

Movers and shakers

Refugees bring plenty from home: structures, leaders, politics. Agencies think they are in charge but the city has its own bureaucracy, chiefs and corridors of power. A hillside of huts is a complex urban community. As Zaire in 1994 showed, camps can become power bases for armies in exile. Lugufu has its Mai Mai sympathizers but is no rebel hiding place. In the bars around its busy market, former Mobutu troops are hungry for news but preoccupied with survival.

Box 9.1 Campaign to control charcoal inspires care for the countryside

The trees were falling around Lugufu. Its new Congolese inhabitants needed firewood, poles for construction, charcoal for cooking. In the bush and along river banks, hunters were stalking hippo and monkey. If it moved and was edible, it was dead.

Humanitarian disasters can cause environmental ones. When Hutus fled Rwanda, the UNESCO-recognized Virunga National Park near Goma was looted by thousands every day. Refugees denuded land around Ngara in western Tanzania, and Ngozi in northern Burundi.

Lugufu might have gone the same way had Charles Ntemi, a CARE environmental protection officer, not been drafted in from Ngara, where around 10 million CARE seedlings are restoring the landscape. This was something else. "Prevention is better than a cure," he says.

Some damage had been done. Ntemi counted 300 charcoal-making sites alone. But with public meetings and grassroots volunteers, an environmental awareness campaign began. Warning signs went up, felling trees brought prosecution, poachers were gaoled.

Alongside enforcement, good environmental practice seemed to have been a hit. CARE has identified areas where wood collecting is permitted, and guides lead people there. Fuel-efficient stoves are promoted, Lugufu has a nursery and tree planting is encouraged.

The campaign's success has spread to the local community. Farmers now know it is unwise to cut trees or cultivate too close to rivers. Ntemi adds: "Success can come fast if you educate people before you begin to prosecute them."

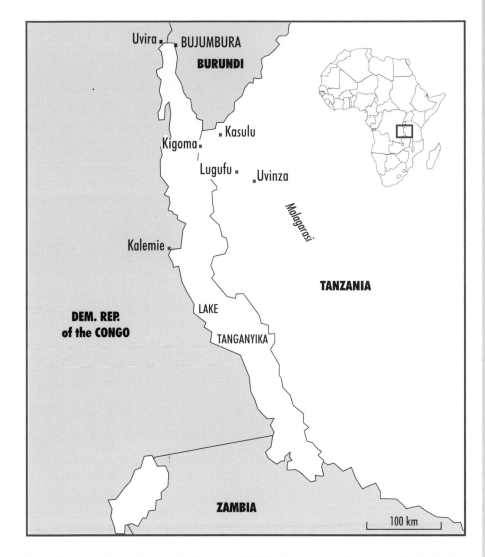

African Great Lakes region. Lugufu – a Refugee City.

It is like any planned town, built on a UNHCR-designed grid system. Each family has a plot, 24 plots make a block, 24 blocks a village. The camp has 28 villages. The people decide how the camp is run. A block leader oversees block affairs and reports to a village leader, who answers to the camp committee, Lugufu's town council. Its chairman is Kilinda M'mangyu.

He is a small, dapper man who wears a collar and tie no matter what the surroundings. There are standards for a man of position, mosquito-infested swamp or not. Back home in Fizi M'mangyu, he is a Bembe clan chief and son of a chief, a traditional leader, chosen by the elders.

He was chosen in Lugufu, and not by any agency. At the start when flooded roads meant food and water were short, young men mobbed an International Federation delegate. M'mangyu cooled tempers, averting a possibly ugly incident. He gathered camp elders and said: "Our young men must behave. We need order in Lugufu." A camp committee evolved; he was chosen as chairman unopposed. What block leaders cannot solve, they take to village leaders. What they cannot solve goes to the committee. Sometimes it's up to M'mangyu. It is the way it was back home.

A burly Irishman named Morris Power acknowledges that. At 30, Power has started and run refugee camps from Burundi to Bosnia. As Lugufu's International Federation team leader, he values the man he refers to as Mister President. "You need the leaders working with you. You must keep to your own agenda but you need dialogue in a place like this."

Statistics make that clear. By Refugee City standards, Lugufu is a small town. Yet at the end of a rutted road to nowhere, it is hard to guarantee the 35,000 daily rations of 17 litres of water, 350 grams of maize, 120 grams of beans, 30 grams of corn/soya blend, and 20 grams of oil per person.

Then there were latrines; 6,748 in all, needing 150,000 square metres of plastic, 143 km of sisal rope, 6,200 kilos of five-inch nails, 910 kilos of two-inch nails, 73,000 four-inch-thick poles, and 90,000 wooden planks. It had all bumped its way over the potholes. What aid staff lacked was enough refugee help to dig and build. The refugees thought the Red Cross should do the work.

With rains imminent and only a third of the latrines completed, Lugufu risked a health crisis. Sanitation delegate Ena Kuang, a Canadian waste management engineer, was blunt: "Cholera. It could leave people dead. It's a disease which doesn't discriminate. It will hit all ages."

The idea had been that the Red Cross made the superstructure, provided materials and tools, and refugees did the rest. Months passed, tools disappeared and progress was too slow. Power went to the camp committee: "Look, Mister President. You have to help us to help you."

Mister President seemed unimpressed. His concern was for plastic sheeting on shelters. Some needed replacing. Power sucked in breath. Some did need replacing, but not all, and plastic thefts from completed latrines had left little in stock. Power went for a deal. He would consider replacing sheeting in villages where all latrines were finished. A murmur of dissent came from the assembly but Mister President nodded. It was the best either of them would get.

Outside, a village leader asked Kuang for gum boots for his children because the rains would wash sewage through the camp. The Canadian, five-feet-nothing of determination, pushed back her spectacles: "Give me 100 per cent latrine coverage and I'll buy yours out of my own pocket."

Swamp fever

Dr August Temmu agonized over the cholera threat. The Tanzania Red Cross health coordinator and his International Federation counterpart are in effect the town's chief medical officers. The well-being of 35,000 people weighed on his shoulders: "This place is a swamp. There is no drainage system." Lugufu needed UNHCR to bring a mechanical digger to excavate ditches between villages so refugees could dig channels to them. But the UN agency would not get there before the rains.

Amid a litany of ills, Lugufu had some hope. The dispensary outpatients department reported 16,200 new cases in September, down from 19,600 the previous month. The diagnosis chart was headed by malaria, then respiratory tract infection, intestinal parasites, watery diarrhoea, scabies, sexually transmitted disease (STD), meningitis and typhoid fever. Perhaps the preventive work of health information teams – all refugee volunteers – was paying off.

Temmu had no problem with clinical facilities. The "dispensary" is an efficient 120-bed regional hospital open to both local villagers and refugees. Besides the out-patient service, there is a mother-and-child clinic, antenatal care, nutritional centre with 24-hour intensive care, pharmacy, and emergency surgical capacity. In October, 600 patients a day were coming in, and up to 200 a day were visiting two satellite health posts.

The environment worried Temmu's counterpart, Australian health delegate Caroline Dunn. She said: "Health-wise, the consequences of putting 35,000 people here are horrendous. What can you do with vector control in a swamp? Poor hygiene and living conditions are contributing to illness. Giving people pills in a place like this is mere sticking plaster."

Refugee behaviour was also worrying. Checking food outlets after some typhoid cases, a health team ran blood tests on staff and also took the opportunity to test samples for syphilis. Over half were positive. A freak sampling or representative of Lugufu's sexual health? What of the incidence of HIV/AIDS? Where syphilis leads, research has shown, HIV is close behind.

After dark, Lugufu is a hot spot, and prostitution is common. Around the market-place, makeshift bars have rooms where women can ply their trade. At one point, Tanzania's Home Affairs Ministry ordered bars to close at 23h00. It did little to curtail nightlife; pursuit of pleasure does not cease when you flee your homeland. In Lugufu, the advice was: love, but love carefully.

The safer-sex slogan came from a programme backed by both UNHCR and the UN Fund for Population Activities (UNFPA). STD, sexual exploitation and sexual violence are big problems in refugee camps everywhere. Yet what agencies refer to as refugee reproductive health care has received little attention.

A pilot project started in Lugufu and Burundian refugee camps in the Kasulu district of western Tanzania. As well as strengthening family planning, STD prevention, safe motherhood and adolescent sexuality programmes, the Tanzania Red Cross moved against sexual violence and the taboos that forced many to suffer in silence. Assured of confidential help, victims of rape and abuse are coming forward in significant numbers.

Death threats

Violence is part of every Refugee City, putting the weak at risk and aid workers in peril. Lugufu does not see the daily killings that haunted some camps, although a refugee visiting from another camp was stoned to death on the mistaken suspicion of being a spy, but crime is pervasive.

Much is due to poverty, some looks like racketeering. Routine UNHCR plans to re-register refugees threatened to expose scams inflating numbers to steal supplies. Under pressure, no refugee turned up for the first registration day. Rumours circulated that UNHCR was conspiring with Kabila's government to force repatriation and anyone cooperating would be killed.

Reliable camp sources deny a mafia gang exists in Lugufu, but how can anything less than organized crime intimidate 35,000 people? In Lugufu, the honest majority are influenced by committee president M'mangyu but he is powerless against young thugs: "They come and threaten the committee. They say nothing can happen to them so they will give us a hard time."

Nothing will happen because there is no effective policing. The camp security – volunteer refugee guards – are not taken seriously. A diligent Tanzanian camp commandant is widely respected, but he has only 10 to 15 policemen to call upon from a base outside the camp.

"A dozen policemen in a city of 35,000 people is a joke," said Denis Masesa, who heads Lugufu's 220-person Tanzania Red Cross team. "We must have more...a younger element...are creating problems. There is sexual harassment, violence, fighting, stealing." A volunteer had just been mugged. Masesa was incensed. "We have learned a great deal in Tanzania's camps. The needs of an urban community do not diminish because it is made up of refugees."

Host costs

Adam Kimbisa, secretary general of the Tanzania Red Cross, likes to quote an African proverb: "The visitor comes; the host benefits." He explains that in a rural community, a visit might lead to the slaughter of a chicken for everyone to share. In the Great Lakes crisis it seemed that the refugees would eat the fowl and leave just the carcass for local people.

It is hard to prevent a new town of 35,000 affecting local people, from higher firewood prices to damaged roads, deforestation and lost markets through free food. The 11,000 inhabitants of Uvinza, Lugufu's nearest town, have seen costs climb. A 50-shilling egg is now 120 shillings, beef is up 50 per cent, and rice has almost doubled in price.

"A few local traders are getting rich," said relief coordinator Joseph Ketto, "Poor people are facing a real problem. It is a question of supply and demand and greedy businessmen."

Many do benefit. Take Muamilla, a 625-strong poor farming village near Lugufu. Its dispensary has staff but no drugs. Before Lugufu began, the nearest medical

---

Box 9.2 **Sex in the city: raising key questions of reproductive health**

Fetching water was the ten-year-old's nightly chore. An older boy and a companion approached her at the tap stand. She was pulled behind a bush and, helped by the friend, the boy raped her.

The girl contracted gonorrhoea and went to a health post complaining of abdominal pains. Saying nothing about rape, she was treated just for her symptoms. She returned with the same complaint, staff became suspicious and the disease was identified. The parents told counsellors from the camp's reproductive health unit they did not know where to turn about the rape.

The girl has recovered, physically. The boy, aged 15, awaits trial. Another case to show that reproductive health is a neglected sector in refugee care.

Sexual assault is common in refugee camps, more than in home communities, evidence suggests. Birth rates are high, affecting the health of women and children. There are limited safe motherhood services and inadequate contraception. These were some of

the reasons the International Federation, backed by UNFPA, UNHCR and a 22-strong inter-agency working group, began a reproductive health pilot project in the Great Lakes region.

Sudanese Red Crescent health staff want the programme expanded to Khartoum's displaced camps. Community health activity already includes reproductive health but a comprehensive approach is essential, says midwife Khamissa Abounowa Souna.

Sexually transmitted disease is one concern. In El Salam it is the fourth most prevalent complaint after malaria, respiratory-tract infections and anaemia. The midwife finds the male response to family planning more worrying. Families of ten or 12 children are common.

Contraception promotion is hard. "These are rural people," she says, "and it is God who decides the number of offspring." When men object, some wives use contraception secretly, risking their husband's wrath.

---

treatment was in Kigoma, a long and expensive journey only for emergencies. The camp brought them a free local hospital.

Some 30 villagers have camp jobs and the village economy is booming. Refugees and villagers buy and sell in each other's markets. Aid staff may be unhappy with a dozen policemen; Muamilla is delighted, it is 12 more than the district had before. Then there is the water. The village source, the Lugufu river, ran dry. Now camp tankers supply clean water to their door.

Suburban Sudan

Thousands of miles north, another city is growing. Southern Sudanese tribes fleeing conflict have created slum suburbs around Khartoum. The capital's population grew from 1.5 million in 1983 to around five million ten years later. Many of the newcomers are northerners escaping drought or looking for work, but two million southerners are also thought to be in Khartoum. When fighting began, census figures showed there were 38,000 southerners in the capital.

Across the Nile from Khartoum, on the outskirts of Omdurman, El Salam disturbs no one. Before 140,000 displaced Dinkas, Nubas, Nuers and Zandis were settled here in featureless desert 30 kilometres from town, the only passers-by were nomads herding livestock to market. Brown huts rise from sandy streets. It is poor, monotonous, harsh.

The mainly Christian and animist population once lived in the lush rural south, a world away from this patch of the largely Muslim and Arab north. War and famine in the south has killed an estimated 1.3 million since 1983. For a government busy with land privatization and a radical housing plan, the 100 squatter settlements created by 1990 by those drifting north were unwelcome. Wreckers moved in, and four official camps opened.

El Salam was one and, if rumours are true, it is here to stay. The displaced may insist they will go home after peace, but the rural are now urban and observers think most will stay. Some camps may become settled areas, with infrastructure added and land sold to residents at nominal prices. A new suburb will emerge alongside one already settled with people displaced by 1980s drought.

Meanwhile, the Sudanese Red Crescent and 15 NGOs meet El Salam's needs. The politics, environment, customs and scale may be different to Lugufu but the challenges are similar. Without a convenient river, the Red Crescent delivers 1.5 million litres of water a day from boreholes. But the population is rising and pressure is on to almost double output.

Malaria is as rampant in El Salam as in Lugufu. Figures for July to September in three neighbouring camps show that of 12,925 patients, almost 4,000 had malaria symptoms. Well over half tested positive. Besides treatment, the Red Crescent launched a health education campaign and ran an environmental clean-up. Homes were sprayed, canals checked, ponds drained.

For this, the Red Crescent tapped into the camp's only natural resource: people. From training health workers to using traditional birth attendants in reproductive health programmes, mobilization is vital. A wealth of human talent – idle, ignored – can be found in Refugee City.

But El Salam isn't working. Casual labouring jobs in nearby markets, construction or industry are scarce, irregular and low-paid. Transport costs eat into low wages. Many seek seasonal employment, leaving families behind to travel to distant harvests.

*Sudan.
El Salam and
Jebel Aulia –
cities for the
displaced.*

The lack of jobs affects every aspect of life. Amira Kafi, 26, a Red Crescent health worker, herself displaced from south Kordofan, encounters tough problems: the handicapped, old and malnourished. But she insists that the worst is the inability of a family to put a meal on its table. People want jobs, not handouts.

As Sudanese citizens, the displaced have the right to work, unlike refugees. They must fend for themselves, with shelter, health care and water provided. Unlike Lugufu, there is no longer a general food distribution, although the malnourished are helped. Agencies report better nutrition but hunger abounds. Its grinding poverty is as bad as any urban slum.

Women's burdens are particularly heavy. Many are heads of households, widows and the wives of men caught up in the conflict. Some spend long days selling tea or groundnuts in the markets. Others turn to prostitution, or producing beer and wine, a risky business in a strict Islamic state.

Abuck, a tall, handsome Dinka widow in her late thirties, made date wine to support her seven children until the police got close. Now she sells tea. Unable to pay court fines, a number of camp women languish in prison. Neighbours care for the children. In a day selling tea, Abuck makes less than the price of just one bottle of good date wine. Work as a cleaner paid more, but travel fares were prohibitive. A feeding centre helps her family survive.

By some estimates, half the camp women make sorghum beer or date wine as their main income. Police raids are hurting and camp chiefs have appealed to the authorities. The law is the law, they have been told.

Turning a dollar

It is possible to make money in Refugee City. Once relocated, businessmen can often start again, but if street markets show the state of the camp economy, El Salam would appear to be in a slump. There are well-stocked traders, but many are outsiders with a branch in El Salam.

Peter, a displaced farmer from Aweil, sits outside his empty store. All his meagre stock is piled on a small stall: a little sugar, some soap, bags of tea, cigarettes. He says the problem is capital. Outsiders with money to invest thrive; the displaced without such funds stay small. El Salam needs a displaced bank. That appeals to Akol, a skilled tailor. He has laboured since 1992 to just break even. "If I had cloth and a better sewing machine, I could sell on the markets in town."

Some agencies have sought remedies for joblessness. None have delivered, so after six years El Salam's focus remains emergency relief. The only big player to have contributed to the displaced is the UN Development Programme. An urban-poor project includes a displaced component.

The Sudanese Red Crescent is looking to existing programmes elsewhere for ideas to help El Salam's endless emergency. With the International Committee of the Red Cross (ICRC), it introduced income-generating fishing ventures in the troubled south. Again with ICRC support, it is out to repeat this with a 50-family pilot project in the Jebel Aulia camp, close to the Nile.

There are other models. Animal loan programmes could help the displaced find their feet. A carpet-weaving venture for women in the western Darfur region, funded by the European Community Humanitarian Office, has become a significant industry. Gaoled beer brewers might find a better direction.

Box 9.3 Desperately seeking something as hunger stalks a burning plain

On the burning plain, the hint of a draught passes through holes in the sacking stretched over the dilapidated shelter's bamboo frame.

Perspiration beads the head of Chol, a 28-year-old Dinka farmer. For three months, he has lived with his wife and six children in the newcomers' quarter in the El Salam camp outside Khartoum. All his possessions hang in two plastic bags from the bamboo.

Chol is depressed. Today he will feed his children one meal of sorghum porridge made with water. Without a feeding centre run by Fellowship for African Relief, he would not know what to do. Since arriving, his children have suffered malnutrition, diarrhoea, malaria and – after rains soaked the shelter – respiratory infections. The Sudanese Red Crescent and Médecins sans Frontières (MSF)-France gave medical care, but Chol is ashamed he cannot take care of his family himself.

Abandoning cattle and goats, the family fled when conflict reached their southern village of Twic. They walked north into Kordofan, got to Khartoum and were transported to El Salam.

Aid agencies are helping. The Adventist Development and Relief Agency gave them two 25-kilogram bags of USAID grain, and two big cans of vegetable oil. The Sudanese Red Crescent and Ireland's Goal gave them materials for a shelter, and MSF-Holland provided two jerrycans.

Chol desperately wants work to buy food, clothes and wood for a better home. Winter is coming. He cannot make ends meet with casual market work. Chol wants his children to go to primary school. Which one: the Islamic Mission or Global Health Foundation, Catholics or Episcopalians, Allelujah Pentacostals or the Sudanese Love and Peace organization? How can he think of school until his children have food? Hunger, schools report, brings absenteeism. UNICEF and Save the Children Fund-UK have been talking to the World Food Programme about giving school breakfasts to the displaced.

Chol has been to his chief, who takes cases to a Popular Committee, one of 23 giving El Salam local government. But no help has come.

As flows of refugees and displaced people have grown in numbers and speed, linked mainly to conflict, the scale and density of their settlements demands greater understanding of their urban dimensions, from their demand for services – water, food, health care – to their real political structures, that have little relation to any aid agency theory of camp management.

The extended duration of many settlements – measured in years if not decades – implies moving beyond emergency-style solutions. Finding ways to free people to work, farm and trade with credit is critical to improving lives and ensuring that Refugee City is not just a holding operation.

If aid agencies' long experience of refugee camps means that further improvements through innovation in delivery of goods and services are unlikely, an urban awareness appears to offer many areas of work where advances are possible, from political management, environmental care and security to information, refugee credit and community mobilization.

Chapter 9 Sources, references and further reading

International Federation of Red Cross and Red Crescent Societies. *Under the Volcanoes.* World Disasters Report special focus. Geneva, 1994.

International Federation *World Disasters Report 1996.* Oxford: Oxford University Press, 1996.

International Federation. *World Disasters Report 1995.* Dordrecht: Martinus Nijhoff Publishers, 1995.

Mintzberg, Henry, with Gullet, Abbas and Omollo, Stephen. *Managing exceptionally.* Paper from an evaluation of International Federation management of a refugee camp. Available from the International Federation.

US Committee for Refugees. *World Refugee Survey 1997.* Washington DC, 1997.

Web sites

International Federation: http://www.ifrc.org

UNHCR: http://www.unhcr.ch

UNDHA ReliefWeb: http://www.reliefweb.int

Columbia sustains multiple disasters: guerrilla war, earthquakes, floods and landslides; refugees and ever-growing shanty towns. Disaster preparedness and response in Columbia has to address the politically difficult, as well as the inevitability of repeating disasters.
Charles Page/International Federation. Colombia, 1997.

Chapter

10 Colombian response aims for the long term

Active volcanoes, severe earthquakes, flash floods and forest fires have killed tens of thousands in Colombia in recent years, a toll of sudden natural-trigger disasters more than enough for any country. But these take place in the context of constantly shifting guerrilla warfare and human rights violations, thousands

Figure 10.1
Not including
disaster
response, traffic
accidents
accounted for
almost 70 per
cent of
Colombian Red
Cross
assistance in
Bogotá in 1997.
Source:
Colombian Red
Cross,

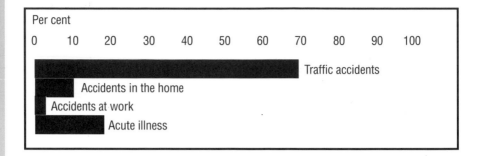

of displaced people, poverty and deep divisions, and multi-billion dollar drug empires.

Such crises and their causes – crime, conflict, underdevelopment, geology – have emphasized the need for a national disaster management infrastructure, especially after the 1985 catastrophe in the small city of Armero, when a volcanic eruption led to the deaths of 23,000 people and rendered many more homeless. Under Interior Ministry supervision, the SNPAD – National System for Prevention and Attention to Disasters – was created to bring together all the relevant national governmental and non-governmental organizations (NGOs).

Playing a key role in SNPAD's development has been the Colombian Red Cross Society, which for 70 years has responded to the needs created by violence and vulnerability. Working in all phases of both natural disasters and conflict, the National Society has a countrywide framework of offices, three national networks – supplies, transportation, telecommunications – and some 70,000 volunteers.

As a member of the International Red Cross and Red Crescent Movement, and supported by international donors, Colombian institutions and private citizens, the National Society also promotes international humanitarian law and human

Box 10.1 Swift pre-hospital care in Bogotá aims to save road casualties

Much of the work of the Colombian Red Cross in Bogotá involves responding to traffic accidents, many of them occurring at weekends with drivers who have been drinking

Financed through vehicle insurance, the Cundinamarca chapter has established an accident rescue programme with doctors from the Emergency Medical Attention Service (SAMU) and volunteers trained in search and rescue, and in pre-hospital care.

A critical factor in good response is coordination with other agencies: police, fire service, hospitals via the mayor's office health secretariat, and private clinics and ambulance companies.

All agencies share information on specific VHF radio frequencies, while cellular phone companies have agreed to handle calls to an emergency number at the Colombian Red Cross. Relief volunteers patrol accident "black spots" and receive crash reports by VHF radio, cellular telephone or pager. Extra volunteers can be called in using a Colombian Red Cross pager system.

In an emergency, the Society mobilizes a four-wheel drive vehicle with a doctor, rescue staff and equipment, and an ambulance with volunteers trained in pre-hospital care.

The doctor carries out initial stabilization and the rescue group extracts the injured, who are taken to the ambulance for advanced stabilization and then to the closest hospital, which has already been alerted by radio with details of the patients' condition.

Agencies are still learning to integrate their actions, and the response capacity is still minuscule compared to the needs of a city of seven million people, but it is an important initiative tackling a key source of death and injury.

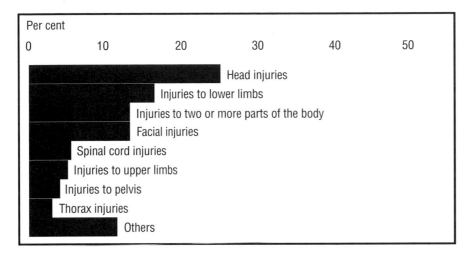

Figure 10.2 Even with Red Cross volunteers patrolling accident "black spots" in Bogotá, one-quarter of all traffic accidents led to serious head injuries.

Source: Colombian Red Cross.

rights, manages blood banks, runs training courses, and gives assistance in traffic accidents.

A vulnerability analysis of threats and capacities by the Colombian Red Cross is bringing changes to make best use of resources for 21st-century disasters. Conflict is an immediate challenge, since it also threatens the security of staff assisting victims. In the longer term, limited resources hamper recovery efforts to stabilize communities so they can better prepare for future crises.

Reviewing five different crises – earthquakes, volcanoes, floods, fires and displaced people – illustrates how each is fostering improvements in disaster management.

Colombia experiences many earthquakes and volcanic eruptions, especially in its Andean zones. These disasters are caused by geological factors, from the Nazca plate in the northern zone to Central America's Pacific Rim fault, and the mountain ranges that form a three-tipped fork as they drop towards the Caribbean Sea.

For disaster managers, this means building detailed knowledge of zones most affected by seismic and volcanic phenomena through improved monitoring,

---

Box 10.2 Training vulnerable communities to prepare for flood hazards

The Colombian Red Cross works closely with vulnerable communities to encourage active participation in preparedness programmes.

After heavy rains led to floods on the country's east coast, the SNPAD has been working with the National Society on a programme called "Training in the prevention of floods along the Caribbean coast".

The aim is to train prevention trainers in vulnerable communities so they can identify risks, alert and inform others about flood hazards, and prepare for and even prevent disasters.

The education programme was carried out in the departments of Cordoba, Sucre, Bolivar, Atlantico, Cesar and Magdalena, training 3,380 trainers, all members of vulnerable communities in 32 of the towns most affected by floods.

The training covered general disaster knowledge, floods information, communication techniques, drafting operational plans, and running local workshops. Practice sessions with the community were also held.

The work is beginning to develop a preventive culture in these vulnerable communities, with a search for better management of natural resources and greater respect for the environment.

ensuring the readiness of both equipment and personnel, and converting technical and operational information into community training programmes, including educational work with young people and the illiterate.

Charles Page/
International Federation

Preparedness through training and close inter-agency liaison, and based on better formal and informal community relations, is vital to reduce impact and improve response. The Colombian Red Cross is fostering expertise in search and rescue groups nationwide, with special equipment to work in confined spaces, aiding rescue from buildings.

Paternalistic approaches have been shown to be unsuccessful. In the Armero disaster, for example, attempts were made to solve all the community's problems from response to recovery. It has become clear that the community must solve its own problems, while the National Society acts as a guide and partner, encouraging wide participation.

Colombia rumbles and shudders more than most countries. There are 16 active volcanoes, and two principal cities - Pasto and Manizales - are located next to volcanoes. Colombia has also had ten serious earthquakes this century.

Among the most recent, an earthquake affected the city of Pereira and the Risaralda, Valle and Quindio areas, causing deaths and destruction. But preparedness programmes involving the vast majority of affected people saved many lives, through training to deal with the earthquake and its aftermath, and by ensuring compliance with seismic building codes. There was a large and immediate response using Red Cross supply, telecommunications and transport networks.

Another major earthquake affected much of the population in the Indian reservation land of the Paez (Cauca) region and Andean Central Range. Nearly 40,000 people were involved in the relief efforts. More than 2,000 tons of medical supplies were transported to distant rural populations via two main cities, Popayan and Neiva, in southern Colombia. Relief for local people was organized through 40 centres, and the operation showed good coordination between the government and organizations belonging to the SNPAD.

Box 10.3 Seismic planning brings Pereira earthquake aid within hours

The Risaralda chapter of the Colombian Red Cross put a pre-planned response system into action on 8 February 1995 when an earthquake hit Pereira, a city in a high-risk zone for seismic events.

The earthquake killed 30 people, injured 300, affected more than 3,000 families and caused losses of US$ 1.5 million, but effective planning and coordination meant the emergency was well managed.

The Red Cross supply network ensured that victims received their first relief items – mattresses, blankets and kitchen kits – in less than four hours. Within five days, all affected families had been identified and were being helped.

More than 150 Red Cross volunteers assisted in the aftermath of the disaster, helping coordinate the activities of more than 400 volunteers from other organizations. First response was from search and rescue groups, including the recently initiated Red Cross search-dog programme.

Preparedness work in schools paid off. Although more than 40 educational centres were seriously affected, only one person died and three were injured. The preparedness programme has been expanded to cover all 240 educational centres in the department of Risaralda.

As well as its effective volunteer force, the Colombian Red Cross has developed networks for supply, transportation and communications that ensure fast and efficient use of external donor resources.

Colombia.
Geological factors
contribute to the
country's frequent
natural disasters.

Flash and slow floods have affected all the lower basins in Colombia. Slow floods on low inclines affect mostly crops, allowing families time to abandon dwellings, but have serious economic and environmental effects, from food supply to water management. Flash floods affect the steeply-sloped valleys of Colombia and can cause landslides and avalanches. Certain urban areas – built on steep inclines, such as Bogotá's eastern suburbs – are also at risk from flash floods and the mudslides and erosion they provoke.

Coordination has been established between several government ministries (agriculture, environment, health and the interior) with the Colombian Red Cross, a range of local and national NGOs, and private companies to create specific flood programmes. These programmes include training for river basin communities to live with and manage the water systems for agriculture while controlling the risks they face from floods.

Figure 10.3
The Colombian
Red Cross set
up its website in
November 1996
- the first Latin
American
Society to do
so. The site, in
English and
Spanish, gives
information on
its relief
activities, its
local chapters,
partners with
whom it works,
as well as
general
information on
the International
Red Cross and
Red Crescent
Movement. It
also has a
photo gallery
portraying the
work of its
street children
programme
(PAMC). The
site can be
accessed on
http://www.crcol.
org.co/

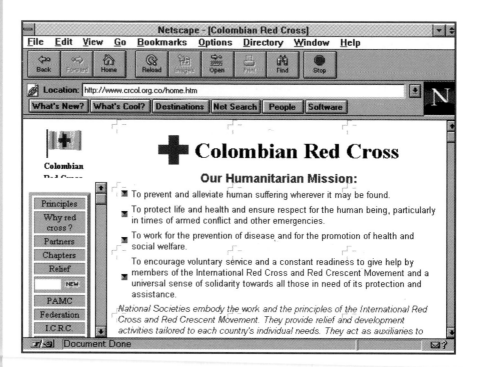

The regions of Atlantico, Cordoba and Sucre show a history of very serious floods, a situation aggravated by the El Niño phenomenon. Floods require a great effort in preparedness, from effective early warning through metereological and hydrological surveillance to pre-positioned stocks. Flood response includes providing food, emergency first aid, portable shelters, and aquatic search and rescue, which means having specialized equipment and personnel ready in flood-prone locations.

In dealing with forest fires and other environmental hazards, the Colombian Red Cross has developed expertise in prevention and environmental conservation. Colombia has made slow progress in coping with environmental problems, such as waste disposal, but the National Society is promoting environmental awareness among children with the slogan: "Let's clean the world and let's clean the region where we live".

As well as offering backup for fire-fighting operations, from first aid to food supplies, the Red Cross offers forest fire management courses with emphasis on prevention, control and extinguishing of fires in the regions of Meta, Risaralda, Valle and the entire Caribbean coast.

Conflict is a major challenge for disaster professionals and volunteers. The continuing conflict between government forces and guerrilla movements has led to large-scale movements of displaced people in various regions, such as Bolivar, particularly southern Bolivar, the Uraba zone of Antioquia, the Darien and Uraba zones of Choco and Caqueta.

In addition to this violence, conflict and displacement, terrorism in main cities – Bogotá, Cali, Medellín, Bucaramanga and Cartagena – has involved bombings and other attacks affecting a large number of people for six or more years. The Colombian Red Cross has developed a 24-hour alert system for both volunteers and experts in cases of large disasters.

The National Society cannot solve these security problems, only treat the symptoms, but under the slogan "May our presence be peace and all our actions be development", it has aimed to promote the importance of the neutrality, impartiality, independence and volunteer work of the Red Cross as fundamental elements in achieving renewed peace and development.

By decentralizing authority while maintaining good management, improved local capacities have been fostered, which in turn has encouraged strong support from the communities in the most affected regions.

Because it is impossible for one organization to meet all needs for disaster preparedness, relief and recovery, cooperation is vital, both in-country and globally. The creation of the SNPAD has led to greater integration and impact by agencies working together in cooperation with affected communities.

Continuity and sustainability are crucial factors in the cooperation with international partners, so that operations contribute to longer-term development and can be maintained by the National Society, other Colombian agencies or local communities.

Recent wide-ranging experience with natural hazards and conflict has brought the Colombian Red Cross to a number of conclusions. Among the most important are:

- Preparedness is essential in disaster management to help vulnerable communities with training and support before disasters take place.

- International and national attention on, and funding for, emergency relief – often substantial immediately after a disaster – makes it very difficult to maintain recovery and stabilization programmes for affected populations.

- Effective relief requires four logistical networks: human resources, supply, transportation, and telecommunications and information.

- Technical and scientific development is necessary to provide adequate preparation and early warning for natural disasters.

- Four elements are crucial to good response: timeliness, efficient management of resources, effective interventions in communities, and maintaining the security of all staff and volunteers.

Chapter 10 Sources, references and further information

Colombian Red Cross Society (see chapter 13).

The Institute of the Americas. Hemisfile. *The Institute of the Americas,* 10111 North Torrey Pinea Road, La Jolla, CA 92037 USA. Fax (1)(619) 453 2165.

Web sites

Colombia Support Network: http://www.igc.apc.org/csn

Colombian Red Cross Society: http://www.crcol.org.co/

International Federation: http://www.ifrc.org

Pan-American Health Organization: http://www.paho.org

Pan-American Development Foundation: http://www.oas.org/EN/PINFO/ar10e.htm

Countries where flooding is a regular occurrence build up local and national coping strategies. Not so in Eastern Europe where the floods devastated villages, farmland and whole towns. The transition economies of the affected countries found it difficult to organize effective response. People lost not just their possessions but their livelihoods, and the catastrophe led to an upsurge in cases of depression. The effect of these floods will be felt for many years to come.

©Petr Hornbuk.
Poland, 1997.

Chapter

11 European floods bring pressures for change

Downpours over Central Europe in 1997 unleashed a devastating natural disaster. From Romania to the Baltic Sea, an abnormal low-pressure weather system brought torrential rains and floods, exacting a heavy toll in human lives, homes, factories, cropland and livestock.

To the south, the Danube burst its banks in Austria, Hungary and Slovakia, causing millions of dollars in damage and prompting evacuation of thousands from nearby villages. Water-surges along the Oder River, which divides Germany from Poland, threatened to inundate the fertile plain east of Berlin. In the end, only the Ziltendorfer Niederung region in Germany's eastern state of Brandenburg was flooded. A swift response of nearly 7,000 troops with 65 helicopters and 100 boats helped the country escape the worst of the region's flooding.

Not so in Poland and the Czech Republic, which bore the full brunt of the catastrophe. Heavy rains over the Krkouose and Jeseniky mountains along the Polish, Czech and Slovak borders caused swelling of the Oder, Vistula and Niesse rivers to the north and the Morava which runs south to the Danube, flooding thousands of towns and villages.

The rains began on July 5 and lasted for two weeks, leaving much of the Czech Republic under water, and flooded 1.5 million acres in south-west Poland. In some places, twice the month's average rainfall fell in a few days. The most devastating surge was along the Oder, ravaging the city of Wroclaw on its way towards the German border and the Baltic Sea. The floods in both countries cut road, rail and telecommunication links, and inundated valuable industrial and cropland. In the Czech Republic, 30,000 business and residential properties and 312,000 acres of cropland were flooded.

Poland suffered even more heavily. In the country's south-west, the flood affected 6,000 square kilometres, including 1,360 towns and villages. Damage was heavy: 45,000 flooded buildings, including 500 schools, more than 3,000 kilometres of damaged roads, almost 2,000 kilometres of damaged rail lines, and hundreds of damaged or destroyed bridges. The floods hit heaviest in the provinces of Wroclaw, Walbrzych and Opole while some smaller cities, such as Klodzko and Raciborz further upstream along the Oder, were inundated.

The floods left behind shattered homes and livelihoods. Graphic television images showed tens of thousands forced to leave their homes, with evacuations by boat and helicopter. More than 100 people were killed, and tens of thousands made

---

Box 11.1 Making the most of the market to find more coping mechanisms

As former communist countries become market economies, commercial insurance is an effective but under-used coping mechanism for families and businesses to protect their assets.

Despite property insurance growth, awareness of risk sharing in Eastern Europe remains low. Only 10 to 15 per cent of Czech and Polish flood victims had any insurance.

Most firms in the region are under-insured, particularly small firms that tend to have minimum cover. Few hold business interruption cover, while use of risk managers and insurance brokers is negligible.

The insured may recover very little. Poland's National Insurance Institute estimates that businesses cover only 25 per cent of assets. Under communism, firms simply had to report the book value

to the sole state insurer. Few upgraded cover to the true asset value.

New Polish and Czech insurance companies are potentially at risk in a big catastrophe through lack of capital, which has also discouraged development of the insurance market.

Even developed insurance markets tend to underestimate natural disaster risks, especially floods. Munich Re, the world's largest reinsurance company, recently reported that flooding is one of the least insured yet most costly natural hazards.

It urged a partnership of policy holders, insurers, reinsurers and governments to cover the floods insurance gap. This could include a government-backed catastrophe reinsurance programme with financial incentives to mitigate risks.

destitute. In total, 160,000 people had been evacuated from their homes in Poland, and another 50,000 in the Czech Republic.

Receding waters ushered in a whole new set of problems as thousands of returning evacuees and survivors were forced to deal with strewn sewage, rubbish and dead farm animals, often while cut off from power and medical aid. Many returned to find a life's work and savings lost or smashed. Health officials broadcast warnings to use bottled water and avoid contaminated food, fearing outbreaks of dysentery, hepatitis, salmonella and typhoid.

The scale of the floods found both countries desperately unprepared. In stark contrast to the huge quantities of money and trained manpower that Germany was able to marshal, the cash-strapped Czech and Polish governments seemed, at times, almost impotent to prevent flooding, organize relief efforts and mobilize funds to rebuild. There was strong public criticism. In Poland, the government's loss of parliamentary elections in September was partly attributed to the disaster. No one could have stopped the floods, critics argued, but its repercussions could have been greatly reduced.

Prevention lacking

Decades of neglect of flood control under the old communist regimes had left the region vulnerable to just such a disaster. In January 1994, Poland's Supreme Board of Inspection reported to the government that 2,000 of the country's 9,000 kilometres of dykes required modernization. The cost of modernization and river regulation was put at 2.6 billion zlotys (US$ 850 million).

Little had been done to rectify the problem. During the floods, Poland's National Flood Control Committee complained they lacked adequate equipment to analyse rainfalls, perform flood simulations or monitor mountain tributaries of flooded rivers.

In addition, the condition of Poland's forests, usually a major factor in flood prevention, had been rapidly deteriorating. Forests occupy 28 per cent of Poland's land surface but much is poorly managed. The Green Federation and other environment groups linked harmful exploitation of highland forests to the floods. There were many other examples of neglect. At Kvasice on the Morava

---

Box 11.2 Assistance offered as suicides rise after the waters subside

Poland is helping flood victims overcome the social and psychological effects.

Its health ministry sent seven teams of psychologists, social workers and doctors to counsel those suffering from stress.

Most victims suffered some degree of post-traumatic stress disorder, which was expected to intensify over the winter.

Common symptoms were recurrent fears, with nightmares, fear of water, and compulsive acts. One woman constantly woke up her husband to check if embankments were leaking. Another became hysterical at the sound of a running tap.

Janusz Czapinski, Poland's psychological aid coordinator, reported 50 flood-linked suicides by the end of August. He said physically and psychologically exhausted people feared they might never recover. Alcohol abuse rose. Feelings of injustice over aid handouts were likely.

Among those badly affected were children who saw the security of their homes swept away, while their parents were powerless against the destruction. Months later, some still suffered repeated nightmares, and many would break down in tears at the sound of helicopters.

The government planned to produce a handbook to help teachers help children, while the Polish Psychological Society aimed to establish a psychosocial assistance programme of seven centres to help victims deal with the aftermath.

River in the Czech Republic, continued use of a gravel pit that should have ceased operation in 1985 weakened river barriers and allowed water to pour into the town.

Critics claimed that both governments relied too heavily on large and expensive reservoir projects, which were insufficient as flood control without smaller reservoir systems to act as cumulative buffers. Poland has 150 water reservoirs, but has lost many of the water mills and ponds that existed before the World War II. According to its Central Statistical Office, Poland is one of the worst countries in Europe in terms of water storage, with 1,600 cubic metres per head in 1996, a third of the 4,500-cubic-metre European average.

The Czech government, conceding that the reservoir system was inadequate, proposed that four new dams being built should including smaller facilities like flood banks to cut future flooding risks.

©Teit Hornbak

Coordination

The Polish and Czech governments were also criticized for delay and mistakes in their efforts to manage the catastrophe and coordinate relief.

Early warning systems were deficient. A report by the United Nations Department of Humanitarian Affairs (UNDHA) showed just how important warning systems were in combating the floods. Czech and Polish cities, given enough time, were able to limit damage with better control of water flows or by diverting floods to non-critical areas. Many towns and villages were not given the option.

The first warnings by Poland's Institute of Meteorology and Water Resources came on July 4. But the towns of Klodzko and Raciborz were still unprepared for flooding which hit on July 7, three days after heavy rains began. Even after the deluge ravaged much of south-west Poland, officials were unclear how far the floods would progress.

On July 10, Feliks Dela, head of the National Civilian Defence, declared that the wave that inundated Opole was not dangerous to 650,000-strong Wroclaw since it was "milder and it was flattening." A high water-surge along the Oder and Wisla rivers 48 hours later swamped Wroclaw's unprepared suburbs and would have done the same to the historic city centre had it not been for a frantic overnight effort by determined citizens building sandbag barriers.

There were many examples of flood alert guidelines being ignored in the Czech Republic, where upstream districts are obliged to warn lower districts of impending water levels.

Czech government officials also acknowledged problems in coordinating state and non-state agencies in flood relief, in response to concern that while a few high-profile communities received substantial help, others got nothing. The country's environment minister, Jiri Skalicky, who was also the reconstruction commissioner, subsequently brought together all agencies involved in flood relief to coordinate operations more efficiently.

An assessment team from the US Bureau for Humanitarian Response and Office of Foreign Disaster Assistance suggested both countries should consider more unified national structures for disaster preparedness, including shared radio frequencies.

Coordination was obstructed by mistrust between government and flood victims, particularly in Poland. Early in the flooding, Poland's then-prime minister, Wlodzimierz Cimoszewicz, blamed flood victims for not having insurance and said that farmers whose land was flooded would not be compensated. He soon retracted the statements, but the damage was done.

Some flood victims even believed that their villages were recklessly sacrificed by officials who destroyed retaining walls to divert waters away from larger communities downstream. Others alleged that relief food had been spoiling in warehouses, or been sold by officials for personal profit.

Lack of trust could bring harsh consequences. Wroclaw might have been spared terrible damage if local villagers had allowed gaps to be blown in upstream dykes. Instead the villagers, fearing they would not be compensated for their homes and farms, lay down on the dykes to prevent the blasting. By the time full payment was offered, it was too late. The deputy president of Wroclaw's council, Stanislaw Huskowski, estimated the costs of compensating the farmers at one-tenth of the damage to the city.

Damage and rebuilding

With receding waters, both governments rolled into action with recovery and reconstruction plans to rebuild infrastructure, find schools for children, and shelter for the homeless. The bills were hard to pay.

Poland's coordinating National Programme of Reconstruction and Modernization estimated flooding caused damage of about 9.8 billion zlotys (approximately $3 billion) or 2.7 per cent of total 1996 GDP. Repairing roads and bridges was expected to cost more than $700 million and take five years. In the Czech Republic, flood damage was estimated at some 60 billion crowns ($1.8 billion) or 3.7 per cent of GDP, with half due to damaged buildings, roads and bridges.

Insurance industry figures show that less than 10 per cent of households and businesses were properly covered for flood damage. Aid from abroad was expected to cover only a small percentage of total costs. Neither country operated a national insurance programme, nor held emergency reserves. Both countries had been in the middle of tough fiscal austerity campaigns to reduce state expenditures and cut government budget deficits.

Box 11.3 Fast response from donors in cash, equipment and teams

The international community's immediate response included cash, equipment and teams for flood relief.

At August 5, the UNDHA recorded $10.3 million in disbursed relief assistance, including $7.5 million in official and non-official German aid.

The EU was a committed supporter of relief and reconstruction. ECHO allotted ECU 2.5 million for aid to the Czech Republic and Poland, and ECU 1.6 million for other flood-affected countries.

The European Investment Bank approved ECU 500 million in loans – ECU 300 million for Poland, ECU 200 million for the Czech Republic – to part-finance repairs to roads, railways, flood protection and water facilities.

The European Bank for Reconstruction and Development offered ECU 100 million in loans to damaged Polish and Czech cities, including ECU 35 million for Wroclaw. The World Bank loaned Poland $300 million for road and bridge repairs.

The EU's PHARE programme planned to provide ECU 36.75 million to help business restoration, particularly smaller companies with limited credit access.

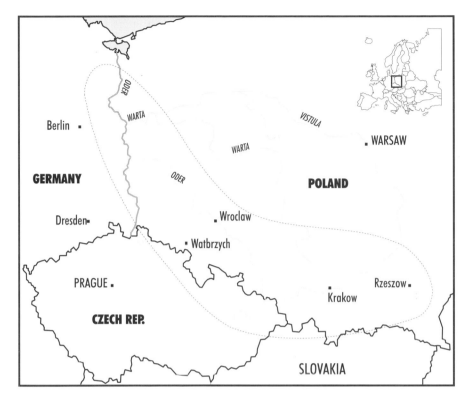

Central Europe 1997. Devasting downpours shatter homes and livelihoods (—— extent of floods.)

Poland's initial response was to find hundreds of millions of dollars by switching budget funds from other purposes and freezing other construction projects. Much of that went to the immediate clean-up. The government also increased its borrowing limit from the central bank by $740 million and increased its foreign borrowing limit.

By October, the Polish government had already spent 1.4 billion zloty ($428 million) in relief and repairs. This figure included funds from emergency organizations and the European Union's (EU) PHARE programme, which provides grants to support the economic and political transformation of would-be EU member states.

With insurance payouts, official funds and foreign aid, spending will approach 3 billion zlotys. The government also plans to raise another 2 billion zlotys from foreign loans. How to finance the remaining 4.6 billion zloty from the state budget is under intense debate.

A financing gap also worries the Czech government. Prague has proposed to provide up to 5 billion crowns in domestic bond issues, another 5 billion from state asset proceeds, such as privatization receipts, and 2.7 billion from the state budget. Insurance companies will cover 5 to 10 billion crowns. This is well short of the estimated cost of 60 billion crowns.

Flood bond sales have gone poorly and very few Czechs seem to favour paying for the rest. In a poll by the Institute for Public Opinion Research in September, just two months after the flooding, only 7 per cent of respondents were ready to find more for flood costs. Another survey in the same month, by the Center for Empirical Research, showed only 10 per cent wanted a special tax to finance rebuilding work. In Poland, the "compassion fatigue" of shrinking support for flood victims set in quite early, raising doubts about the government's ability to honour flood cost pledges.

Official damage figures do not include the enormous, but hard to estimate, losses in production, wages and jobs. The Polish Agriculture Ministry put damage to agricultural infrastructure at 1.1 billion zlotys, while production losses that could reach 25 to 30 billion zlotys. Czech farmers, eligible for compensation, complained that they received less than 20 per cent of the costs of machinery, property and lost production.

Any central government finance gaps will have to be filled by individuals, firms and local authorities.

New approach

Government officials blamed the problems on the disaster's unprecedented scale and unpredictability. How could they forecast flood paths when surges changed direction so rapidly? With roads and railroad tracks demolished, how could relief shipments arrive on time? Financing reconstruction would have to go cautiously or jeopardize economic stability.

The disaster was extreme and unusual: rainfall four times the July average, floods one-and-a-half times higher than those anticipated by dyke builders, rivers two metres above flood warning levels. There were at least as many acts of competence and resolve as there were failures and mismanagement but the problems exemplified the inexperience of institutions tackling the risks and costs of natural disasters, and exposed how incomplete the transformation from centrally run economies is in Poland and the Czech Republic.

Transformation involves all aspects of economic and social life, but in particular how the state manages resources. The old decision making was inherently centralized, including the management of natural disasters, from flood defence

Box 11.4 International Federation coordinates international aid

The International Federation of Red Cross and Red Crescent Societies was one of the first international organizations to respond to the floods.

On July 14, the International Federation launched an Emergency Appeal seeking CHF 6,960,000 in cash, kind and services to assist 257,000 flood victims in Poland, the Czech Republic, Slovakia and Hungary.

National Societies in each country coordinated their relief work with governments, local authorities and NGOs. Local branches in Poland were active members of district Anti-Flood Task Force Units, while the Czech Red Cross worked through Local Crisis Units.

The initial focus was on immediate relief: food, hygiene and bedding items, as well as drinking water tanks. National Societies and volunteers in local branches packaged and distributed emergency aid items. Staff and volunteers helped evacuate citizens to shelters while National Societies coordinated collection of public donations.

As the flood waters retreated, National Societies began to identify rehabilitation needs to facilitate the return of those evacuated. These included providing basic household equipment, minor repair materials, detergent and disinfectants for the clean-up operation and insecticides to combat mosquitoes. Summer camps were organized for flood-affected children.

Relief and reconstruction efforts were supported by National Societies throughout Europe, including in-kind donations from the Belgian and Spanish Red Cross Societies towards food and hygiene needs. German and Austrian Red Cross Emergency Response Units carried out water purification operations in affected areas.

systems to coordinating response efforts, compensating victims and rebuilding infrastructure after disasters.

Insurance was nationalized in both the Czech Republic and Poland. Flood cover was almost universal. All premiums went back into state funds, claims were paid from the state budget and any gaps were met by the state controlling resource allocations. Since then, decentralization and democratization have weakened state power.

Transition, however, remains incomplete. Despite considerable political liberalization, both Poland and the Czech Republic maintain centralized government structures, but without the old communist state's political and financial strength. Devolution has yet to catch up with democracy. Over-centralization and an elderly crisis management system were much to blame for the delays, shortages, poor logistics and general disorganization during the floods.

Likewise, new institutions, such as private insurance, have yet to fill the void of the departing state. If families, farmers, businesses and local governments end up bearing the costs of natural disasters, they must begin preparing to manage these risks.

Under such conditions, the importance and benefits of insurance are vast. Awareness, however, remains low. Insurance premiums in Poland account for only 2 to 3 per cent of GDP, compared to 13 per cent in Britain, for example. People tend to underestimate hazards. Flood risk is difficult to measure, loss potentials are high, insurance against it is sometimes hard to find and the cost may be unaffordable for the average home-owner or small business.

A report from the global reinsurance giant Munich Re, Floods and Insurance – Old Questions, New Solutions?, has urged a partnership of policy holders, insurers, reinsurers and the state, "in which each party assumes a portion of the overall risk for some costs of the precautions taken", as "the only feasible way of providing more comprehensive cover for flood risks" since both governments and insurers have a role to play in loss prevention.

In this "stakeholders" approach to natural disaster risks, governments and insurers can help by identifying high-risk communities, fostering scientific examination of flood processes, mapping areas by flood exposure and motivating mitigation through financial incentives. Governments can monitor environmental conditions and enforce land use policies, zoning and river regulation. Insurers can contribute loss analysis and risk inspections. Both can work together promoting awareness campaigns to develop better understanding of disaster risks.

For Poland and the Czech Republic, other partners might be useful, such as aid agencies. In the US, the American Red Cross and an insurance industry association are joining forces to educate communities about the benefits of disaster mitigation planning.

Pooling risks is another possible avenue for both countries. European insurance industry officials have been promoting the establishment of government-backed catastrophe reinsurance programmes, like those available in Spain or France.

Better yet, both countries can begin experimenting with decentralized programmes – perhaps modelled on the US National Flood Insurance Program – that make insurance or other financial incentives available to flood-prone communities. In return, communities agree to guide future floodplain development themselves, taking responsibility for mitigation efforts to protect infrastructure and buildings before disaster strikes.

Local initiatives will happen, with or without government help. Barum Continental Ostrokovice, the giant Czech tyre manufacturer, has already suggested raising the banks of the Drevnice River or building a one-metre-high concrete wall to protect the company and a neighbouring heating facility from the swollen river. The company has proposed sharing the costs with regional and municipal governments.

A stakeholder, decentralized approach marks new opportunities not only in mitigation but in disaster response. In both the Czech Republic and Poland, centralized relief coordination often made response slow and incomplete. Local councils and other organizations could not properly respond without a "signal" from Warsaw or Prague, while central government had no administrative mechanisms with which to respond to the disaster quickly or exhaustively.

In mid-July, Czech First Deputy Interior Minister Jaroslav Kopriva admitted that "better communication at all levels, and improved legislation to define the authority of public officials in an emergency are needed".

Local government

Local authorities argued that the disaster illustrated the extreme costs and inefficiency of central decision-making and complained about a lack of proper powers – or clear responsibility – to act in emergency situations. No plans existed for coordination between regional officials, local figures and anti-flood committees. Local authorities did not know or understand what could be done without consulting higher authorities. When they did, no funds existed to respond adequately. In Poland, for example, local government has access to only 14 per cent of total state income. Many believe neglect of local government reform was at the root of inefficient flood rescue operations.

In Poland, no administrative unit exists between the regional voivods, consisting of millions of people, and the gminas consisting of a few thousand. In disasters, gminas are probably too small for effective response, while voivods are too distant from local problems. An intermediate administrative unit is also missing in the Czech Republic, which has only one level of elected local government, the community.

To be effective, administrative reform will need to be accompanied by restructuring of government finances to allocate more at regional level. This is a major change; Prague and Warsaw had so far shown very little enthusiasm for deregulating power to local authorities. Poland's new centre-right government has since accelerated government debate on administrative reform, promising to create intermediate levels of government and allocate about 40 per cent of total budgetary funds to locally elected authorities. A countrywide referendum on a new administrative structure was scheduled for some time in 1998.

A highly decentralized disaster response, involving a diverse range of personnel and organizations, allows organizations to adapt to rapidly changing disaster environments. This rejects the "command and control" model of a single unified structure for emergency action. Central to the new approach is the assumption that local people know the most about local needs. For this to work, however, both countries need to devolve power and resources.

Prague or Warsaw would still play an important role in mitigation and control of natural disasters, which tend to involve many organizations and require effective coordination of diverse resources. Central government can promote mitigation, shared planning and response strategies between affected communities, organizations and individuals. This, however, should not mean extinguishing the creativity, experience and flexibility offered by so many other legitimate partners in society.

Chapter 11 Sources, references and further reading

Blaikie, et al. *At Risk: Natural Hazards, People's Vulnerability, and Disasters*. London: Routledge, 1996.

Corps of Engineers' Institute for Water Resources. *Internaional Cost Effectiveness Analysis for Environmental Planning: Nine Easy Steps*. IWR Report 94-PS2, October 1994. Corps of Engineers' Institute for Water Resources, Water Resources Support Center, Casey Building, 7701 Telegraph Road, Alexandria, Va., USA.

Drabek, T. and Hoetmer, G. *Emergency Management: Principles and Practice for Local Government*. Washington, DC: International City Management Association, 1991.

Dynes, R. and Tierney, K. (eds.) *Disasters, Collective Behaviour and Social Organizations*. Newark: University of Delaware Press, 1994.

Gow, Gordon A. *New Approaches In Disaster Communications: Towards a Global Communications Lifeline Infrastructure*. Graduate Programme in Communications Studies, University of Calgary, 1997.

Kent, Randolph C. *Anatomy of Disaster Relief: The International Network in Action*. New York: Pinter, 1987. ISBN: 0-86187-294-0.

Koehler, Gus A. (ed.) *What Disaster Response Management Can Learn from Chaos Theory*. Conference Proceedings, May 18-19, 1995. Sacramento: California Research Bureau, 1996.

McLuckie, Benjamin F. *Italy, Japan, and the United States: Effects of Centralization on Disaster Response 1964-1969*. 1977.

Quarantelli, E.L. *Organizational Behavior in Disasters and Implications for Disaster Planning*. FEMA Monograph Series, 1984.

United Nations International Decade for Natural Disaster Reduction (IDNDR). *Planning for a Safer World in the 21st Century. Development and Implementation Notes*. Geneva: UN IDNDR Secretariat, 1995.

Web sites

AlertNet: http://www.alertnet.org

Disaster   Relief: http://www.disasterrelief.org

Disaster   Research   Center: http://www.udel.edu/DRC

Disaster   Resources: http://www.uiuc.edu/~disaster/disaster.html

Flood   Disaster   in   Poland: http://www.flooding.pl

Flooding   in   Poland: http://www.polishworld.com/flooding

Floodplain   Management   Association: http://www.floodplain.org

Natural   Hazards   Information   Center: http://www.colorado.edu/hazards

UN   IDNDR: http://hoshi.cic.sfu.ca/~idndr/IDPLANDR.html.

UNDHA   ReliefWeb: http://www.reliefweb.int

University   of   Calgary: http://www.sfu.ca/~gagow/capcom/thesis.htm

Volunteers   in   Technical   Assistance: http://www.vita.org

Warsaw   Voice: http://www.warsawvoice.com.pl

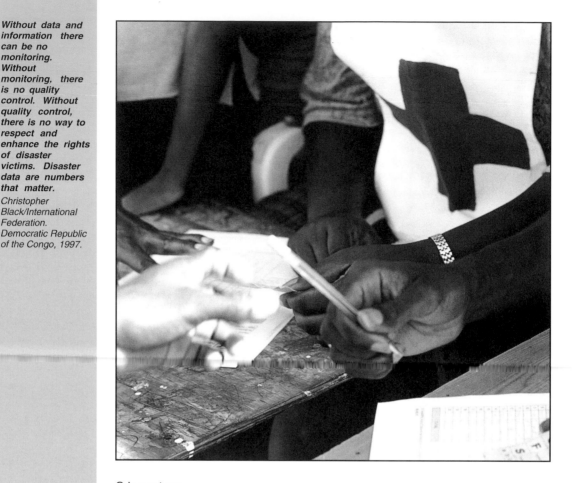

Chapter

12 Using key statistics for improved response

Data on disaster occurrence, its effect upon people and its cost to countries remain, at best, patchy. The *World Disasters Report* draws upon five main sources of information for the data presented here: the Centre for Research on the Epidemiology of Disasters (CRED); the US Committee for Refugees (USCR); the PIOOM Foundation, based at Leiden University in the Netherlands; the Organisation for Economic Co-operation and Development's (OECD) Development Assistance Committee (DAC); and INTERFAIS, a World Food Programme (WFP) information system. Each organization is described in more detail below.

One of the key problems today with disaster data collection is the lack of standard, accepted definitions. Problems exist over such loose categories as "internally displaced" people or even people "affected" by disaster.

Much of the data in this chapter, except that on government humanitarian spending, is culled from a variety of public sources: newspapers, insurance reports, aid agencies, etc. The original information is not specifically gathered for statistical purposes and so, inevitably, even where the compiling organization applies strict definitions for disaster events and parameters, the original suppliers of the information may not.

The figures therefore should be regarded as indicative. Relative changes and trends are more useful to look at than absolute, isolated figures.

CRED

Based at the Department of Public Health, Catholic University of Louvain (Belgium), CRED has developed a system of databases for global disaster management, drawing on its existing disaster documentation, information network and computer system. Tables 1 to 12 of this database section were derived from the EM-DAT, a disaster events database developed by CRED and sponsored by the International Federation of Red Cross and Red Crescent Societies, World Health Organization (WHO), United Nations Department for Humanitarian Affairs (UNDHA), European Community Humanitarian Office (ECHO) and the International Decade for Natural Disaster Reduction. USAID's Office of Foreign Disaster Assistance also collaborated in getting this database started.

EM-DAT is now fully operational, with more than 11,500 records of disaster events from 1900 onward, and its own menu for updates, modification and retrieval. Designed to have the right level of detail for wide use, the entries are constantly reviewed for redundancies, inconsistencies and the completion of missing data.

USCR

The US Committee for Refugees (USCR), which supplied the data for tables 13 to 15, is the public information and advocacy arm of Immigration and Refugee Services of America, a non-governmental organization (NGO). USCR's activities are twofold: It reports on issues affecting refugees, asylum seekers and internally displaced people; and it encourages the public, policy makers and the international community to respond appropriately and effectively to the needs of uprooted populations.

USCR travels to the scene of refugee emergencies to gather testimony from uprooted people, to assess their needs, and to gauge governmental and international response. The committee conducts public briefings to present its findings and recommendations, testifies before the US Congress, communicates concerns directly to governments, and provides first hand assessments to the media. USCR publishes the annual *World Refugee Survey,* the monthly *Refugee Reports,* and issue papers.

PIOOM

Data for tables 16 to 19 were provided by PIOOM – the Interdisciplinary Research Programme on the Root Causes of Human Rights Violations. Based at Leiden University in the Netherlands, PIOOM was established in 1988 to study violence and human rights. PIOOM's researchers at Leiden and Utrecht universities collaborate with the London-based FEWER (Forum on early warning and early response) consortium and other associates worldwide.

The violation of human rights often acts as an indicator for escalating conflicts, and is frequently the result of armed disputes, so the monitoring of conflict dynamics is central to PIOOM's effort to understand the root causes of human rights violations. PIOOM hopes that by studying, and promoting the study of, human rights and violence it may help reduce worldwide human rights violations.

OECD/DAC

The data in table 20 have been supplied by the OECD's Development Assistance Committee, which is the principal body through which OECD deals with issues related to cooperation with developing countries. The committee is concerned with support for efforts in developing countries to strengthen local capacities to pursue integrated development strategies, and studies the financial aspects of development assistance, statistical problems, aid evaluation, and women in development.

INTERFAIS/WFP

The source of information for table 21 is INTERFAIS (the International Food Aid Information System), a system funded by WFP. It is a dynamic system, which involves the interaction of all users, represented by donor governments, international organizations, NGOs, recipient governments and WFP country offices. All information is cross-checked before being disseminated. Its comprehensive and integrated database allows the monitoring of food-aid allocations and shipments for the purpose of improving food aid management, coordination and statistical analysis. The database is updated on a continuing basis, and data can therefore change as allocation plans and delivery schedules are subject to modifications. Data is available from 1988.

Disaster data

Information systems have improved vastly in the last 25 years and statistical data as a result are much more easily available. An increase in the number of disaster victims, for example, does not necessarily mean that disasters, or their impact, are increasing, but may simply be a reflection of better reporting. However, the lack of systematic and standardized data collection from disasters, man-made or natural, in the past is now revealing itself as a major weakness for any developmental planning. Cost-benefit analyses, impact analyses of disasters or rationalization of preventive actions are severely compromised by unavailability and inaccuracy of data or even field methods for collection. Fortunately, as a result of increased pressures for accountability from various sources, many donor and development agencies have started placing priority on data collection and its methodologies.

Tables 1 to 12

CRED's data have appeared in each edition of the *World Disasters Report* since the pilot issue in 1993. This year, however, the presentation has been updated:

■ Tables 1 to 8 show the annual average number of victims and types of disaster over the last 25 years, in five-year periods, to allow for clear trends analysis. They give an idea of the number of people killed, made homeless, affected or injured by natural and non-natural disasters by region (tables 1 to 4) and by type of disaster (tables 5 to 8).

■ Table 9 presents the annual average number of disasters and victims for a ten-year period (1987 to 1996). This approach modifies considerably the analysis possible on the consequences of natural disasters. Earthquakes and volcanic eruptions, for example, occur infrequently and national or even continental statistics are very different if a ten-year, rather than a 25-year, period is considered. Floods and high wind, on the other hand, are disasters affecting certain states on an almost annual basis, and therefore ten-year statistics can give as good an idea of impact as 25-year statistics. Droughts, however, seem to have been less frequent in the past ten years, which will influence the statistics.

■ Figures in table 11 (annual average number of people reported killed or affected by disaster by country) are shown as a ten-year average. Estimates for 1997 have also been shown.

■ Average estimated damage has been calculated over ten years (rather than five years as was the case in previous editions).

Despite efforts to verify, cross-check and review data, its quality can only be as good as the reporting system. If field agencies were to adhere to standard reporting methods, it would be far easier – and much less costly – to assemble essential data from numerous sources. Data presented in these tables are recorded at CRED; while no responsibility can be taken for a figure, its source can always be provided.

The criteria for entry of an event is ten deaths, and/or 100 affected, and/or an appeal for assistance. In cases of conflicting information, priority is given to data from governments of affected countries, followed by UNDHA, and then the US Office for Foreign Disaster Assistance. Agreement between any two of these sources takes precedence over the third. This priority is not a reflexion on the quality or value of the data, but the recognition that most reporting sources have vested interests, and figures may be affected by socio-political considerations.

Dates can be a source of ambiguity. The declared date for a famine, for example, is both necessary and meaningless – famines do not occur on a single day. In such cases, the date the appropriate body declares an official emergency has been used.

Figures for those "killed" in disasters should include all confirmed dead, and all missing and presumed dead. Frequently, in the immediate aftermath of a disaster, the number of "missing" is not included, but it may be added later. Without international standards, definitions vary from source to source, so each entry is checked for clarification.

People "injured" covers those with physical injury, trauma or illness requiring medical treatment as a direct result of disaster. First aid and other care by volunteers or medical personnel is often the main form of treatment provided at the disaster site, but it has not been defined whether people receiving these services should be included as "injured".

"Homeless" is defined as the number of people needing immediate assistance with shelter. Discrepancies may arise when source figures refer to either individuals or families. Average family sizes for the disaster region are used to reach consistent figures referring to individuals.

Defining "people affected" is extremely arduous. Figures will always rely on estimates, as there are many different standards, especially in major famines and in the complex disasters of the former Soviet Union and Eastern Europe.

In this chapter, both the numbers of people affected, and those made homeless, are given by disaster. However, to obtain a more realistic idea of the numbers involved, the number of homeless for the last five years should be added to the number of people affected.

Disparities in reporting units can create dilemmas, such as the monetary value of damages expressed in either US dollars or local currencies. While it is easier to leave currencies as they are reported and convert them only when the event is of interest, this procedure effectively slows the comparison and computations often required by data users.

In addition, inflation and currency fluctuation are not taken into account when calculating disaster-related damages. At present, estimating the monetary value of disasters is far from precise. Multi-standard reporting makes estimations difficult, as does the lack of standardization of estimate components. For example, one estimation may include only damage to livestock, crops and infrastructure, while another may also include the cost of human lives lost. It is not always clear whether estimations are based on the cost of replacement or on the original value. Insurance figures, while using standard methodology, include only those people that have been insured, which in most developing countries represent a minor proportion of the losses. A standard methodology for the estimation of the economic damages is urgently required to justify prevention and preparedness programmes.

Disaster information from four different sources is reported regularly to CRED, and the register updated daily. The sources are: UNDHA situation reports; International Federation situation reports; *Lloyd's Casualty Week* (published by Lloyd's of London with information on weather events, earthquakes, volcanic eruptions and different types of accidents worldwide); and some World-Wide Web pages on the Internet which provide daily news on disasters in specific regions (for example, the Pan-American Health Organization page).

Each new event is entered with date, type of disaster and country. Data on human or economic impact are consolidated at CRED at three-month intervals the first year. Annual updating is undertaken the following year.

Information is cross-checked each year, and occasionally new events added, using data from reinsurance companies, the World Meteorological Organization, the UN Economic and Social Commission for Asia and the Pacific, as well as articles in specialized journals and unpublished university research. Finally, the annual list of disasters is sent for control to a focal point in countries affected by the disasters.

Changes in national boundaries can cause ambiguities in the data, most notably the break-up of the Soviet Union and Yugoslavia, and the unification of Germany. In such cases, no attempt has been made to retrospectively desegregate or combine data. Statistics are presented for the country as it existed at the time the data were recorded.

Tables 13 to 15

The data in these tables were provided by the US Committee for Refugees (USCR), and concern three categories of uprooted people: refugees, asylum seekers and internally displaced people. Data concerning these populations are often controversial, for they involve judgements about why people have left their home areas. Differing definitions of the groups in question often promote confusion about the meaning of reported estimates.

USCR itself does not conduct censuses of these populations. Instead, the committee evaluates population estimates circulated by governments, UN agencies and humanitarian assistance organizations, attempting to discern which of the various estimates appear to be most reliable. The estimates reproduced in these tables are USCR's preliminary year-end figures for 1997.

The quality of the data in these tables is affected by the less-than-ideal conditions often associated with flight. Unsettled conditions, the biases of governments and opposition groups, and the need to use population estimates to plan for providing humanitarian assistance can each contribute to inaccurate estimates.

Tables 13 and 14 concern refugees and asylum seekers: table 13 lists refugees and asylum seekers by country of origin, while table 14 lists the two groups by host country. The totals in the two tables are not equal because many governments do not report country-of-origin data or because of rounding.

Refugees are people who are outside their home country and are unable or unwilling to return to that country because they fear persecution or armed conflict. Asylum seekers are people who claim to be refugees; many are awaiting a determination of their refugee status. While not all asylum seekers are refugees, they are nonetheless entitled to certain protections under international refugee law, at least until they are determined not to be refugees.

Different standards for refugee status exist in different countries or regions. Recognition of refugee status, however, does not make someone a refugee, but rather declares her or him to be one. "He does not become a refugee because of recognition, but is recognized because he is a refugee," the UN High Commissioner for Refugees (UNHCR) has noted. Not all refugees are recognized as such by governments.

USCR has not included in tables 13 and 14 people who appear to have been granted permanent protection, even if they have not yet officially become citizens of their adopted country. This method of record-keeping differs from that employed by UNHCR.

Table 15 concerns "internally displaced people". Like refugees and asylum seekers, internally displaced people have fled their homes; unlike refugees and asylum seekers, however, they remain within their home country.

No universally accepted definition of an "internally displaced person" exists. USCR generally considers people who are uprooted within their country because of armed conflict or persecution – and thus would be refugees if they were to cross an international border – to be internally displaced. Broader definitions are employed by some agencies, however, which sometimes include people who are uprooted by natural or human-induced disasters or other causes not directly related to human rights.

Internally displaced people often live in war-torn areas and may be subject to ongoing human rights abuse, sometimes at the hands of their own government.

Most internally displaced people are neither registered nor counted in any systematic way. Estimates of the size of internally displaced populations are frequently subject to great margins of error.

Tables 16 to 18

Since 1945, only 63 countries have not been affected by armed conflict and some 200 major conflicts have occurred, more than 90 per cent of them in developing countries, mainly in Africa and Asia. An estimated 45 million people died in fighting between 1945 and 1995.

The classic image of war as a clash between two state-controlled armies has, in large parts of the world, given way to hybrid forms of fighting where "war" crimes and politics often go hand in hand.

In recent years, war between states (about 12 per cent of the 102 wars fought between 1985 and 1994) has been replaced to a large extent by civil and ethnic wars, where the majority of people killed are civilians – 84 per cent according to the winter 1997 edition of the PIOOM Newsletter. With so many civilians becoming victims of armed conflict, the borderline between war and genocide has also become fuzzy. 'Ethnic cleansing' – which sometimes borders on genocide – has become a tactic of internal warfare.

The steep decline of inter-state war has contributed to a reduction in the number of high intensity (high fatality) conflicts (HICs) since 1993, but the number of low-intensity conflicts (LICs) – with less than 1,000 deaths in a 12-month period – has been rising. Also increasing are violent political conflicts (VPCs), the term used to describe conflicts where there are less than 100 fatalities in a 12-month period.

At the end of 1997, there were 17 HICs (compared to 20 in 1995 and 19 in 1996); 70 LICs (39 in 1995 and 42 in 1996); and 74 VPCs (40 in 1995 and 75 in 1996).

PIOOM's tables 16 to 18 show data over a 12-month period for HICs, LICs and VPCs. There is some divergence between the data in the tables and the figures mentioned in the paragraph above, as table data show mid-year figures, while figures in the preceding paragraph are end-of-year figures. Other factors that contribute to variations are a more complete count in some regions, and a disaggregation of conflict in one country into several separate conflicts.

The data presented in tables 16 to 18 have been obtained from various sources, including newspapers (in particular the International Herald Tribune), NGO reports, and academic studies. As estimates of the number of deaths vary widely, minimum and maximum figures have been given, although estimates that are considered excessive and serve propaganda purposes only have been avoided. Estimates for the number of fatalities refer to both direct combat deaths and indirect conflict-induced mortality. The cumulative number of deaths since the beginning of a conflict is based on past monitoring (since 1980) and academic literature. The escalation trend estimates have been calculated by comparing annual codings and a checklist of 13 escalation indicators.

Table 19

In recent years the world has had to cope with an increasing number of humanitarian emergencies. From 1978 to 1985, there were an average of five ongoing emergencies each year, in 1989 the number rose to 14, and increased to 24 in 1996.

Given the scarcity of resources that can be allocated, a tragic triage process of sorting disasters according to severity becomes necessary. In order to establish whether the worst catastrophes receive – as should be the case – most attention, some form of quantification is necessary. It has been noted that some of the worst crises are the result of a cumulation of cross-impacting crises: warfare, a collapse of the health system, a deterioration of the food situation and massive displacement.

Based on 1995-1997 data, PIOOM has used this methodology in table 19 to "classify" 39 humanitarian emergencies.

The following indicators were utilized:

■ War – fatalities from violent and armed conflict, expressed in the number of people killed in political violence in 1997. The following scale was used to calculate the degree of violence: 1 = <315; 2 = 316-999; 3 = 1,000-3,162; 4 = 3,163-10,000; 5 = >10,000.

■ Displacement – number of refugees and internally displaced people, based on 1996 USCR data. The following scale was used: 1 = <100,000; 2 = 100,000-316,199; 3 = 316,200-999,999; 4 = 1,000,000-3,161,999; 5 = >3,162,000.

■ Hunger – calorie intake per capita, expressed in calorie supply as a percentage of requirements (based on 1992-1996 FAO/UNICEF data). Scale: 1 = 141-157; 2 = 124-140; 3 = 107-123; 4 = 90-106; 5 = 72-89.

■ Disease – expressed in terms of under-five mortality rate per 1,000 live births, based on 1995 UNICEF data. The following scale was used: 1 = 5-68; 2 = 69-131; 3 = 132-194; 4 = 195-257; 5 = 258-320.

(In the following tables, some totals may not correspond due to rounding.)

Chapter 12 Data sources

Catholic University of Louvain
School of Public Health
Clos Chapelle aux Champs
30-34
1200 Brussels
Belgium
Tel.: (32)(2) 764 3327
Fax: (32)(2) 764 3328
E-mail: mis-son@epid.ucl.ac.be

US Committee for Refugees
1717 Massachusetts Ave NW
Suite 701
Washington DC 20036
USA
Tel.: (1)(202) 347 3507
Fax: (1)(202) 347 3418
E-mail: targent@irsa-uscr.org

PIOOM
Department of Political
Sciences
Leiden University
Wassenaarseweg 52
2333 AK Leiden
Netherlands
Tel.: (3)(71) 527 3861
Fax: (3)(71) 527 3788
E-mail: schmid@rulfsw.leidenuniv.nl

OECD/DAC
2, rue André-Pascal
75775 Paris Cedex 16
France
Tel.: (33)(1) 4524 9035
Fax: (33)(1) 4524 1980
E-mail: claire.shewbridge@oecd.org

Food Aid Information Group
World Food Programme
Via Cristoforo Colombo 426
00145 Rome
Italy
Tel.: (39)(6) 5228 2796
Fax: (39)(6) 513 2879
E-mail: george.simon@wfp.org

Tables 1 and 2 Annual average number of people killed or affected by region and by period (1972 to 1996)

People killed by disaster

	AFRICA	AMERICAS	ASIA	EUROPE	OCEANIA	TOTAL
1972 to 1976	254,051	25,259	67,148	2,089	83	**348,631**
1977 to 1981	1,512	2,486	16,631	1,861	56	**22,547**
1982 to 1986	114,415	9,925	14,690	1,757	183	**140,971**
1987 to 1991	11,686	5,994	114,990	7,560	151	**140,381**
1992 to 1996	7,595	3,104	18,305	2,352	66	**31,422**
1972 to 1996	77,852	9,354	46,353	3,124	108	**136,790**

People affected by disaster

	AFRICA	AMERICAS	ASIA	EUROPE	OCEANIA	TOTAL
1972 to 1976	3,744,901	1,904,177	61,061,699	267,165	45,889	**67,023,832**
1977 to 1981	9,137,642	2,645,235	81,550,558	380,640	27,620	**93,741,694**
1982 to 1986	17,487,252	8,400,440	116,286,138	326,552	231,230	**142,731,613**
1987 to 1991	13,546,675	4,010,491	217,771,500	1,023,310	69,746	**236,421,721**
1992 to 1996	15,556,453	2,058,314	153,792,164	1,568,139	4,666,887	**177,641,958**
1972 to 1996	11,894,585	3,803,731	126,092,412	713,161	1,008,274	**143,512,164**

The last five-year period (1992 to 1996) has seen a decline in both the numbers of people killed in disaster and the numbers affected. Asia, in particular, has seen reduced deaths due to better flood preparedness. Africa is the only continent showing a rise in the numbers of people affected by disaster, reflecting the ongoing tensions in the Great Lakes region. Source: CRED.

Tables 3 and 4 Annual average number of people made homeless or injured by region and by period (1972 to 1996)

People made homeless by disaster

	AFRICA	AMERICAS	ASIA	EUROPE	OCEANIA	TOTAL
1972 to 1976	44,970	381,577	2,020,205	69,200	240	**2,516,192**
1977 to 1981	213,706	190,660	1,565,719	73,441	4,722	**2,048,248**
1982 to 1986	211,758	405,693	2,440,833	17,360	24,340	**3,099,984**
1987 to 1991	396,423	349,401	9,102,567	145,557	9,627	**10,003,575**
1992 to 1996	555,858	324,252	5,566,715	54,820	32,170	**6,533,815**
1972 to 1996	284,543	330,317	4,139,208	72,076	14,220	**4,840,363**

People injured by disaster

	AFRICA	AMERICAS	ASIA	EUROPE	OCEANIA	TOTAL
1972 to 1976	63	20,882	43,200	4,181	257	**68,583**
1977 to 1981	2,129	3,433	18,282	5,375	139	**29,358**
1982 to 1986	985	18,269	31,239	1,537	2,260	**54,290**
1987 to 1991	645	5,297	51,552	3,905	54	**61,453**
1992 to 1996	6,641	4,896	125,548	4,800	460	**142,345**
1972 to 1996	2,093	10,555	53,964	3,960	634	**71,206**

> *Figures for people made homeless as a result of disaster have declined in all regions except Africa. Here mass displacements in and around the Great Lakes region have inflated the continent's total. Asia has witnessed a tremendous rise in reported injuries from 1992 to 1996. Most of this increase is associated with earthquakes in the region, which are well reported as well as causing high injury-to-death ratios. Source: CRED.*

Table 5 Annual average number of people killed by type of disaster and by period (1972 to 1996)

People killed by disaster

	EARTH-QUAKE	DROUGHT & FAMINE	FLOOD	HIGH WIND	LANDSLIDE	VOLCANO	TOTAL
1972 to 1976	64,170	253,800	7,232	4,977	1,142	9	**331,330**
1977 to 1981	5,821	56	4,900	6,729	343	129	**17,979**
1982 to 1986	3,210	111,832	4,269	6,494	488	4,740	**131,033**
1987 to 1991	15,548	1,852	39,787	57,803	1,184	151	**116,325**
1992 to 1996	4,826	489	7,293	3,797	807	56	**17,268**
1972 to 1996	18,715	73,606	12,696	15,960	793	1,017	**122,787**

	ACCIDENT	TECHNOLOGICAL ACCIDENT	FIRE	TOTAL
1972 to 1977	851	191	14,870	**15,913**
1977 to 1981	1,685	418	343	**2,446**
1982 to 1986	3,450	929	450	**4,829**
1987 to 1991	8,326	1,049	540	**9,914**
1992 to 1996	6,877	542	593	**8,011**
1972 to 1996	4,238	626	3,359	**8,223**

There is no discernible time trend in the numbers of people killed by disasters. Famine remains the biggest killer but improved food security measures and more rapid local disaster response may cause a reduction in numbers dying. Source: CRED.

Table 6 Annual average number of people affected by type of disaster and by period
(1972 to 1996)

People affected by disaster

	EARTH-QUAKE	DROUGHT & FAMINE	FLOOD	HIGH WIND	LANDSLIDE	VOLCANO	TOTAL
1972 to 1976	1,341,084	43,563,400	18,867,313	3,116,419	17,600	34,500	**66,940,317**
1977 to 1981	614,626	52,122,671	31,609,232	8,199,291	1,802	28,400	**92,576,021**
1982 to 1986	484,431	103,246,778	28,693,409	6,399,549	4,461	106,269	**138,934,898**
1987 to 1991	5,071,710	75,851,888	119,779,115	22,664,204	630,750	156,740	**224,154,407**
1992 to 1996	753,477	21,480,303	130,433,416	18,235,163	34,914	144,685	**171,081,957**
1972 to 1996	1,653,066	59,253,008	65,876,497	11,722,925	137,905	94,119	**138,737,520**

	ACCIDENT	TECHNOLOGICAL ACCIDENT	FIRE	TOTAL
1972 to 1977	22	8,940	8,163	**17,125**
1977 to 1981	77,481	106,720	44,933	**229,134**
1982 to 1986	653	114,700	33,119	**148,472**
1987 to 1991	1,004	26,302	73,693	**100,999**
1992 to 1996	10,810	13,296	68,613	**92,719**
1972 to 1996	17,994	53,992	45,704	**117,690**

Disasters always affect many more than they kill. Numbers killed make the headlines but numbers affected give a far better indication of the long-term consequences of disaster. Affected people may need emergency support, and help to rebuild their livelihoods and lives. Source: CRED.

Table 7 Annual average number of people made homeless by type of disaster and by period (1972 to 1996)

People made homeless by disaster

	EARTH-QUAKE	DROUGHT & FAMINE	FLOOD	HIGH WIND	LANDSLIDE	VOLCANO	TOTAL
1972 to 1976	344,457	0	2,041,583	89,629	300	1,000	**2,476,969**
1977 to 1981	166,070	0	238,838	1,630,400	3,420	3,500	**2,042,228**
1982 to 1986	188,056	100,000	1,548,438	729,856	501,316	11,220	**3,078,886**
1987 to 1991	337,048	9,600	8,058,439	1,522,708	18,051	33,325	**9,979,171**
1992 to 1996	205,204	0	4,895,072	1,372,519	14,228	25,753	**6,512,776**
1972 to 1996	248,167	21,920	3,356,474	1,069,022	107,463	14,960	**4,818,006**

	ACCIDENT	TECHNOLOGICAL ACCIDENT	FIRE	TOTAL
1972 to 1977	0	38,000	1,223	**39,223**
1977 to 1981	12	0	6,008	**6,020**
1982 to 1986	0	540	8,558	**9,098**
1987 to 1991	4,327	1,320	18,357	**24,004**
1992 to 1996	541	3,727	12,770	**17,039**
1972 to 1996	976	8,717	9,383	**19,077**

Floods and earthquakes are the most consistent cause of homelessness from disasters, though acting in very different ways. With flooding, there is usually ample warning for people to leave their homes, to which they can return later. Not so with earthquakes. Lack of warning and the direct destruction of property turns disaster homelessness into a long-term problem. Source: CRED.

Table 8 Annual average number of people injured by type of disaster and by period (1972 to 1996)

People injured by disaster

	EARTH-QUAKE	DROUGHT & FAMINE	FLOOD	HIGH WIND	LANDSLIDE	VOLCANO	TOTAL
1972 to 1976	62,251	0	378	3,828	203	1	**66,660**
1977 to 1981	10,489	0	8,591	6,733	18	207	**26,038**
1982 to 1986	13,911	0	5,593	7,708	25	1,100	**28,337**
1987 to 1991	29,035	0	16,947	9,/18	916	66	**56,682**
1992 to 1996	19,372	0	77,861	36,131	160	51	**133,576**
1972 to 1996	27,012	0	21,874	12,824	264	285	**62,259**

	ACCIDENT	TECHNOLOGICAL ACCIDENT	FIRE	TOTAL
1972 to 1977	83	1,790	49	**1,922**
1977 to 1981	1,587	1,360	369	**3,316**
1982 to 1986	1,641	21,670	2,613	**25,925**
1987 to 1991	2,931	1,535	247	**4,712**
1992 to 1996	3,906	3,843	684	**8,433**
1972 to 1996	2,029	6,040	793	**8,862**

> *Flooding, high winds and earthquakes dominate the league table for injuries. For technological disasters, the devastating effect of the Chernobyl nuclear accident of the mid-1980s can clearly be seen. Source: CRED.*

Table 9 Annual average number of disasters by region and by type (1987 to 1996)

Disasters with a natural trigger

	AFRICA	AMERICAS	ASIA	EUROPE	OCEANIA	TOTAL
Earthquake	2	6	11	4	2	25
Drought & famine	7	2	3	1	0	13
Flood	11	22	36	9	5	84
Landslide	1	5	7	1	1	15
High wind	4	28	35	11	7	84
Volcano	0	2	2	0	1	6
Other	17	8	13	7	1	45
Total	43	73	107	33	16	271

Disasters with a non-natural trigger

	AFRICA	AMERICAS	ASIA	EUROPE	OCEANIA	TOTAL
Accident	24	30	68	27	2	151
Technological accident	2	4	10	7	0	23
Fire	2	9	13	14	1	38
Total	28	43	90	48	3	212

> *The historical data of the last decade clearly show the predominance of flooding and traffic accidents as the most frequently reported disasters. Both disaster types are set to increase in number over the next decade as traffic density, particularly in the South, and climatic change caused by global warning start to manifest themselves. Source: CRED.*

Table 10 Total number of disasters by region and by type in 1997

Disasters with a natural trigger

	AFRICA	AMERICAS	ASIA	EUROPE	OCEANIA	TOTAL
Earthquake	0	4	8	1	0	13
Drought & famine	5	2	4	1	2	14
Flood	17	20	20	10	2	69
Landslide	1	3	5	1	2	12
High wind	2	12	18	5	6	43
Volcano	0	2	1	0	0	3
Other	12	2	6	5	0	25
Total	37	45	62	23	12	179

Disasters with a non-natural trigger

	AFRICA	AMERICAS	ASIA	EUROPE	OCEANIA	TOTAL
Accident	7	6	24	20	1	58
Technological accident	0	1	10	3	0	14
Fire	3	8	13	7	3	34
Total	10	15	47	30	4	106

> *In 1997, Asia headed the league table for numbers of disasters reflecting a combination of natural hazards (floods and earthquakes), rapid industrial development and the simple issue of population numbers. The Americas suffered from a high number of disasters in 1997, but through improved disaster preparedness was able to keep death tolls and injury numbers well down. Source: CRED.*

Table 11 Annual average number of people killed or affected by disaster by country over ten years (1987 to 1996) and in 1997

Country	Killed	Affected	Killed 1997	Affected 1997
AFRICA				
Nigeria	1,561	50,491	20	-
Ethiopia	951	4,026,399	297	1,051,200
Mozambique	725	629,167	252	32,176
Niger	578	278,400	13	8,500
Burkina Faso	415	290,592	1,953	16,775
Angola	369	321,220	-	-
Sudan	358	1,489,703	-	-
Zambia	301	379,773	-	-
Egypt	296	11,066	18	-
Cameroon	253	61,691	-	-
Congo, DR of	251	1,648	96	-
Kenya	249	1,020,007	25	1,900,000
Mauritania	247	72,267	-	221,400
South Africa	226	301,216	24	300
Tanzania	194	440,157	114	608,288
Zimbabwe	194	1,010,443	-	-
Chad	189	40,900	-	256,000
Malawi	171	1,446,171	-	400,000
Somalia	109	62,900	1,904	717,000
Uganda	93	98,513	120	150,000
Madagascar	88	213,707	174	520,000
Guinea	80	3,010	-	-
Morocco	68	9,000	10	-
Sierra Leone	58	0	-	-
Congo, PR of	51	0	-	-
Algeria	51	6,536	4	-
Benin	45	34,814	-	-
Ghana	36	50,296	1,191	13,063
Mali	34	31,695	587	13,063
Burundi	33	567	-	-
Gambia	31	400	119	856
Libyan A.J.	31	0	-	-
Rwanda	30	8,173	-	-
Togo	28	52,207	600	5,000
Comoros	25	45	-	-
Botswana	21	80,112	-	-
Côte d'Ivoire	19	716	-	-
Djibouti	18	40,101	-	-
Mauritius	17	400	-	-
Gabon	14	1,018	-	-
Eritrea	13	632	-	-
Senegal	13	500	20	-
Namibia	12	41,320	-	-
Swaziland	11	37,723	-	-
Tunisia	10	4,800	-	-
Reunion	9	16,020	-	-
Cape Verde Is.	8	430	-	-
Cen. African Rep.	6	1,838	-	-
Liberia	6	0	-	-
Lesotho	4	60,173	-	-
Sao Tomé/Prin.,	3	106	-	-
Eq. Guinea	2	31	-	-
Guinea Bissau	0	2,470	701	21,200
Seychelles	0	0	5	250
TOTAL	**8,601**	**12,731,564**	**8,327**	**5,935,170**
AMERICAS				
Peru	1,313	626,819	479	32,800
USA	516	182,699	160	306,390
Brazil	420	459,641	46	600
Ecuador	355	39,332	62	35,000
Colombia	349	30,042	16	-
Haiti	342	341,711	-	-
Mexico	294	73,910	472	622,955
El Salvador	141	5,733	4	34,000
Venezuela	110	6,397	99	15,000
Dominican Rep.	93	122,770	-	-
Chile	92	35,005	44	108,350
Guatemala	85	13,074	-	-
Cuba	78	130,366	56	7,000
Honduras	68	36,380	-	-
Bolivia	64	51,077	-	108,000
Nicaragua	51	95,703	-	290,000
Argentina	41	538,470	-	12,500
Canada	34	5,457	-	30,600

Country	Killed	Affected	Killed 1997	Affected 1997
Costa Rica	25	64,814	-	-
Panama	24	3,998	-	-
Suriname	17	0	-	-
Puerto Rico	12	986	-	-
Jamaica	7	108,217	-	-
St. Lucia	5	78	-	-
Bermuda	3	0	-	-
Paraguay	2	40,858	36	60,000
Uruguay	2	770	75	-
Trinidad/Tobago	1	20	-	-
Montserrat	1	1,000	32	4,000
Martinique	1	150	-	-
Virgin Is.	1	0	-	-
Guadeloupe	1	0	-	-
Antigua	0	6,500	-	-
St Vincent	0	100	-	-
St Martin/Saba	0	4,000	-	-
Dominica	0	300	-	-
St Kitts	0	180	-	-
Guyana	0	2,848	-	-
TOTAL	**4,547**	**3,029,403**	**1,581**	**1,667,195**

ASIA

Country	Killed	Affected	Killed 1997	Affected 1997
Bangladesh	44,014	18,574,280	463	3,468,738
India	5,063	56,563,631	2,540	392,690
Iran	4,293	40,725	2,754	151,658
China, P. Rep.	4,135	99,073,268	1,389	16,832,527
Philippines	2,556	3,690,032	119	486,765
Afghanistan	1,207	18,129	54	20,000
Indonesia	848	153,898	1,262	215,000
Nepal	783	200,768	20	-
Pakistan	748	1,407,065	528	837,228
Japan	676	124,347	49	68,200
Viet Nam	618	1,302,381	492	4,900
Thailand	383	1,677,378	160	50,000
Tajikistan	315	38,371	12	-
Korea, Rep. of	265	38,439	25	130,000
Myanmar	208	430,764	89	104,383
Saudi Arabia	184	0	343	-
Korea, DPR of	121	851,465	-	1,740,000
Iraq	87	80,810	-	-
Sri Lanka	87	504,297	-	-

Country	Killed	Affected	Killed 1997	Affected 1997
Laos	81	155,164	-	-
Malaysia	74	8,703	10	5,000
Cambodia	74	733,040	64	-
Taiwan	73	2	70	-
Yemen Arab Rep.	57	26,000	-	-
Hong Kong	42	966	7	-
Mongolia	28	10,511	-	-
Kazakhstan	28	4,286	-	8,000
Kyrgyzstan	26	27,857	-	-
Yemen, P. D. Rep.	21	47,700	-	-
Uzbekistan	14	714	-	-
Israel	7	8	13	-
Lebanon	7	5,150	-	-
Bhutan	4	6,557	-	-
Jordan	3	1,800	-	-
Bahrain	1	0	-	-
Cyprus	0	14	-	-
Singapore	0	0	-	1,200
Kuwait	0	0	2	200
Macao	0	120	-	-
Turkmenistan	0	43	-	-
Maldives	0	30	-	-
United Arab Emir.	0	0	86	-
TOTAL	**67,130**	**185,798,713**	**10,551**	**24,516,489**

EUROPE

Country	Killed	Affected	Killed 1997	Affected 1997
Soviet Union	6,794	284,189	-	-
Russian Federat.	1,022	36,774	252	-
Turkey	305	23,584	-	-
Estonia	152	23	-	-
Greece	130	1,750	70	-
United Kingdom	112	351,296	20	1,000
Finland	92	0	-	-
Ukraine	83	69,112	16	-
Georgia	76	17,717	-	-
Poland	75	0	115	162,500
France	74	31,172	46	10,000
Azerbaijan	72	275,045	31	75,000

Country	Killed	Affected	Killed 1997	Affected 1997
Norway	61	400	55	-
Italy	58	1,780	52	130,000
Romania	50	1,550	39	-
Spain	47	2,051	46	750
Yugoslavia	42	5	-	-
Macedonia	39	2,000	-	-
Denmark	37	10	-	-
Germany	32	10,380	30	15,000
Belgium	27	142	10	-
Portugal	27	305	11	-
Sweden	24	0	-	-
Azores	17	6	29	-
Armenia	15	216,667	4	7,000
Netherlands	12	26,200	2	-
Czechoslovakia	10	0	-	-
Moldova	8	4,167	-	-
Croatia	7	0	-	-
Bulgaria	7	0	-	-
Albania	6	362,511	-	-
Switzerland	5	720	-	-
German Dem. Rep.	5	0	-	-
Ireland	4	350	-	-
Austria	4	0	-	-
Iceland	3	6	-	-
Slovak Rep.	3	0	-	-
Belarus	2	6,714	5	-
Malta	1	0	-	-
Hungary	1	0	-	-
Lithuania	1	0	-	-
Czech Rep.	0	0	29	87,725
Bosnia and Herzegovina	0	0	12	-
TOTAL	**9,542**	**1,717,626**	**874**	**488,975**

Country	Killed	Affected	Killed 1997	Affected 1997
OCEANIA				
Papua New Guinea	47	25,940	102	703,000
Australia	39	2,283,391	41	400
Vanuatu	6	5,610	-	-
Solomon Islands	4	8,852	-	-
New Zealand	3	1,626	3	340
Fiji	3	15,537	25	3,500
Samoa	3	0	-	-
Western Samoa	2	25,500	-	-
Cook Islands	1	200	19	700
French Polynesia	1	0	-	-
Wallis & Futuna	1	0	-	-
Tonga	0	260	-	-
Guam	0	0	228	1,400
Tokelau	0	170	-	-
Tuvalu	0	30		
Pacific Islands	0	1,200	-	-
TOTAL	**109**	**2,368,316**	**418**	**709,340**

> The ratio of killed to affected in disasters reflects the type of disaster and the degree of disaster preparedness in a country; more preparedness means less lives lost. Floods affect many but kill few. The ratio of killed to affected is far greater for earthquakes. Source: CRED.

Table 12 Annual average estimated damage by region and by type over ten years (1987-1996) in thousands US dollars

Disasters with a natural trigger

	AFRICA	AMERICAS	ASIA	EUROPE	OCEANIA	TOTAL
Earthquake	30,920	2,913,486	12,006,577	47,213,990	146,763	**62,311,736**
Drought & famine	9,874	314,440	8,276	218,860	520,840	**1,072,289**
Flood	157,577	2,463,027	13,522,541	8,806,790	34,860	**24,984,795**
Landslide	0	2,620	28,330	50,000	0	**80,950**
High wind	69,297	7,474,687	5,603,058	7,520,826	318,388	**20,986,255**
Volcano	0	1,000	22,089	1,650	40,000	**64,739**
Other	4,700	465,290	189,889	281,039	0	**940,918**
Total	**737,488**	**18,737,071**	**49,532,435**	**66,506,395**	**1,120,130**	**136,633,519**

Disasters with a non-natural trigger

	AFRICA	AMERICAS	ASIA	EUROPE	OCEANIA	TOTAL
Accident	194,400	1,726,980	8,137,280	170,160	10,840	**10,239,660**
Technological accident	14,850	300,106	32,665	403,930	3,800	**755,351**
Fire	23,310	524,175	905,893	632,530	15,000	**2,100,908**
Total	**232,560**	**2,551,261**	**9,075,838**	**1,206,620**	**29,640**	**13,095,919**

> *Estimates of damage, recorded as financial loss, need to be treated with caution. Earthquakes and technological disasters always rate high on such listings, as figures reflect the cost of rebuilding infrastructure or damage reported through insurance companies. Economic damage to individual households is badly under-reported, hence the very low figures for famine and drought. Source: CRED.*

Table 13 Refugees and asylum seekers by country of origin

	1991	1992	1993	1994	1995	1996	1997
AFRICA	**5,321,500**	**5,730,600**	**5,812,400**	**5,857,650**	**5,191,200**	**3,623,200**	**2,878,000**
Angola	443,200	404,200	335,000	344,000	313,000	220,000	214,000
Burundi	208,500	184,000	780,000	330,000	290,000	285,000	285,000
Chad	34,800	24,000	33,400	29,000	16,000	15,500	12,000
Congo, DR of**	66,700	66,900	79,000	56,000	58,600	116,800	132,000
Congo, PR of	—	—	—	—	—	—	40,000
Djibouti	—	—	7,000	10,000	10,000	10,000	5,000
Eritrea	*	*	373,000	384,500	342,500	343,100	310,000
Ethiopia	752,400	834,800	232,200	190,750	110,700	58,000	47,000
Ghana	—	—	—	—	—	10,000	10,000
Liberia	661,700	599,200	701,000	784,000	725,000	755,000	470,000
Mali	53,000	81,000	87,000	115,000	90,000	80,000	25,000
Mauritania	66,000	65,000	79,000	75,000	80,000	65,000	55,000
Mozambique	1,483,500	1,725,000	1,332,000	325,000	970,000	—	—
Niger	500	5,000	6,000	20,000	20,000	15,000	15,000
Rwanda	203,900	201,500	275,000	1,715,000	1,545,000	257,000	75,000
Senegal	27,000	15,000	18,000	17,000	17,000	17,000	17,000
Sierra Leone	181,000	200,000	260,000	260,000	363,000	350,000	295,000
Somalia	717,600	864,800	491,200	457,400	480,300	467,100	395,000
South Africa	23,700	11,100	10,600	—	—	—	—
Sudan	202,500	263,000	373,000	510,000	448,100	433,700	375,000
Togo	15,000	6,000	240,000	140,000	95,000	30,000	6,000
Uganda	14,900	15,100	20,000	15,000	10,000	15,000	10,000
Western Sahara	165,000	165,000	80,000	80,000	80,000	80,000	85,000
EAST ASIA AND PACIFIC	**811,450**	**502,000**	**797,400**	**690,050**	**640,950**	**648,200**	**718,000**
Cambodia	392,700	148,600	35,500	30,250	26,300	34,400	96,000
China (Tibet)	114,000	128,000	133,000	139,000	141,000	128,000	130,000
Indonesia	6,900	5,500	9,400	9,700	9,500	10,000	8,000
Laos	63,200	43,300	26,500	12,900	8,900	3,500	1,300
Myanmar	112,000	86,700	289,500	203,300	160,400	184,300	201,000
Viet Nam	122,650	89,900	303,500	294,900	294,850	288,000	282,000
SOUTH AND CENTRAL ASIA	**6,900,800**	**4,715,400**	**3,899,050**	**3,319,200**	**2,809,400**	**3,184,100**	**3,172,000**
Afghanistan	6,600,800	4,286,000	3,429,800	2,835,300	2,328,400	2,628,550	2,639,000
Bangladesh	65,000	50,000	53,500	48,300	48,000	53,000	44,000
Bhutan	25,000	95,400	105,100	116,600	118,600	121,800	122,000
India	—	—	—	—	—	13,000	13,000
Sri Lanka	210,000	181,000	106,650	104,000	96,000	100,150	105,000
Tajikistan	*	52,000	153,000	165,000	170,400	215,600	197,000

Source: US Committee for Refugees

	1991	1992	1993	1994	1995	1996	1997
Uzbekistan	*	51,000	51,000	50,000	48,000	52,000	52,000
MIDDLE EAST	**2,792,500**	**2,849,300**	**2,975,000**	**3,826,950**	**3,958,500**	**4,373,100**	**4,418,000**
Iran	50,000	65,400	39,000	54,250	49,500	46,100	35,000
Iraq	217,500	125,900	134,700	635,900	622,900	608,500	585,000
Palestine	2,525,000	2,658,000	2,801,300	3,136,800	3,266,100	3,718,500	3,798,000
EUROPE	**120,000**	**2,529,800**	**1,952,650**	**1,775,800**	**1,805,600**	**1,875,150**	**1,406,000**
Armenia	*	202,000	200,000	229,000	185,000	197,000	197,000
Azerbaijan	*	350,000	290,000	374,000	390,000	238,000	218,000
Bosnia and Herzegovina#	*	n.a.	n.a.	863,300	905,500	1,006,450	577,000
Croatia #	*	n.a.	n.a.	136,900	200,000	300,000	293,000
Georgia	*	130,000	143,000	106,800	105,000	105,000	107,000
Moldova	*	80'000	—	—	—	—	—
Turkey	—	—	—	13,000	15,000	15,000	11,000
Yugoslavia #	120,000	1,767,800	1,319,650	52,800	5,100	13,700	3,100
AMERICAS & CARIBBEAN	**118,250**	**104,250**	**97,500**	**120,550**	**68,400**	**65,700**	**61,000**
Colombia	4,000	—	450	100	200	—	300
Cuba	1,400	1,650	1,400	30,600	4,000	850	600
El Salvador	24,200	22,800	21,900	16,200	12,400	12,000	12,000
Guatemala	46,700	45,750	49,200	45,050	34,150	34,650	29,000
Haiti	6,950	1,600	1,500	5,850	1,500	—	—
Nicaragua	25,400	30,850	23,050	22,750	16,150	18,200	19,000
Suriname	9,600	1,600	—	—	—	—	—
WORLD TOTAL	**16,064,500**	**16,431,350**	**15,534,000**	**15,590,200**	**14,479,850**	**13,769,450**	**12,653,000**

Notes: — indicates zero or near zero; * country did not exist as of reporting date; n.a. not available, or reported estimates unreliable; # for 1992-93, refugees from Croatia and Bosnia included in Yugoslavia total, for 1994-95, Yugoslavia total includes only refugees from Serbia and Montenegro; ** formerly Zaire.

Nearly half of the world's refugees and asylum seekers in 1997 were either Palestinians or Afghans. The number of Bosnian refugees still in need of durable solutions declined significantly during the year. Repatriation and refugee censuses in host countries resulted in lower estimates of the Liberian refugee population. (Note: In part because asylum states do not always report country-of-origin data, this table understates the number of refugees and asylum seekers from many countries.) Source: US Committee for Refugees.

TABLE 14 Refugees and asylum seekers by host country

	1991	1992	1993	1994	1995	1996	1997
AFRICA	**5,339,950**	**5,697,650**	**5,824,700**	**5,879,700**	**5,222,300**	**3,682,700**	**3,002,000**
Algeria	204,000	210,000	121,000	130,000	120,000	114,000	112,000
Angola	10,400	9,000	11,000	11,000	10,900	9,300	9,000
Benin	15,100	4,300	120,000	50,000	25,000	11,000	3,000
Botswana	1,400	500	500	—	—	—	—
Burkina Faso	400	6,300	6,000	30,000	21,000	26,000	2,000
Burundi	107,000	107,350	110,000	165,000	140,000	12,000	12,000
Cameroon	6,900	1,500	2,500	2,000	2,000	1,000	1,000
Cent. African Rep.	9,000	18,000	41,000	42,000	34,000	36,400	38,000
Chad	—	—	—	—	—	—	300
Congo, DR of**	482,300	442,400	452,000	1,527,000	1,332,000	455,000	330,000
Congo, PR of	3,400	9,400	13,000	16,000	15,000	16,000	25,000
Côte d'Ivoire	240,400	195,500	250,000	320,000	290,000	320,000	200,000
Djibouti	120,000	96,000	60,000	60,000	25,000	22,000	22,000
Egypt	7,750	10,650	11,000	10,700	10,400	46,000	46,000
Eritrea	—	—	—	—	—	—	1,000
Ethiopia	304,000	110,000	158,000	250,000	308,000	328,000	293,000
Gabon	800	200	200	—	1,000	1,000	1,000
Gambia	1,500	3,300	2,000	1,000	5,000	5,000	7,000
Ghana	6,150	12,100	133,000	110,000	85,000	35,000	15,000
Guinea	566,000	485,000	570,000	580,000	640,000	650,000	430,000
Guinea-Bissau	4,600	12,000	16,000	16,000	15,000	15,000	5,000
Kenya	107,150	422,900	332,000	257,000	225,000	186,000	166,000
Lesotho	300	200	100	—	—	—	—
Liberia	12,000	100,000	110,000	100,000	120,000	100,000	100,000
Libya	—	—	—	—	28,100	27,200	27,000
Malawi	950,000	1,070,000	700,000	70,000	2,000	—	—
Mali	13,500	10,000	13,000	15,000	15,000	15,000	17,000
Mauritania	40,000	40,000	46,000	55,000	35,000	15,000	5,000
Mozambique	500	250	—	—	—	—	—
Namibia	30,200	150	5,000	1,000	1,000	1,000	1,000
Niger	1,400	3,600	3,000	3,000	17,000	27,000	12,000
Nigeria	4,600	2,900	4,400	5,000	8,000	8,000	9,000
Rwanda	32,500	24,500	370,000	—	—	20,000	30,000
Senegal	53,100	55,100	66,000	60,000	68,000	51,000	41,000
Sierra Leone	17,200	7,600	15,000	20,000	15,000	15,000	15,000
Somalia	35,000	10,000	—	—	—	—	—
South Africa	201,000	250,000	300,000	200,000	90,000	22,500	30,000
Sudan	717,200	750,500	633,000	550,000	450,000	395,000	355,000
Swaziland	47,200	52,000	57,000	—	—	—	—
Tanzania	251,100	257,800	479,500	752,000	703,000	335,000	315,000

Source: US Committee for Refugees

	1991	1992	1993	1994	1995	1996	1997
Togo	450	350	—	5,000	10,000	10,000	10,000
Tunisia	—	—	—	—	500	300	300
Uganda	165,450	179,600	257,000	323,000	230,000	225,000	197,000
Zambia	140,500	155,700	158,500	123,000	125,400	126,000	118,000
Zimbabwe	198,500	265,000	200,000	20,000	—	1,000	1,000
EAST ASIA AND PACIFIC	**688,500**	**398,600**	**467,600**	**444,100**	**452,850**	**449,600**	**483,000**
Australia	23,000	24,000	2,950	5,300	7,500	7,400	4,600
China##	14,200	12,500	296,900	297,100	294,100	294,100	289,000
Hong Kong##	60,000	45,300	3,550	1,900	1,900	1,300	n.a.
Indonesia	18,700	15,600	2,400	250	—	—	100
Japan	900	700	950	7,350	9,900	300	300
Korea	200	200	150	—	—	—	—
Macau	100	—	—	—	—	—	—
Malaysia	12,700	16,700	8,150	6,100	5,300	5,200	5,200
Papua New Guinea	6,700	3,800	7,700	9,700	9,500	10,000	8,200
Philippines	18,000	5,600	1,700	250	450	50	100
Singapore	150	100	—	—	—	—	—
Solomon Islands	—	—	—	3,000	1,000	1,000	800
Taiwan	150	150	—	—	—	—	—
Thailand	512,700	255,000	108,300	83,050	98,200	95,850	171,000
Viet Nam	21,000	19,000	35,000	30,100	25,0000	34,400	34,000
EUROPE	**578,400**	**3,210,400**	**2,542,100**	**2,421,500**	**2,520,700**	**2,479,100**	**1,919,000**
Armenia	*	300,000	290,000	295,800	304,000	150,000	219,000
Austria	27,300	82,100	77,700	59,000	55,900	80,000	11,000
Azerbaijan	*	246,000	251,000	279,000	238,000	249,150	249,000
Belarus	*	3,700	10,400	18,800	7,000	10,800	35,000
Belgium	15,200	19,100	32,900	19,400	16,400	18,200	18,000
Bulgaria	—	—	—	900	500	550	2,000
Croatia	*	420,000	280,000	188,000	189,500	167,000	53,000
Cyprus	—	—	—	—	—	—	50
Czechoslovakia	2,800	2,200	*	*	*	*	*
Czech Republic	*	*	6,300	4,700	2,400	2,900	700
Denmark	4,600	13,900	23,300	24,750	9,600	24,600	7,500
Estonia	*	—	—	100	—	—	—
Finland	2,100	3,500	3,700	850	750	1,700	1,600
France	46,800	29,400	30,900	32,600	30,000	29,200	7,400
Germany	256,100	536,000	529,100	430,000	442,700	436,400	277,000
Greece	2,700	1,900	800	1,300	3,200	5,600	2,800
Hungary	5,200	40,000	10,000	11,200	9,100	5,400	3,400
Ireland	—	—	—	—	—	1,800	4,200
Italy	31,400	19,100	33,550	31,800	60,700	10,600	11,000

Source: US Committee for Refugees

	1991	1992	1993	1994	1995	1996	1997
Latvia	*	—	—	150	150	—	—
Lithuania	*	—	—	—	400	—	—
Macedonia	*	32,700	12,100	8,200	7,000	5,100	5,100
Netherlands	21,600	24,600	35,400	52,600	39,300	46,200	6,300
Norway	4,600	5,700	14,200	11,600	11,200	12,700	2,600
Poland	2,500	1,500	600	500	800	3,200	1,200
Portugal	200	—	2,250	600	350	200	200
Romania	500	—	1,000	600	1,300	600	600
Russian Federation	*	460,000	347,500	451,000	500,000	484,000	325,000
Slovak Republic	*	*	1,900	2,000	1,600	2,000	100
Slovenia	*	68,900	38,000	29,000	24,000	10,300	10,000
Spain	8,100	12,700	14,000	14,500	4,300	7,200	2,200
Sweden	27,300	88,400	58,800	61,000	12,300	60,500	9,200
Switzerland	41,600	81,700	27,000	23,900	29,000	41,700	31,000
Turkey	31,500	31,700	24,600	30,650	21,150	13,000	5,000
Ukraine	*	40,000	—	5,000	6,000	8,000	10,000
United Kingdom	44,700	24,600	28,100	32,000	44,000	40,500	58,000
Yugoslavia #	1,600	621,000	357,000	300,000	450,000	550,000	550,000
AMERICAS & CARIBBEAN	**218,800**	**249,000**	**272,450**	**297,300**	**256,400**	**232,800**	**611,000**
Argentina	1,800	—	—	—	—	400	400
Bahamas	—	—	—	—	200	—	—
Belize	12,000	8,700	8,900	8,800	8,650	8,700	8,700
Bolivia	100	—	600	600	600	550	500
Brazil	200	200	1,000	2,000	2,000	2,200	2,200
Canada	30,500	37,700	20,500	22,000	24,900	26,100	49,000
Chile	—	—	100	200	300	200	200
Colombia	700	400	400	400	400	200	200
Costa Rica	24,300	34,350	24,800	24,600	20,500	23,150	23,000
Cuba	1,100	1,100	—	—	1,800	1,650	1,600
Dominican Republic	—	—	1,300	1,350	900	600	600
Ecuador	4,200	200	100	100	100	200	200
El Salvador	250	250	150	150	150	150	100
French Guiana	9,600	1,600	—	—	—	—	—
Guatemala	8,300	4,900	4,700	4,700	2,500	1,200	1,200
Honduras	2,050	150	100	100	50	—	—
Mexico	48,500	47,300	52,000	47,700	38,500	34,450	29,000
Nicaragua	2,800	5,850	4,750	300	450	900	900
Panama	1,300	850	950	900	800	650	600
Peru	600	400	400	700	700	300	—
United States	68,800	103,700	150,400	181,700	152,200	129,600	491,000

Source: US Committee for Refugees

	1991	1992	1993	1994	1995	1996	1997
Venezuela	1,700	1,350	1,300	1,000	700	1,600	1,600
MIDDLE EAST	**5,770,200**	**5,586,850**	**4,923,800**	**5,447,750**	**5,499,100**	**5,840,550**	**5,888,000**
Gaza Strip	528,700	560,200	603,000	644,000	683,600	716,900	746,000
Iran	3,150,000	2,781,800	1,995,000	2,220,000	2,075,500	2,020,000	2,015,000
Iraq	48,000	64,600	39,500	120,500	115,200	114,400	109,000
Jordan	960,200	1,010,850	1,073,600	1,232,150	1,294,800	1,362,500	1,414,000
Kuwait	—	—	—	25,000	55,000	42,000	30,000
Lebanon	314,200	322,900	329,000	338,200	348,300	355,100	362,000
Saudi Arabia	34,000	27,400	25,000	17,000	13,200	257,850	254,000
Syria	293,900	307,500	319,200	332,900	342,300	384,400	360,000
United Arab Emirates	—	—	—	150	400	400	500
West Bank	430,100	459,100	479,000	504,000	517,400	532,400	543,000
Yemen	11,100	52,500	60,500	13,850	53,400	54,600	54,000
SOUTH AND CENT. ASIA	**4,050,750**	**2,341,700**	**2,151,400**	**1,776,450**	**1,386,300**	**1,794,800**	**1,767,000**
Afghanistan	—	52,000	35,000	20,000	18,400	18,900	—
Bangladesh	30,150	245,300	199,000	116,200	55,000	40,000	41,000
India	402,600	378,000	325,600	327,850	319,200	352,200	350,000
Kazakhstan	*	—	6,500	300	6,500	14,000	14,000
Kyrgyzstan	*	—	3,500	350	7,600	17,000	17,000
Nepal	24,000	89,400	99,100	104,600	106,600	109,800	110,000
Pakistan	3,594,000	1,577,000	1,482,300	1,202,650	867,500	1,215,700	1,203,000
Tajikistan	*	—	400	2,500	2,500	2,200	1,000
Turkmenistan	*	—	—	—	—	22,000	28,000
Uzbekistan	*	—	—	2,000	3,000	3,000	3,000
WORLD TOTAL	**16,646,60**	**17,484,200**	**16,182,05**	**16,266,800**	**15,337,650**	**14,479,550**	**13,670,000**

Notes: — indicates zero or near zero; * country did not exist as of reporting date; n.a. not available, or reported estimates unreliable; # beginning in 1992, includes only Serbia and Montenegro; ** formerly Zaire; ## as of 1997, figures for Hong Kong are included in total for China.

> The total number of refugees and asylum seekers continued its general downward trend in 1997, reaching a nine-year low, according to USCR. That trend is due, in part, to the unwillingness of many states, especially those in the developed world, to accept new refugees and asylum seekers. The overwhelming majority of the world's refugees and asylum seekers continued to seek protection in the countries of the developing world. Nearly half of the world's refugees and asylum seekers were found in just five countries or territories: Iran, Jordan, Pakistan, the Gaza Strip and the West Bank, and the Federal Republic of Yugoslavia. Source: US Committee for Refugees.

TABLE 15 Significant populations of internally displaced people

	1991	1992	1993	1994	1995	1996	1997
AFRICA	**14,222,000**	**17,395,000**	**16,890,000**	**15,730,000**	**10,185,000**	**8,805,000**	**8,170,000**
Algeria	—	—	—	—	—	10,000	n.a.
Angola	827,000	900,000	2,000,000	2,000,000	1,500,000	1,200,000	1,200,000
Burundi	—	—	500,000	400,000	300,000	400,000	400,000
Congo, DR of**	—	100,000	700,000	550,000	225,000	400,000	200,000
Congo, PR of	—	—	—	—	—	—	250,000
Djibouti	—	—	140,000	50,000	—	25,000	—
Eritrea	*	*	200,000	—	—	—	—
Ethiopia	1,000,000	600,000	500,000	400,000	—	—	—
Ghana	—	—	—	20,000	150,000	20,000	20,000
Kenya	—	45,000	300,000	210,000	210,000	100,000	100,000
Liberia	500,000	600,000	1,000,000	1,100,000	1,000,000	1,000,000	500,000
Mozambique	2,000,000	3,500,000	2,000,000	500,000	500,000	—	—
Nigeria	—	—	—	—	—	30,000	30,000
Rwanda	100,000	350,000	300,000	1,200,000	500,000	—	—
Sierra Leone	145,000	200,000	400,000	700,000	1,000,000	800,000	1,000,000
Somalia	500,000	2,000,000	700,000	500,000	300,000	250,000	200,000
South Africa	4,100,000	4,100,000	4,000,000	4,000,000	500,000	500,000	500,000
Sudan	4,750,000	5,000,000	4,000,000	4,000,000	4,000,000	4,000,000	3,500,000
Togo	—	—	150,000	100,000	—	—	—
Uganda	300,000	—	—	—	—	70,000	270,000
AMERICAS & CARIBBEAN	**1,221,000**	**1,354,000**	**1,400,000**	**1,400,000**	**1,280,000**	**1,220,000**	**1,565,000**
Colombia	150,000	300,000	300,000	600,000	600,000	600,000	1,000,000
El Salvador	150,000	154,000	—	—	—	—	—
Guatemala	150,000	150,000	200,000	200,000	200,000	200,000	200,000
Haiti	200,000	250,000	300,000	—	—	—	—
Honduras	7,000	—	—	—	—	—	—
Mexico	—	—	—	—	—	—	15,000
Nicaragua	354,000	—	—	—	—	—	—
Panama	10,000	—	—	—	—	—	—
Peru	200,000	500,000	600,000	600,000	480,000	420,000	350,000
SOUTH AND CENTRAL ASIA	**2,685,000**	**1,810,000**	**880,000**	**1,775,000**	**1,600,000**	**2,400,000**	**2,054,000**
Afghanistan	2,000,000	530,000	n.a.	1,000,000	500,000	1,200,000	1,000,000
India	85,000	280,000	250,000	250,000	250,000	250,000	250,000
Sri Lanka	600,000	600,000	600,000	525,000	850,000	900,000	800,000
Tajikistan	*	400,000	30,000	—	—	50,000	3,500

Source: US Committee for Refugees

	1991	1992	1993	1994	1995	1996	1997
EUROPE	**1,755,000**	**1,626,000**	**2,765,000**	**5,195,000**	**5,080,000**	**4,735,000**	**2,760,000**
Armenia	*	*	—	—	75,000	50,000	70,000
Azerbaijan	*	216,000	600,000	630,000	670,000	550,000	550,000
Bosnia and Herzegovina	*	740,000	1,300,000	1,300,000	1,300,000	1,000,000	800,000
Croatia	*	340,000	350,000	290,000	240,000	185,000	100,000
Cyprus	268,000	265,000	265,000	265,000	265,000	265,000	265,000
Georgia	*	15,000	250,000	260,000	280,000	285,000	275,000
Moldova	*	20,000	—	—	—	—	—
Russian Federation	*	—	n.a.	450,000	250,000	400,000	350,000
Soviet Union	900,000	*	*	*	*	*	*
Turkey	30,000	30,000	n.a.	2,000,000	2,000,000	2,000,000	350,000
Yugoslavia #	557,000	—	—	—	—	—	—
MIDDLE EAST	**1,450,000**	**800,000**	**1,960,000**	**1,710,000**	**1,700,000**	**1,475,000**	**1,475,000**
Iran	—	—	260,000	—	—	—	—
Iraq	700,000	400,000	1,000,000	1,000,000	1,000,000	900,000	900,000
Lebanon	750,000	400,000	700,000	600,000	400,000	450,000	450,000
Syria	—	—	—	—	—	125,000	125,000
Yemen	—	—	—	110,000	300,000	—	—
EAST ASIA AND PACIFIC	**680,000**	**699,000**	**595,000**	**613,000**	**555,000**	**1,102,000**	**525,000**
Cambodia	180,000	199,000	95,000	113,000	55,000	32,000	—
Myanmar	500,000	500,000	500,000	500,000	500,000	1,000,000	500,000
Papua New Guinea	—	—	—	—	—	70,000	25,000
WORLD TOTAL	**22,013,000**	**23,684,000**	**24,490,000**	**26,423,000**	**20,400,000**	**19,737,000**	**16,549,000**

Notes: — indicates zero or near zero; * country did not exist as of reporting date; n.a. not available, or reported estimates unreliable; # for 1992-93, refugees from Croatia and Bosnia included in Yugoslavia total, for 1994-95, Yugoslavia total includes only refugees from Serbia and Montenegro; ** formerly Zaire.

Large internally displaced populations remained in Sudan, Afghanistan, Angola, Iraq and elsewhere in 1997. Significant new displacement occurred in the People's Republic of Congo, Colombia and Sierra Leone, while important numbers of internally displaced people were able to return home in Liberia. About half of the world's internally displaced people were in Africa. Estimates of the size of internally displaced populations are often imprecise. Source: US Committee for Refugees.

Table 16 Survey of current high-intensity conflicts (mid-1996 to mid-1997)

	Intensity of conflict*	Deaths (1996/1997)	Cumulative no. of deaths
AMERICAS			
Colombia	3	>2,500	>100,000
EUROPE			
Turkey	3	>4,000	25-30,000
Albania	1	>1,700	>1,700
Total Europe		>5,700	>26,700
AFRICA			
Algeria	5	>10,000	70-100,000
Angola	1,4	>1,000	500-900,000
Burundi	2	>10,000	170-200,000
Congo (DR of)	3	50-100,000	70-160,000
Congo (PR of)	3	1-2,000	3-5,000
Rwanda	3	>20,000	>800,000
Sudan	3	>6,000	1,500,000
Total Africa		>98,000	>3,113,000
MIDDLE EAST			
Iraq (Kurds)	3	>1,000	>200,000
ASIA AND FAR EAST			
Afghanistan	3	>10,000	1-2,000,000
Cambodia	3	>1,000	1-3,000,000
India-Pakistan (Kashmir)	4	>1,500	30-50,000
India (Assam)	3	>1,000	>5,000
India (Bihar)	3	>10,000	>1,000
Indonesia (W. Kalimantan)	5	>1,000	>1,000
Pakistan (Sindh)	4	>1,000	>14,000
Sri Lanka	3	>4,000	48-60,000
Tajikistan	4	>1,000	30-100,000
Total Asia and Far East		>21,500	2,129,000
WORLD TOTAL		128,700	>5,568,700

Notes: * 1 = Conflict more or less terminated: ceasefire or post-conflict phase; 2 = Conflict has remained more or less at same level of violence; 3 = Conflict has escalated in 12-month period shown; 4 = Conflict has de-escalated in 12-month period shown; 5 = Conflict has both escalated and de-escalated in 12-month period shown.

Most ongoing armed conflicts have escalated in scale in 1997 causing more than 120,000 directly attributable deaths. Source: PIOOM.

Table 17 Survey of current low-intensity conflicts (mid-1996 to mid-1997)

	Intensity of conflict*	Deaths (1996/1997)	Cumulative no. of deaths
AMERICAS			
Guatemala	1,2	>100	100-160,000
Haiti	3,1	>100	4-5,000
Mexico (Guerrero)	3	>100	?
Mexico (Oaxaca)	3	>100	?
Mexico (Chiapas)	3	>100	150-500
Peru	3	>100	28-30,000
Total Americas		>600	>132,150
EUROPE			
Azerbaijan/Armenia (Nagorny Karabakh)	4	>300	25-50,000
Bosnia and Herzegovina	1,4	>100	60-263,000
Daghestan	4	>100	?
Georgia (Abkhazia)	1,4	>100	3-10,000
Italy (Camorra)	3	>100	?
Croatia	1,4	>100	10-50,000
Chechnya	1,4	>100	40-90,000
Total Europe		>900	>138,000
AFRICA			
Angola (Cabinda)	3	>100	?
Central African Republic (Yakoma)	3	>500	500
Chad (South)	1,4	>200	
Ethiopia (Oromo)	2	>100	
Ethiopia (Amhara)	2	>100	?
Ethiopia (Ogaden)	2	>100	?
Ethiopia (Afar)	2	>100	?
Ethiopia (Harar)	2	>100	?
Ethiopia/Somalia (Ittihad)	3	>300	?
Cameroon (NW province)	2	>100	?
Kenya (Turkana Samburu)	3	>100	?
Liberia	1,4	>100	200,000
Libya (Islamists)	3	>300	?
Mozambique (Shona Shangaan)	1,4	>100	100,000
Nigeria (opposition)	3	>150	?
Nigeria (Ijaw Itsekiri Urhobo)	3	>100	?
Uganda (LRA)	3	>700	12,000
Uganda (WNLF)	3	>100	?
Uganda (ADF)	3	>100	?
Senegal (Casamance)	4	>100	500
Sierra Leone (RUF Kamajohs)	1,4	>100	15-20,000
Somalia (inter-clan)	2	>150	350-500,000
Somalia (Somaliland)	2	>100	?

South Africa (Kwazulu Natal)	1,4	>500	15-20,000
Total Africa		>4,400	>1,697,000
MIDDLE EAST			
Egypt (Islamists)	4	>150	1,150
Iraq (Shi'ites)	3	>100	30-100,000
Iran (NLA)	3	>100	100,000
Iran (Kurds)	3	>100	5,500
Israel (Occupied Territory)	3	>100	2,500
Lebanon (South)	2	>100	16,250
Total Middle East		>650	>155,400
ASIA AND FAR EAST			
Bangladesh (CHT)	1,4	>100	24,500
China (Xinjiang)	5	>500	?
Philippines (Moros)	3	>170	30-50,000
India (Maharashtra)	2	>100	?
India (Manipur)	2	>100	?
India (Nagaland)	2	>100	?
India (Punjab)	4	>100	10-150,000
India (Tripura)	3	>200	30,000
Indonesia (Atjeh)	4	>100	10-20,000
Pakistan (Punjab)	3	>100	?
Pakistan (NWFP)	2	>100	?
Laos (Hmong)	2	>100	1,000
Myanmar (Karen)	2	>500	130-500,000
Myanmar (Shan)	2	>100	?
Myanmar (Karenni)	3	>100	?
Nepal (Maoists)	3	>100	?
Total Asia and Far East		>2,570	>2,355,500

Notes: * 1 = Conflict more or less terminated: ceasefire or post-conflict phase; 2 = Conflict has remained more or less at same level of violence; 3 = Conflict has escalated in 12-month period shown; 4 = Conflict has de-escalated in 12-month period shown; 5 = Conflict has both escalated and de-escalated in 12-month period shown.

> Low-intensity conflicts are present on every continent of the world. Death tolls per year from such conflicts may not be high, only few hundred, but the accumulative effect over years, as conflict ebbs and flows, can mount to hundreds of thousands. Source: PIOOM.

Table 18 Survey of current violent political conflicts (mid-1996 to mid-1997)

	Intensity of conflict*	Deaths (1996/1997)	Cumulative no. of deaths
AMERICAS			
Bolivia (Chaparé)	3	>10	?
Brazil (MST)	3	<100	>1,000
Cuba (exiles)	2	<10	?
El Salvador	4,1	>50	75-85,000
Honduras	2	<10	?
Mexico (Veracruz)	3	>10	?
Nicaragua (re-contras)	4.1	>10	30-45,000
Total Americas		>200	>106,000
EUROPE			
Cyprus	2	<10	>5,000
France (Corsica)	3	>40	>500
Georgia (S. Ossetia)	4	>10	?
Macedonia (Albanians)	3	>10	?
N. Ireland (IRA)	3	>10	>3,200
Russian Fed. (Cossacks)	3	>10	?
Serbia (Kosovo)	3	>10	>200
Serbia (opposition)	3	>10	?
Spain (Basques)	2	>10	800
Uzbekistan (Fergana Valley)	3	>10	>100
Total Europe		>130	>10,000
AFRICA			
Djibouti (Afar)	2	>10	>150
Eritrea (Islamists)	3	10	150,000
Ghana (north)	4	>10	2-5,000
Cameroon-Nigeria (Bakassi)	4,1	>10	>50
Kenya (Rift Valley)	4	>10	2-10,000
Mali (Tuareg)	4,1	>40	>1,000
Mauritania	4	?	>500
Morocco (W. Sahara)	4,1	?	>15,000
Niger (Tuareg)	4,1	>10	>150
Nigeria (Islamists)	2	>40	>1,000
Nigeria (Ogoni)	4	?	>1,000
Togo	4	>10	>200
Total Africa		>150	>173,050
MIDDLE EAST			
Bahrain (Islamists)	3	>30	30
Palestine, territories under authority of	3	>10	?
Saudi Arabia (Islamists)	5	>50	?
Total Middle East		>90	>30

	Intensity of conflict*	Deaths (1996/1997)	Cumulative no. of deaths
ASIA AND FAR EAST			
Bhutan (Lotshampas)	2	?	?
China (Inner Mongolia)	2	>10	?
China (Tibet)	3	>10	?
Philippines (Communists)	4,1	>10	50,000
India (West Bengal)	2	>10	?
India (Orissa)	2	>10	?
India (Madhya Pradesh)	2	>10	?
India (Andra Pradesh)	4	>10	?
Indonesia (opposition)	3	>300	?
Indonesia (West Irian)	2	>10	10-30,000
Indonesia (East Timor)	3	>40	50-200,000
Korea, DPK/Korea, Rep. of	3	>10	1,300
Papua New Guinea	3	>10	15,000
Total Asia and Far East		>440	>126,300

Notes: * 1 = Conflict more or less terminated: ceasefire or post-conflict phase; 2 = Conflict has remained more or less at same level of violence; 3 = Conflict has escalated in 12-month period shown; 4 = Conflict has de-escalated in 12-month period shown; 5 = Conflict has both escalated and de-escalated in 12-month period shown.

Violent political conflict seems to be a fact of live in many countries today. Often dissent never rises above this threshold. Governments, and their people, come to accept low-level violence as the norm, as part of modern living. Source: PIOOM.

Table 19 (page 165)

Figures in this table represent a ranking on a scale of 1 to 5 of the degree of war, displacement, hunger or disease prevalent in a country (see scale indicators on page 139). Given that over 90 per cent of war victims today are civilians, it is no coincidence that humanitarian emergencies follow war. Displacement, hunger and increased public health problems are all part of the collateral damage of today's conflicts. Source: PIOOM.

Table 19 Current 'official' and de facto humanitarian emergencies

	War	Displacement (1996/1997)	Hunger	Disease
Afghanistan (HIC)	5	5	5	4
Burundi (HIC)	5	3	5	3
Angola (LIC)	3	4	5	5
Congo, DR of (HIC)	5	3	4	3
Rwanda (HIC)	5	2	5	3
Sudan (HIC)	4	5	5	2
Sri Lanka (HIC)	4	4	4	1
Sierra Leone (LIC)	1	4	5	5
Turkey (HIC)	4	4	2	1
Algeria (HIC)	5	1	3	1
Iraq (HIC)	3	4	2	2
Mozambique (LIC)	1	2	5	5
Liberia (HIC)	1	4	4	4
Ethiopia (LIC)	2	1	5	4
Somalia (LIC)	1	3	5	4
India (HIC)	3	2	4	2
Myanmar (Karen) (HIC)	2	3	3	3
Colombia (HIC)	3	3	4	1
Congo, PR of (HIC)	3	1	4	2
Tajikistan (HIC)	3	2	2	2
Eritrea (LIC)	1	3	4	4
Zambia (VPC)	1	1	5	4
Uganda (LIC)	2	1	4	3
Cambodia (LIC)	2	1	4	3
Armenia/Azerbaijan (LIC)	1	4	2	1
Albania (HIC)	3	1	3	1
Chad (LIC)	1	1	5	3
Kenya (LIC)	1	2	5	2
Madagascar (–)	1	1	4	3
Tanzania (–)	1	1	4	3
Peru (LIC)	1	3	5	1
Haiti (LIC)	1	1	5	2
Bosnia and Herzegovina (LIC)	1	4	2	1
Central African Republic (LIC)	2	1	5	3
Russian Federation (Chechnya) (LIC)	1	3	2	1
Viet Nam (VPC)	1	2	4	1
Georgia (LIC)	1	3	2	1
Guatemala (LIC)	1	2	4	1
DPR Korea (VPC)	1	1	3	1

Notes: HIC = high-intensity conflict; LIC = low-intensity conflict; VPC = violent political conflict.

TABLE 20 Non-food emergency and distress relief, grant disbursements in millions US$ from 1987 to 1996

DONOR	1987	1988	1989	1990	1991	1992	1993	1994	1995	1996
Australia	17.31	7.94	6.78	12.23	13.23	29.56	26.56	25.49	35.80	32.44
Austria	5.92	14.07	22.68	43.96	93.87	145.83	123.45	127.04	114.72	92.17
Belgium	1.21	1.75	1.59	4.59	5.71	13.18	19.05	14.02	15.75	23.99
Canada	26.44	55.86	29.69	45.76	85.14	78.86	273.96	228.45	164.72	174.38
Denmark	—	—	—	108.27	52.83	104.85	77.14	78.62	71.38	54.15
Finland	26.21	19.74	31.96	70.54	102.24	61.55	21.61	27.48	22.64	38.85
France	—	—	—	—	—	25.88	125.08	122.223	138.43	96.38
Germany	28.16	35.82	30.68	45.21	415.31	680.32	549.52	392.53	438.71	294.20
Ireland	1.06	1.22	1.33	2.09	2.89	2.10	5.15	8.53	8.34	16.34
Italy	124.88	145.21	84.15	104.06	456.33	137.39	341.69	105.40	87.89	96.68
Japan	2.22	8.90	19.61	26.46	20.48	14.93	40.37	31.08	60.08	71.94
Luxembourg	0.40	1.50	2.00	3.80	10.30	7.21	8.49	5.09	7.03	9.05
Netherlands	28.96	33.99	24.40	63.58	109.74	197.45	303.29	302.37	350.42	340.88
New Zealand	1.24	0.61	—	3.85	1.51	5.12	4.96	2.68	1.84	3.86
Norway	20.37	41.74	50.38	88.62	77.60	86.48	113.21	180.75	183.78	198.76
Portugal	—	—	—	—	0.11	0.11	8.35	3.70	3.52	5.56
Spain	—	—	1.20	5.00	8.42	6.43	7.74	5.04	19.53	12.91
Sweden	133.29	110.28	214.50	124.49	181.65	342.56	277.28	334.17	269.75	268.61
Switzerland	64.53	40.87	46.49	46.75	67.78	68.61	66.85	80.98	97.20	81.34
United Kingdom	21.49	32.36	31.72	37.95	116.48	56.83	187.27	260.52	181.76	194.73
United States	183.00	170.00	210.00	221.00	596.00	521.00	669.00	1,132.00	789.00	585.00
TOTAL	**686.69**	**721.86**	**809.16**	**1,058.21**	**2,417.62**	**2,586.25**	**3,250.02**	**3,468.17**	**3,062.29**	**2,692.23**
Proportion for refugees	130.30	177.47	225.76	348.21	1,052.41	1,713.30	1,976.28	1,976.28	1,799.49	1,489.06

> *Total government donations to humanitarian assistance peaked in 1994. The figures for 1996 – the last year for which full figures are available – shows a definite drop in donations across the board. Provisional figures for 1997 confirm this trend. Humanitarian agencies, and governments, are now asking if ways need to be found to fund disaster assistance. Should funding always be so reactive, or can more sustainable proactive ways be found to channel finance into international humanitarian efforts? Source: OECD/DAC.*

Table 21 Breakdown of food aid deliveries by category per year from 1989 to 1997 in thousand tonnes – cereals in grain equivalent

	1989	1990	1991	1992	1993	1994	1995	1996	1997*
Emergency	2,389	2,767	3,540	4,991	4,202	4,208	3,451	2,351	2,461
Project	2,872	2,837	2,980	2,578	2,498	2,779	2,408	1,683	2,126
Programme	6,473	8,038	6,650	7,663	10,170	5,730	4,046	2,846	1,630
World total	11,734	13,642	13,170	15,232	16,870	12,717	9,905	6,880	6,217

Figures for 1997 are provisional.

Quantities of food aid disbursed around the world have dropped dramatically in the last few years. World trade agreements mean that grain surpluses are no longer produced in the quantities available in the early 1990s, and are no longer held by governments. Food aid, like other commodities, now has to be bought with the aid dollar and agencies need to gauge if food provides as high a return on investment as other possible uses of that dollar. Source: WFP.

The International Federation's 175 National Societies, with their 122 million volunteers, are dedicated to alleviating the suffering of the most vulnerable people around the world.

Christopher Black/International Federation. Democratic Republic of the Congo, 1997.

Chapter

13 National Societies: protecting life and health

Contact details for the members of the International Red Cross and Red Crescent Movement.

INTERNATIONAL RED CROSS AND RED CRESCENT MOVEMENT

International Federation of Red Cross and Red Crescent Societies

P.O. Box 372
1211 Geneva 19
SWITZERLAND
Tel. (41)(22) 730 42 22
Fax (41)(22) 733 03 95
Tlx (045) 412 133 FRC CH
Tlg. LICROSS GENEVA
E-mail secretariat@ifrc.org
WWW http://www.ifrc.org

International Committee of the Red Cross

19 avenue de la Paix
1202 Geneva
SWITZERLAND
Tel. (41)(22) 734 60 01
Fax (41)(22) 733 20 57
Tlx 414 226 CCR CH
Tlg. INTERCROIXROUGE GENEVE
E-mail icrc.gva@gwn.icrc.org
WWW http://www.icrc.org

NATIONAL RED CROSS AND RED CRESCENT SOCIETIES

National Red Cross and Red Crescent Societies are listed alphabetically by International Organization for Standardization Codes for the Representation of Names of Countries, English spelling.

Details correct as of 31 March 1998. Please forward any changes to the International Federation's Information Resource Centre in Geneva (e-mail: irc@ifrc.org).

Afghan Red Crescent Society

Pul Artel
Kabul
Postal address:
P.O. Box 3066
Shahre - Naw Kabul
AFGHANISTAN
Tel. 32357 / 32211
Tlx arcs af 24318
Tlg. SERAMIASHT KABUL

Albanian Red Cross

Rruga "Muhammet
Gjollesha"
Sheshi "Karl Topia"
Tirana
Postal address: C.P. 1511
Tirana
ALBANIA
Tel. (355)(42) 25855;
22037
Fax (355)(42) 25855
Tlg. ALBCROSS TIRANA

Algerian Red Crescent

15 bis, Boulevard
Mohammed V
Alger
ALGERIA
Tel. (213) 2645727;
2645728;
Fax (213) 2649787
Tlx 56056 HILAL ALGER
Tlg. HILALAHMAR ALGER

Andorra Red Cross

Prat de la Creu 22
Andorra la Vella
ANDORRA
Tel. (376) 825225
Fax (376) 828630
Tlx AND 208 "Att. CREU
ROJA"
E-mail creuroja@andor-
net.ad

Angola Red Cross

Rua 1 Congresso no 21
Luanda
Postal address:
Caixa Postal 927
Luanda
ANGOLA
Tel. (244)(2) 336543;
333991
Fax (244)(2) 345065
Tlx 3394 CRUZVER AN

Antigua and Barbuda Red Cross Society

Red Cross House
Old Parham Road
St. Johns, Antigua W.I.
Postal address:
P.O. Box 727
St. Johns, Antigua W.I.
ANTIGUA AND BARBUDA
Tel. (1)(809) 4620800
Fax (1)(809) 4620800
Tlx 2195 DISPREP "For
Red Cross"
E-mail   redcross@candw.ag

Argentine Red Cross

Hipólito Yrigoyen 2068
1089 Buenos Aires
ARGENTINA
Tel. (54)(1) 9511391;
9511854
Fax (54)(1) 9527715
Tlx 21061 CROJA AR
Tlg. ARGENCROSS
BUENOS AIRES

Armenian Red Cross Society

Antarain str. 188
Yerevan 375019
ARMENIA
Tel. (374)(2) 560630;
583630
Fax (374)(2) 583630
Tlx 243345 ODER SU,
Country code 64

Australian Red Cross

155 Pelham Street
Carlton South, VIC 3053
Postal address:
Locked Bag 4
Carlton South, VIC 3053
AUSTRALIA
Tel. (61)(3) 93451800
Fax (61)(3) 93482513
E-mail
redcross@nat.redcross.org.
au

Austrian Red Cross

Wiedner Hauptstrasse 32
Wien 4
Postal address: Postfach
39
1041 Wien 4
AUSTRIA
Tel. (43)(1) 58900-0
Fax (43)(1) 58900-199
Tlx oerk a 133111
Tlg. AUSTROREDCROOS
WIEN
E-mail oerk@redcross.or.at
WWW
http://www.redcross.or.at/

Red Crescent Society of Azerbaijan

Prospekt Azerbaidjan 19
Baku
AZERBAIJAN
Tel. (994)(12) 931912;
938481
Fax (994)(12) 931578

The Bahamas Red Cross Society

John F. Kennedy Drive
Nassau
Postal address:
P.O. Box N-8331
Nassau
BAHAMAS
Tel. (1)(242) 3237370;
3237371
Fax (1)(242) 3237404
Tlx 20657
BAHREDCROSS
Tlg. BAHREDCROSS
NASSAU

Bahrain Red Crescent Society

P.O. Box 882
Manama
BAHRAIN
Tel. (973) 293171
Fax (973) 291797
Tlg. HILAHAMAR
MANAMA

Bangladesh Red Crescent Society

684-686 Bara Maghbazar
Dhaka - 1217
Postal address:
G.P.O. Box 579
Dhaka
BANGLADESH
Tel. (880)(2) 407908;
406902
Fax (880)(2) 831908
Tlx 632232 BDRC BJ
Tlg. RED CRESCENT
DHAKA

The Barbados Red Cross Society

Red Cross House
Jemmotts Lane
Bridgetown
BARBADOS
Tel. (1)(246) 4262052
Fax (1)(246) 426-2052
"For Red Cross"
Tlx 2201 P.U.B. T.L.X.
W.B.
Tlg. REDCROSS
BARBADOS

Belarusian Red Cross

35, Karl Marx Str.
220030 Minsk
BELARUS
Tel. (375)(17) 2272620
Fax (375)(17) 2272620
Tlx 252290 KREST SU

Belgian Red Cross

Ch. de Vleurgat 98
1050 Bruxelles
BELGIUM
Tel. (32)(2) 6454411
Fax (32)(2) 6460439
(French); 6460441
(Flemish)
Tlx 24266 BELCRO B
Tlg. CROIXROUGE
BELGIQUE BRUXELLES
E-mail belgian.redcross@
infoboard.be
WWW http://redcross.be/

Belize Red Cross Society

1 Gabourel Lane
Belize City
Postal address:
P.O. Box 413
Belize City
BELIZE
Tel. (501)(2) 73319
Fax (501)(2) 30998
Tlx BTL BOOTH 211 Bze
attn. Red Cross
E-mail bzercsha@btl.net

Red Cross of Benin

B.P. No. 1
Porto-Novo
BENIN
Tel. (229) 212886
Fax (229) 214927
Tlx 1131 CRBEN

Bolivian Red Cross

Avenida Simón Bolívar
N 1515
La Paz
Postal address:
Casilla No. 741
La Paz
BOLIVIA
Tel. (591)(2) 340948;
326568
Fax (591)(2) 359102
Tlx 2220 BOLCRUZ
Tlg. CRUZROJA - LA PAZ

Botswana Red Cross Society

135 Independance Avenue
Gaborone
Postal address:
P.O. Box 485
Gaborone
BOTSWANA
Tel. (267) 352465; 312353
Fax (267) 312352
Tlg. THUSA GABORONE

Brazilian Red Cross

Praça Cruz Vermelha No.
10
20230-130 Rio de Janeiro
RJ
BRAZIL
Tel. (55)(21) 5075543;
5075544
Fax (55)(21) 5071538
Tlx (38) 2130532 CVBR BR
Tlg. BRAZCROSS RIO DE
JANEIRO

Brunei Darussalam Red Crescent Society

P.O. Box 3065
Bandar Seri Begawan 1930
BRUNEI DARUSSALAM
Tel. (673)(2) 339774
Fax (673)(2) 339572

Bulgarian Red Cross

61, Dondukov Boulevard
1527 Sofia
BULGARIA
Tel. (359)(2) 9434868;
441443
Fax (0u0)(u) 010101/
Tlx 23248 B CH K BG
Tlg. BULGAREDCROSS
SOFIA
E-mail
redcross@mail.bol.bg
WWW
http://www.usd.edu/dmhi/brc
/brcindex.html

Burkinabe Red Cross Society

01 B.P. 4404
Ouagadougou 01
BURKINA FASO
Tel. (226) 300877
Fax (226) 363121
Tlx LSCR 5438 BF
OUAGADOUGOU

Burundi Red Cross

18, Av. de la Croix-Rouge
Bujumbura
Postal address: B.P. 324
Bujumbura
BURUNDI
Tel. (257) 223159; 223576
Fax (257) 23159
Tlx 5081 CAB PUB BDI

Cambodian Red Cross Society

17, Vithei de la
Croix-Rouge
Cambodgienne
Phnom-Penh
CAMBODIA
Tel. (855)(23) 362140;
362876
Fax (855)(23) 362140

Cameroon Red Cross Society

Rue Henri Dunant
Yaoundé
Postal address: B.P. 631
Yaoundé
CAMEROON
Tel. (237) 224177
Fax (237) 224177
Tlx (0970) 8884 KN

The Canadian Red Cross Society

1800 Alta Vista Drive
Ottawa, Ontario KIG 4J5
CANADA
Tel. (1)(613) 7393000
Fax (1)(613) 7311411
Tlx CANCROSS 05-33784
Tlg. CANCROSS OTTAWA
E-mail
cancross@redcross.ca
WWW
http://www.redcross.ca/

Red Cross of Cape Verde

Rua Andrade Corvo
Caixa Postal 119
Praia
CAPE VERDE
Tel. (238) 611701; 614169
Fax (238) 614174
Tlx 6004 CV CV

Central African Red Cross Society

Avenue Koudoukou Km, 5
Bangui
Postal address: B.P. 1428
Bangui
CENTRAL AFRICAN
REPUBLIC
Tel. (236) 612223; 502130
Fax (236) 612223
Tlx DIPLOMA 5213 "Pour
Croix-Rouge"

Red Cross of Chad

B.P. 449
N'djamena
CHAD
Tel. (235) 523434
Tlg. CROIXROUGE
N'DJAMENA

Chilean Red Cross

Avenida Santa María
No. 150 Providencia
Santiago de Chile
Postal address: Correo
21, Casilla 246 V
Santiago de Chile
CHILE
Tel. (56)(2) 7771448
Fax (56)(2) 7370270
Tlx 340260 PBVTR CK
Tlg. "CHILECRUZ"

Red Cross Society of China

53 Ganmian Hutong
100010 Beijing
CHINA
Tel. (86)(10) 65124447;
65135838
Fax (86)(10) 65124169
Tlx 210244 CHNRC CN
Tlg. HONGHUI BEIJING
E-mail
hq@chineseredcross.org.
cn
WWW
http://www.chinatoday.com
/org/rcsc/a.htm

Colombian Red Cross Society

Avenida 68 N 66-31
Santafé de Bogotá D.C.
Postal address:
Apartado Aéreo 11-10
Bogotá, D.C.
COLOMBIA
Tel. (57)(1) 2506611
Fax (57)(1) 2319208
E-mail scrcol@col1.tele-
com.
com.co
WWW
http://www.crcol.org.co/

Congolese Red Cross

Place de la Paix
Brazzaville
Postal address:
B.P. 4145
Brazzaville
CONGO
Tel. (242) 824410
Fax (242) 828825
Tlx UNISANTE 5364
Pour "Croix-Rouge"

Red Cross of the Democratic Republic of the Congo

41, Avenue de la Justice
Zone de la Gombe
Kinshasa I
Postal address:
B.P. 1712
Kinshasa I
CONGO, DEMOCRATIC
REPUBLIC OF
Tel. (243)(12) 34897

Costa Rican Red Cross

Calle 14, Avenida 8
San José 1000
Postal address:
Apartado 1025
San José 1000
COSTA RICA
Tel. (506) 2337033;
2553761
Fax (506) 2237628
Tlx 2547 COSTACRUZ
SAN JOSÉ
Tlg. COSTACRUZ SAN
JOSÉ
E-mail
bcrcsn@sol.rasca.co.cr

Red Cross Society of Côte d'Ivoire

P.O. Box 1244
Abidjan 01
COTE D'IVOIRE
Tel. (225) 321335
Fax (225) 225355
Tlx 24122 SICOGI CI

Croatian Red Cross

Ulica Crvenog kriza 14
10000 Zagreb
CROATIA
Tel. (385)(1) 4655809;
4655814
Fax (385)(1) 4550072
E-mail redcross@hck.hr
WWW http://www.hck.hr/

Cuban Red Cross

Calle Calzada No. 51
Vedado
Ciudad Habana
C.P. 10400
CUBA
Tel. (53)(7) 326005
Fax (53)(7) 662057
Tlx 511149 MSP CU para
Cruz Roja
Tlg. CRUROCU HABANA
E-mail
crsn@infomed.sld.cu

Czech Red Cross

Thunovska 18
CZ-118 04 Praha 1
CZECH REPUBLIC
Tel. (420)(2) 57320196;
57320207
Fax (420)(2) 57320207
Tlx 122 400 csrc c
Tlg. CROIX PRAHA

Danish Red Cross

Blegdamsvej 27
2100 København Ö
Postal address:
P.O. Box 2600
DK-2100 København Ö
DENMARK
Tel. (45) 35259200
Fax (45) 35259292
Tlg. DANCROIX
KÖBENHAVN
E-mail drc@redcross.dk
WWW
http://www.redcrossdk.dk/

Red Crescent Society of Djibouti

B.P. 8
Djibouti
DJIBOUTI
Tel. (253) 352451
Fax (253) 355049
Tlx 5871 PRESIDENCE DJ

Dominica Red Cross Society

Federation Drive
Goodwill
DOMINICA
Tel. (1)(767) 4488280
Fax (1)(767) 4487708
Tlg. DOMCROSS
E-mail redcross@tod.dm

Dominican Red Cross

Calle Juan E. Dunant No.
51
Ens. Miraflores
Santo Domingo
Postal address:
Apartado Postal 1293
Santo Domingo, D.N.
DOMINICAN REPUBLIC
Tel. (1)(809) 6823793;
6897344
Fax (1)(809) 6822837
Tlx rca sdg 4112 "PARA
CRUZ ROJA DOM."
Tlg. CRUZ ROJA
DOMINICANA, SANTO
DOMINGO
E-mail
cruz.roja@codetel.net.do

Ecuadorian Red Cross

Av. Colombia y Elizalde
Esq.
Quito
Postal address:
Casilla 17-01-2119
Quito
ECUADOR
Tel. (593)(2) 514587
Fax (593)(2) 570424
Tlx CRUZRO 2662
Tlg. CRUZ ROJA QUITO
E-mail
crequito@uio.satnet.net

Egyptian Red Crescent Society

29, El Galaa Street
Cairo
EGYPT
Tel. (20)(2) 5750558;
5750397
Fax (20)(2) 5740450
Tlx 93249 ERCS UN
Tlg. 124 HELALHAMER
E-mail
erc@brainzl.ie-eg.com

Salvadorean Red Cross Society

17 C. Pte. y Av. Henri
Dunant
San Salvador
Postal address:
Apartado Postal 2672
San Salvador
EL SALVADOR
Tel. (503) 2227743;
2227749
Fax (503) 2227758
Tlx 20550 cruzalva
Tlg. CRUZALVA SAN
SALVADOR

Red Cross of Equatorial Guinea

Alcalde Albilio Balboa 92
Malabo
Postal address:
Apartado postal 460
Malabo
EQUATORIAL GUINEA
Tel. (240)(9) 3701
Fax (240)(9) 3701
Tlx 099/1111 EG.PUB
MBO "Favor Transmetien
Cruz Roja Tel. 2393"

Estonia Red Cross

Lai Street 17
EE-0001 Tallinn
ESTONIA
Tel. (372) 6411643
Fax (372) 6411641
Tlx 173491

Ethiopian Red Cross Society

Ras Desta Damtew
Avenue
Addis Ababa
Postal address:
P.O. Box 195
Addis Ababa
ETHIOPIA
Tel. (251)(1) 519364;
159074
Fax (251)(1) 512643
Tlx 21338 ERCS ET
Tlg. ETHIOCROSS
ADDISABABA
E-mail
ercs@padis.gn.apc.org

Fiji Red Cross Society

22 Gorrie Street
Suva
Postal address:
GPO Box 569
Suva
FIJI
Tel. (679) 314133;
314138
Fax (679) 303818
Tlx 2279 Red Cross (Public facility)
Tlg. REDCROSS SUVA

Finnish Red Cross

Tehtaankatu 1 a
FIN-00140 Helsinki
Postal address:
P.O. Box 168
FIN-00141 Helsinki
FINLAND
Tel. (358)(9) 12931
Fax (358)(9) 1293352
Tlx 121331 FINCR FI
Tlg. FINCROSS HELSINKI
E-mail
forename.surname@
redcross.fi
WWW
http://www.redcross.fi/

French Red Cross

1, Place Henry-Dunant
F-75384 Paris Cedex 08
FRANCE
Tel. (33)(1) 44431100
Fax (33)(1) 44431101
Tlx CR PARIS 642760 F
CRPAR
Tlg. CROIROUGE PARIS
086

The Gambia Red Cross Society

Kanifing Industrial Area -
Banjul
Postal address:
P.O. Box 472, Banjul
GAMBIA
Tel. (220) 392405; 393179
Fax (220) 394921
Tlx 2338 REDCROSS GV
Tlg. GAMREDCROSS
BANJUL

Red Cross Society of Georgia

15, Krilov Street
Tbilisi
GEORGIA
Tel. (995)(32) 953304;
953826
Tlx 212167 RED

German Red Cross

Friedrich-Ebert-Allee 71
D-53113 Bonn
Postal address:
Postfach 1460
53004 Bonn
GERMANY
Tel. (49)(228) 5411
Fax (49)(228) 541290
Tlx 886619 DKRB D
Tlg.
DEUTSCHROTKREUZ
BONN
E-mail drk@drk.de
WWW
http://www.rotkreuz.de

Ghana Red Cross Society

Ministries Annex Block A3
Off Liberia Road Extension
Accra
Postal address:
P.O. Box 835
Accra
GHANA
Tel. (233)(21) 662298
Fax (233)(21) 667226
Tlx 2008 GRBS GH
Tlg. GHANACROSS
ACCRA
E-mail ifrcsrc@ghana.com

Hellenic Red Cross

Rue Lycavittou 1
Athens 106 72
GREECE
Tel. (30)(1) 3646005;
3628648
Fax (30)(1) 3613564
Tlx 225156 EES GR
Tlg. HELLECROIX
ATHENES
E-mail
hcr@netmode.ntua.gr

Grenada Red Cross Society

Upper Lucas Street
St. George's
Postal address:
P.O. Box 551
St. George's
GRENADA
Tel. (1)(473) 4401483
Fax (1)(473) 4401829
E-mail grercs@ca-
ribsurf.com

Guatemalan Red Cross

3a Calle 8 - 40, Zona 1
Guatemala, C.A.
GUATEMALA
Tel. (502)(2) 532026;
532027
Fax (502)(2) 324649
E-mail crg@guate.net

Red Cross Society of Guinea

B.P. 376
Conakry
GUINEA
Tel. (224) 443825
Fax (224) 414255
Tlx 22101

Red Cross Society of Guinea-Bissau

Avenida Unidade Africana,
No. 12
Bissau
Postal address: Caixa
postal 514-1036 BIX,
Codex
Bissau
GUINEA BISSAU
Tel. (245) 212405
Tlx 251 PCE BI

The Guyana Red Cross Society

Eve Leary
Georgetown
Postal address:
P.O. Box 10524
Georgetown
GUYANA
Tel. (592)(2) 65174
Fax (592)(2) 77099
Tlx 2226 FERNA GY "For
Guyana Red Cross"
Tlg. GUYCROSS
GEORGETOWN

Haitian National Red Cross Society

1, rue Eden
Bicentenaire
Port-Au-Prince
Postal address: CRH
B.P. 1337
Port-Au-Prince
HAITI
Tel. (509) 225553; 225554
Fax (509) 231054
Tlg. HAITICROSS PORT
AU PRINCE

Honduran Red Cross

7a Calle
entre 1a. y 2a. Avenidas
Comayagüela D.C.
HONDURAS
Tel. (504) 2378876;
2374628
Fax (504) 2380185
Tlx 1437 CRUZ R HO
Tlg. HONDUCRUZ
COMAYAGUELA
E-mail
honducruz@datum.hn

Hungarian Red Cross

Arany János utca 31
1051 Budapest V.
Postal address:
Magyar Vöröskereszt
1367 Budapest 5, Pf. 121
HUNGARY
Tel. (36)(1) 3313950;
3317711
Fax (36)(1) 1533988
Tlx 224943 REDCR H
Tlg. REDCROSS
BUDAPEST
E-mail intdept@hrc.hu

Icelandic Red Cross

Efstaleiti 9
103 Reykjavik
ICELAND
Tel. (354) 5704000
Fax (354) 5704010
E-mail
central@redcross.is
WWW
http://www.redcross.is

Indian Red Cross Society

Red Cross Building
1 Red Cross Road
New Delhi 110001
INDIA
Tel. (91)(11) 3716441;
3716442
Fax (91)(11) 3717454
Tlx 3166115 IRCS IN
Tlg. INDCROSS NEW
DELHI
E-mail ircs@irc.unv.er-
net.in

Indonesian Red Cross Society

Jl. Jenderal Datot Subroto
Kav. 96
Jakarta 12790
Postal address:
P.O. Box 2009
Jakarta
INDONESIA
Tel. (62)(21) 7992325
Fax (62)(21) 7995188
Tlx 66170 MB PMI IA
Tlg. INDONCROSS JKT

Red Crescent Society of the Islamic Republic of Iran

Ostad Nejatolahi Ave.
Tehran
IRAN, ISLAMIC
REPUBLIC OF
Tel. (98)(21) 8849077;
8849078
Fax (98)(21) 8849079
Tlx 224259 RCIA-IR
Tlg. CROISSANT-ROUGE
TEHERAN

Iraqi Red Crescent Society

Al-Mansour
Baghdad
Postal address:
P.O. Box 6143
Baghdad
IRAQ
Tel. (964)(1) 8862191;
5343922
Fax (964)(1) 8840872
Tlx 213331 HELAL IK
Tlg. REDCRESCENT
BAGHDAD

Irish Red Cross Society

16, Merrion Square
Dublin 2
IRELAND
Tel. (353)(1) 6765135;
6765136
Fax (353)(1) 6614461
Tlx 32746 IRCS EI
E-mail info@redcross.ie
WWW http://www.swor-
dpoint.com/
irishredcross.htm

Italian Red Cross

12, Via Toscana
I - 00187 Roma
ITALY
Tel. (39)(6) 47591
Fax (39)(6) 4759223
Tlx 613421 CRIROM I
Tlg. CRIROM 00187
WWW http://www.cri.it/

Jamaica Red Cross

Central Village
Spanish Town
St. Catherine
Postal address:
76 Arnold Road
Kingston 5
JAMAICA West Indies
Tel. (1)(876) 98478602
Fax (1)(876) 9848272
Tlx COLYB JA 2397 "For
Red Cross"
Tlg. JAMCROSS
KINGSTON
WWW http://www.
infochan.com/
ja-red-cross/

Japanese Red Cross Society

1-3 Shiba Daimon,
1-Chome, Minato-ku
Tokyo-105
JAPAN
Tel. (81)(3) 34381311
Fax (81)(3) 34358509
Tlx JARCROSS J 22420
Tlg. JAPANCROSS
TOKYO
E-mail
rcjpn@ppp.bekkoame.or.jp
WWW
http://www.sphere.ad.jp/
redcross/

Jordan National Red Crescent Society

Madaba Street
Amman
Postal address:
P.O. Box 10001
Amman 11151
JORDAN
Tel. (962)(6) 773141;
773142
Fax (962)(6) 750815
Tlx 22500 HILAL JO
Tlg. HALURDON AMMAN

Kenya Red Cross Society

Nairobi South "C"
(Belle Vue), off Mombasa
Road
Nairobi
Postal address:
P.O. Box 40712
Nairobi
KENYA
Tel. (254)(2) 503781;
503789
Fax (254)(2) 503845
Tlx 25436 IFRC KE
Tlg. KENREDCROSS
NAIROBI

Kiribati Red Cross Society

P.O. Box 213
Bikenibeu
Tarawa
KIRIBATI
Tel. (686) 28128
Fax (686) 28128

Red Cross Society of the Democratic People's Republic of Korea

Ryonwa 1, Central District
Pyongyang
KOREA, DEMOCRATIC
PEOPLE'S REPUBLIC OF
Tel. (850)(2) 18111 (ask
for 3818048)
Fax (850)(2) 3814644
Tlx 5355 DAEMUN KP
Tlg. KOREACROSS
PYONGYANG

The Republic of Korea National Red Cross

32 - 3ka, Namsan-dong
Choong-Ku
Seoul 100 - 043
KOREA, REPUBLIC OF
Tel. (82)(2) 7559301
Fax (82)(2) 7740735
Tlx ROKNRC K28585
Tlg. KORCROSS SEOUL
E-mail krchq@chollian.net

Kuwait Red Crescent Society

Al-Jahra St.
Shuweek
Postal address:
P.O. Box 1359
13014 Safat
KUWAIT
Tel. (965) 4839114;
4815478
Fax (965) 4839114
Tlx 22729

Lao Red Cross

Avenue Sethathirath
Vientiane
Postal address: B.P. 650
Vientiane
LAO PEOPLE'S
DEMOCRATIC
REPUBLIC
Tel. (856)(21) 216610;
212036
Fax (856)(21) 215935
Tlx 4491 TE via PTT
LAOS
Tlg. CROIXLAO
VIENTIANE

Latvian Red Cross

1, Skolas Street
Riga LV-1010
LATVIA
Tel. (371)(7) 310902;
2275635
Fax (371)(7) 310902

Lebanese Red Cross

Rue Spears
Beyrouth
LEBANON
Tel. (961)(1) 372802;
372803
Fax (961)(1) 378207
Tlx CROLIB 20593 LE
Tlg. LIBACROSS
BEYROUTH

Lesotho Red Cross Society

23 Mabile Road
Maseru 100
Postal address:
P.O. Box 366
Maseru 100
LESOTHO
Tel. (266) 313911
Fax (266) 310166
Tlx 4515 LECROS LO
Tlg. LESCROSS
MASERU
E-mail lrcs@wn.apc.org

Liberian Red Cross Society

107 Lynch Street
1000 Monrovia 20
Postal address:
P.O. Box 20-5081
1000 Monrovia 20
LIBERIA
Tel. (231) 225172
Fax (231) 226231
Tlx 44210

Libyan Red Crescent

P.O. Box 541
Benghazi
LIBYAN ARAB
JAMAHIRIYA
Tel. (218)(61) 9095152;
9095202
Fax (218)(61) 9095829
Tlx 40341 HILAL PY
Tlg. LIBHILAL BENGHAZI

Liechtenstein Red Cross

Heiligkreuz 25
FL-9490 Vaduz
LIECHTENSTEIN
Tel. (41)(75) 2322294
Fax (41)(75) 2322240
Tlg. ROTESKREUZ
VADUZ

Lithuanian Red Cross Society

Gedimino ave. 3a
2600 Vilnius
LITHUANIA
Tel. (370)(2) 628037
Fax (370)(2) 619923

Luxembourg Red Cross

Parc de la Ville
L - 2014 Luxembourg
Postal address: B.P. 404
L - 2014 LUXEMBOURG
Tel. (352) 450202; 450201
Fax (352) 457269

The Red Cross of The Former Yugoslav Republic of Macedonia

No. 13
Bul. Koco Racin
91000 Skopje
MACEDONIA
Tel. (389)(91) 114355
Fax (389)(91) 230 542

Malagasy Red Cross Society

1, rue Patrice Lumumba
Tsaralalaba
Antananarivo
Postal address: B.P. 1168
Antananarivo
MADAGASCAR
Tel. (261)(20) 2222111
Fax (261)(20) 2235457
Tlg. ficrts.mg

Malawi Red Cross Society

Red Cross House (along
Presidential Way)
Lilongwe
Postal address:
P.O. Box 30096
Capital City
Lilongwe 3
MALAWI
Tel. (265) 732877; 732878
Fax (265) 730210
Tlx 44276
E-mail mrcs@
unima.wn.apc.org

Malaysian Red Crescent Society

JKR 32, Jalan Nipah
Off Jalan Ampang
55000 Kuala Lumpur
MALAYSIA
Tel. (60)(3) 4578122;
4578236
Fax (60)(3) 30166
Tlx MACRES MA 30166
Tlg. MALREDCRES
KUALA LUMPUR
E-mail mrcs@po.jaring.my

Mali Red Cross

Route Koulikoro
Bamako
Postal address: B.P. 280
Bamako
MALI
Tel. (223) 244569
Fax (223) 240414
Tlx 2611 MJ

Malta Red Cross Society

104 St Ursola Street
Valletta 15400
MALTA
Tel. (356) 222645
Fax (356) 243664
E-mail
mltredcr@keyworld.net

Mauritanian Red Crescent

Avenue Gamal Abdel
Nasser
Nouakchott
Postal address: B.P. 344
Nouakchott
MAURITANIA
Tel. (222)(2) 51249
Fax (222)(2) 58352
Tlx 5830 CRM

Mauritius Red Cross Society

Ste. Thérèse Street
Curepipe
MAURITIUS
Tel. (230) 6763604
TlxYBRAT IW 4258 "For
Mauritius Red Cross"
Tlg. MAUREDCROSS
CUREPIPE

Mexican Red Cross

Calle Luis Vives 200
Colonia Polanco
México, D.F. 11510
MEXICO
Tel. (52)(5) 3951111;
5800070
Fax (52)(5) 3951598
Tlx 01777617 CRMEME
Tlg. CRUZROJA MEXICO
WWW
http://www.cruz-roja.org.mx

Red Cross of Monaco

27, Boulevard de Suisse
Monte Carlo
MONACO
Tel. (377)(93) 506701
Fax (377)(93) 159047
Tlg. CROIXROUGE
MONTECARLO

Mongolian Red Cross Society

Central Post Office
Post Box 537
Ulaanbaatar
MONGOLIA
Tel. (976)(1) 320635
Fax (976)(1) 320934
Tlx 79358 MUIW
Tlg. MONRECRO
E-mail
redcross@magicnet.mn

Moroccan Red Crescent

Palais Mokri
Takaddoum
Rabat
Postal address: B.P. 189
Rabat
MOROCCO
Tel. (212)(7) 650898;
651495
Fax (212)(7) 759395
Tlx ALHILAL 319-40 M
RABAT
Tlg. ALHILAL RABAT

Mozambique Red Cross Society

Avenida Agostinhoaero
284
Maputo
Postal address:
Caixa Postal 2986
Maputo
MOZAMBIQUE
Tel. (258)(1) 490943;
497721
Fax (258)(1) 497725
Tlx 6-169 CV MO

Myanmar Red Cross Society

Red Cross Building
42 Strand Road
Yangon
MYANMAR
Tel. (95)(1) 296552;
295238
Fax (95)(1) 296551
Tlx 21218 BRCROS BM
Tlg. MYANMARCROSS
YANGON

Namibia Red Cross

Red Cross House
Erf 2128, Independence
Avenue
Katutura
Windhoek
Postal address:
P.O. Box 346
Windhoek
NAMIBIA
Tel. (264)(61) 235216;
235226
Fax (264)(61) 228949
E-mail
namcross@iafrica.com.na

Nepal Red Cross Society

Red Cross Marg
Kalimati
Kathmandu
Postal address:
P.O. Box 217
Kathmandu
NEPAL
Tel. (977)(1) 270650;
270167
Fax (977)(1) 271915
Tlx 2569 NRCS NP
Tlg. REDCROSS
KATHMANDU
E-mail nrcs@
kalimati.mos.com.np

The Netherlands Red Cross

Leeghwaterplein 27
2521 CV The Hague
Postal address:
P.O. Box 28120
2502 KC The Hague
NETHERLANDS
Tel. (31)(70) 4455666;
4455755
Fax (31)(70) 4455777
Tlx 32375 NRCS NL
Tlg. ROODKRUIS THE
HAGUE
E-mail hq@redcross.nl
WWW
http://www.redcross.nl/
nrcs

New Zealand Red Cross

Red Cross House
14 Hill Street
Wellington 1
Postal address:
P.O. Box 12140
Thorndon, Wellington
NEW ZEALAND
Tel. (64)(4) 4723750
Fax (64)(4) 4730315
E-mail
sep@redcross.org.nz
WWW
http://www.redcross.org.nz

Nicaraguan Red Cross

Reparto Belmonte
Carretera Sur
Managua
Postal address:
Apartado 3279
Managua
NICARAGUA
Tel. (505)(2) 652082;
652084
Fax (505)(2) 651643
Tlx 2363 NICACRUZ
Tlg.
NICACRUZ-MANAGUA
E-mail
nicacruz@ibw.com.ni

Red Cross Society of Niger

B.P. 11386
Niamey
NIGER
Tel. (227) 733037
Fax (227) 723244
Tlx CRN GAP NI 5371

Nigerian Red Cross Society

11, Eko Akete Close
off St. Gregory's Road
South West Ikoyi
Lagos
Postal address:
P.O. Box 764
Lagos
NIGERIA
Tel. (234)(1) 2695188;
2695189
Fax (234)(1) 2691599
Tlx 21470 NCROSS NG
Tlg. NIGERCROSS
LAGOS

Norwegian Red Cross

Hausmannsgate 7
0133 Oslo
Postal address: Postbox
1. Gronland
0133 Oslo
NORWAY
Tel. (47) 22054000
Fax (47) 22054040
Tlx 76011 NORCR N
Tlg. NORCROSS OSLO
E-mail post-
man@redcross.no
WWW
http://www.redcross.no

Pakistan Red Crescent Society

Sector H-8
Islamabad
PAKISTAN
Tel. (92)(51) 854885;
856420
Fax (92)(51) 280530
Tlx 54103 PRCS PK
Tlg. HILALAHMAR
ISLAMABAD

Palau Red Cross Society

P.O. Box 6043
Koror
REPUBLIC OF PALAU
96940
Tel. (680) 4885780;
4885781
Fax (680) 4884540

Red Cross Society of Panama

Albrook, Areas Revertidas
Calle Prinicpal
Edificio # 453
Panamá
Postal address:
Apartado 668
Zona 1 Panamá
PANAMA
Tel. (507) 2325589;
2325559
Fax (507) 2327450
Tlx 2661 STORTEXPA
Tlg. PANACRUZ PANAMA
E-mail
cruzroja@pan.gbm.net
WWW
http://www.cruzroja.org.pa/

Papua New Guinea Red Cross Society

Taurama Road
Port Moresby
Boroko
Postal address:
P.O. Box 6545
Boroko
PAPUA NEW GUINEA
Tel. (675) 3258577;
3258759
Fax (675) 3259714
Tlx PNG RC NE 23292

Paraguayan Red Cross

Brasil 216 esq. José
Berges
Asunción
PARAGUAY
Tel. (595)(21) 22797;
208199
Fax (595)(21) 211560
Tlg. CRUZ ROJA
PARAGUAYA
E-mail
cruzroja@pla.net.py

Peruvian Red Cross

Av. Arequipa No. 1285
Lima
Postal address:
Apartado 1534
Lima
PERU
Tel. (51)(1) 2658784;
2658785
Fax (51)(1) 2658788
Tlg. CRUZROJA
PERUANA LIMA
E-mail
scrperu@mail.iaxis.com.pe

The Philippine National Red Cross

Bonifacio Drive
Port Area
Manila 2803
Postal address:
PO Box 280
Manila 2803
PHILIPPINES
Tel. (63)(2) 5278384;
5278397
Fax (63)(2)5270857
Tlx 27846 PNRC PH
Tlg. PHILCROSS
MANILA
E-mail
pnrcnhq@pdx.rpnet.com

Polish Red Cross

Mokotowska 14
00-561 Warszawa
Postal address:
P.O Box 47
00-950 Warszawa
POLAND
Tel. (48)(22) 6285201-7
Fax (48)(22) 6284168
Tlx 813561 PCK PL
Tlg. PECEKA VARSOVIE
E-mail pck@ids.pl
WWW
http://www.pck.org.pl

Portuguese Red Cross

Jardim 9 de Abril, 1 a 5
1293 Lisboa Codex
PORTUGAL
Tel. (351)(1) 3905571;
3905650
Fax (351)(1) 3951045
Tlx 14369 PORCRS P
Tlg. CRUZVERMELHA

Qatar Red Crescent Society

P.O. Box 5449
Doha
QATAR
Tel. (974) 435111
Fax (974) 439950
Tlx 4753 qrcs dh
Tlg. hilal doha

Romanian Red Cross

Strada Biserica Amzei, 29
Sector 1
Bucarest
ROMANIA
Tel. (40)(1) 6593385;
6506233
Fax (40)(1) 3128452
Tlx 10531 romcr r
Tlg. ROMCROIXROUGE
BUCAREST

The Russian Red Cross Society

Tcheryomushkinski Proezd
5
117036 Moscow
RUSSIAN FEDERATION
Tel. (7)(095) 1265731;
1265831
Fax (7)(095) 2302867
Tlx 411400 IKPOL SU
Tlg. IKRESTPOL
MOSKWA

Rwandan Red Cross

B.P. 425
Kigali
RWANDA
Tel. (250) 74402
Fax (250) 73233
Tlx 22663 CRR RW

Saint Kitts and Nevis Red Cross Society

Red Cross House
Horsford Road
Basseterre
Postal address:
P.O. Box 62
Basseterre
SAINT KITTS AND NEVIS
Tel. (1)(869) 4652584
Fax (1)(869) 4652584

Saint Lucia Red Cross

Vigie
Castries St Lucia, W.I.
Postal address:
P.O. Box 271
Castries St Lucia, W.I.
SAINT LUCIA
Tel. (1)(758) 4525582
Fax (1)(758) 4537811
Tlx 6256 MCNAMARA LC
Attn. Mrs Boland

Saint Vincent and the Grenadines Red Cross

Halifax Street
Ministry of Education
Compound
Kingstown
Postal address:
P.O. Box 431
SAINT VINCENT AND
THE GRENADINES
Tel. (1)(809) 4561888
Fax (1)(809) 4856210
E-mail
svgredcross@caribsurf.com

Western Samoa Red Cross Society

P.O. Box 1616
Apia
SAMOA
Tel. (685) 23686
Fax (685) 22676
Tlx 779 224 MORISHED
SX (Attention Red Cross)

Red Cross of San Marino

Via Scialoja, Cailungo
Repubblica di San Marino,
47031
SAN MARINO
Tel. (37)(8) 994360
Fax (37)(8) 994360
Tlg. CROCE ROSSA
REPUBBLICA DI
SAN MARINO

Sao Tome and Principe Red Cross

Avenida 12 de Julho No.11
Sao Tomé
Postal address: B.P. 96
Sao Tome
SAO TOME AND
PRINCIPE
Tel. (239)(12) 22305;
22469
Fax (239)(12) 21365
publico ST
Tlx 213 PUBLICO ST
"Pour Croix-Rouge"

Saudi Arabian Red Crescent Society

General Headquarters
Riyadh 11129
SAUDI ARABIA
Tel. (966)(1) 4740027
Fax (966)(1) 4787453
Tlx 400096 HILAL SJ

Senegalese Red Cross Society

Boulevard F. Roosevelt
Dakar
Postal address: B.P. 299
Dakar
SENEGAL
Tel. (221) 8233992
Fax (221) 8225369

Seychelles Red Cross Society

B.P. 53
Victoria
Mahé
SEYCHELLES
Tel. (248) 322122; 322220
Fax (248) 322122
Tlx 2302 HEALTH SZ
E-mail
excel@seychelles.net

Sierra Leone Red Cross Society

6 Liverpool Street
Freetown
Postal address:
P.O. Box 427
Freetown
SIERRA LEONE
Tel. (232)(22) 222384
Fax (232)(22) 229083
Tlx 3692 SLRCS
Tlg. SIERRA RED CROSS

Singapore Red Cross Society

Red Cross House
15 Penang Lane
Singapore 0923
SINGAPORE
Tel. (65) 3373587; 3360269
Fax (65) 3374360
Tlx SRCS RS 33978
Tlg. REDCROS SINGA-
PORE
WWW
http://vhp.nus.sg/redcross/

Slovak Red Cross

Grösslingova 24
814 46 Bratislava
SLOVAKIA
Tel. (421)(7) 325305;
323576
Fax (42)(7) 323279

Slovenian Red Cross

Mirje 19
Ljubljana
Postal address:
P.O. Box 236
SI-1000 Ljubljana
SLOVENIA
Tel. (386)(61) 1261200
Fax (386)(61) 1252142

The Solomon Islands Red Cross

P.O. Box 187
Honiara
SOLOMON ISLANDS
Tel. (677) 22682
Fax (677) 25299
Tlx 66347 WING HQ

Somali Red Crescent Society

c/o ICRC Box 73226
Nairobi
KENYA
Tel. Mogadishu (871 or
873) 131 2646; Nairobi
(254)(2) 723963
Fax 1312647
(Mogadishu); 715598
(Nairobi)
Tlx 25645 ICRC KE

The South African Red Cross Society

25 Erlswold Way
Saxonwold
Johannesburg 2196
Postal address:
P.O. Box 2829
Parklands 2121
SOUTH AFRICA
Tel. (27)(11) 4861313;
4861314
Fax (27)(11) 4861092
Tlg. REDCROSS JO-
HANNESBURG

Spanish Red Cross

Rafael Villa, s/n (Vuelta Ginés Navarro)
28023 El Plantio
Madrid
SPAIN
Tel. (34)(1) 3354444;
3354545
Fax (34)(1) 3354455
Tlx 23853 OCCRE E
Tlg. CRUZ ROJA
ESPANOLA MADRID
E-mail informa@cruzroja.es
WWW
http://www.cruzroja.es/

The Sri Lanka
Red Cross Society

106, Dharmapala Mawatha
Colombo 7
Postal address:
P.O. Box 375
Colombo
SRI LANKA
Tel. (94)(1) 691095;
699935
Fax (94)(1) 695434
Tlx 23312 SLRCS CE
Tlg. RED CROSS
COLOMBO

The Sudanese Red
Crescent

P.O. Box 235
Khartoum
SUDAN
Tel. (249)(11) 772011
Fax (249)(11) 772877
Tlx 23006 LRCS SD
Tlg. EL NADJA
KHARTOUM

Suriname Red Cross

Gravenberchstraat 2
Paramaribo
Postal address: Postbus
2919
Paramaribo
SURINAME
Tel. (597) 498410
Fax (597) 464780

Baphalali Swaziland
Red Cross Society

104 Johnstone Street
Mbabane
Postal address:
P.O. Box 377
Mbabane
SWAZILAND
Tel. (268) 42532
Fax (268) 46108
Tlx 2260 WD
Tlg. BAPHALALI
MBABANE
E-mail bsrcs@wn.apc.org

Swedish Red Cross

Östhammarsgatan 70
Stockholm
Postal address: Box 27316
S-102 54 Stockholm
SWEDEN
Tel. (46)(8) 6655600
Fax (46)(8) 66228877
Tlx 19613 SWECROS S
Tlg. SWEDCROS
STOCKHOLM
E-mail
postmaster@redcross.se
WWW
http://www.redcross.se

Swiss Red Cross

Rainmattstrasse 10
3001 Bern
Postal address: Postfach
3001 Bern
SWITZERLAND
Tel. (41)(31) 3877111
Fax (41)(31) 3877122
Tlx 911102 CRSB CH
Tlg. CROIXROUGE
SUISSE BERNE
E-mail info@redcross.ch
WWW
http://www.redcross.ch

Syrian Arab Red
Crescent

Al Malek Aladel Street
Damascus
SYRIAN ARAB REPUBLIC
Tel. (963)(11) 4429662
Fax (963)(11) 4425677
Tlx 412857 HLAL
Tlg. CROISSANROUGE
DAMAS

Red Crescent Society
of Tajikistan

120, Umari Khayyom Str.
734017, Dushanbe
TAJIKISTAN
Tel. (7)(3772) 240374
Fax (7)(3772) 245378
E-mail
rcstaj@rcstaj.td.silk.glas.
apc.org

Tanzania Red Cross
National Society

Upanga Road
Dar es Salaam
Postal address:
P.O. Box 1133
Dar es Salaam
TANZANIA, UNITED
REPUBLIC OF
Tel. (255)(51) 116514;
151236
Tlx TACROS 41878
E-mail
redcross@unidar.gn.apc.or

The Thai Red Cross
Society

Paribatra Building
Central Bureau
1873, Rama IV Road
Bangkok-10330
THAILAND
Tel. (66)(2) 2564037;
2564038
Fax (66)(2) 2553727
Tlx 82535 threcso th
Tlg. THAICROSS
BANGKOK
E-mail
trcs@md2.md.chula.ac.th
WWW
http://kanchanapisek.or.th/
kp7/

Togolese Red Cross

51, rue Boko Soga
Amoutivé
Lome
Postal address: B.P. 655
Lome
TOGO
Tel. (228) 212110
Fax (228) 215228
Tlx UNDERVPRO
5261/5145
"pour Croix-Rouge"
Tlg. CROIX-ROUGE
TOGOLAISE LOME

Tonga Red Cross
Society

P.O. Box 456
Nuku'Alofa
South West Pacific
TONGA
Tel. (676) 21360; 21670
Fax (676) 24158
Tlx 66222 CW ADM TS
Attn. Redcross
Tlg. REDCROSS
TONGA

The Trinidad and
Tobago Red Cross
Society

Lot 7A, Fitz Blackman
Drive
Wrightson Road
Port of Spain, West
Indies
Postal address:
P.O. Box 357
Port of Spain
TRINIDAD AND
TOBAGO
Tel. (1)(868) 6278215;
6278128
Fax (1)(868) 6278215
Tlx (294) 9003 "for Red
Cross"
Tlg. TRINREDCROSS

Tunisian Red
Crescent

19, Rue d'Angleterre
Tunis 1000
TUNISIA
Tel. (216)(1) 320630;
325572
Fax (216)(1) 320151
Tlx 12524 HILAL TN
Tlg. HILALAHMAR
TUNIS

Turkish Red
Crescent Society

Atac Sokak 1 No. 32
Yenisehir
Ankara
TURKEY
Tel. (90)(312) 4302300;
4311158
Fax (90)(312) 4300175
Tlx 44593 KZLY TR
Tlg. KIZILAY ANKARA

Red Crescent Society of Turkmenistan

48 A. Novoi str.
744000 Ashgabat
TURKMENISTAN
Tel. (933)(12) 395512
Fax (933)(12) 351750
E-mail
nrcst@nrcst.ashgabad.
su

The Uganda Red Cross Society

Plot 97, Buganda Road
Kampala
Postal address:
P.O. Box 494
Kampala
UGANDA
Tel. (256)(41) 258701;
258702
Fax (256)(41) 258184
Tlx (0988) 62118 redcrosug
Tlg. UGACROSS
KAMPALA
WWW http://www.
geocities.com/
RainForest/Vines/3997/

Ukrainian Red Cross Society

30, Pushkinskaya St.
252004 Kiev
UKRAINE
Tel. (380)(44) 2250157;
2465658
Fax (380)(44) 2251096
Tlx 131329 LICRO SU
E-mail
root@redcross.freenet.kiev.
ua

Red Crescent Society of the United Arab Emirates

P.O. Box 3324
Abu Dhabi
UNITED ARAB EMIRATES
Tel. (9)(712) 219000
Fax (9)(712) 212727
Tlx 23582 RCS EM
Tlg. HILAL AHMAR
ABU DHABI

British Red Cross

9 Grosvenor Crescent
London SW1X 7EJ
UNITED KINGDOM
Tel. (44)(171) 2355454
Fax (44)(171) 2456315
Tlx 918657 BRCS G
Tlg. REDCROS, LONDON,
SW1
E-mail
information@redcross.org.uk
WWW
http://www.redcross.org.uk/

American Red Cross

17th Street, NW
Washington, DC 20006
UNITED STATES
Tel. (1)(202) 7286630;
7286600
Fax (1)(202) 7750733
Tlx ARC TLX WSH 892636
Tlg. AMCROSS
WASHINGTON DC
E-mail
postmaster@usa.redcross.
org
WWW
http://www.redcross.org

Uruguayan Red Cross

Avenida 8 de Octubre,
2990
11600 Montevideo
URUGUAY
Tel. (598)(2) 802112
Fax (598)(2) 800714
Tlg. CRUZ ROJA
URUGUAYA
MONTEVIDEO

Red Crescent Society of Uzbekistan

30, Yusuf Hos Hojib St.
700031 Tashkent
UZBEKISTAN
Tel. (7)(3712) 563741
Fax (7)(3712) 561801

Vanuatu Red Cross Society

P.O. Box 618
Port Vila
VANUATU
Tel. (678) 27418
Fax (678) 22599
Tlx VANRED
Tlg. VANRED

Venezuelan Red Cross

Avenida Andrés Bello, 4
Caracas 1010
Postal address:
Apartado 3185
Caracas 1010
VENEZUELA
Tel. (58)(2) 5714380;
5712143
Fax (58)(2) 5761042
Tlx 27237 CRURO VC
Tlg. CRUZ ROJA
CARACAS

Red Cross of Viet Nam

68, Rue Ba Triêu
Hanoï
VIET NAM
Tel. (844)(8) 262315;
264868
Fax (844)(8) 266285
Tlx 411415 VNRC VT
Tlg. VIETNAMCROSS
HANOI
E-mail
vnrchq@netnam.org.vn

Yemen Red Crescent Society

Head Office, Building
N 10
26 September Street
Sanaa
Postal address:
P.O. Box 1257
Sanaa
YEMEN
Tel. (967)(1) 283132;
283133
Fax (967)(1) 283131
Tlx 3124 HILAL YE
Tlg. SANAA HELAL
AHMAR

Yugoslav Red Cross

Simina 19
11000 Belgrade
YUGOSLAVIA, FEDERAL
REPUBLIC OF
Tel. (381)(11) 623564
Fax (381)(11) 622965
Tlx 11587 YU CROSS
Tlg. YUGOCROSS
BELGRADE

Zambia Red Cross Society

2837 Los Angeles
Boulevard
Longacres
Lusaka
Postal address:
P.O. Box 50001
(Ridgeway 15101)
Lusaka
ZAMBIA
Tel. (260)(1) 250607;
254798
Fax (260)(1) 252219
Tlx ZACROS ZA 45020
Tlg. REDRAID LUSAKA
E-mail zrcs@zamnet.zm

Zimbabwe Red Cross Society

Red Cross House
98 Cameron Street
Harare
Postal address:
P.O. Box 1406
Harare
ZIMBABWE
Tel. (263)(4) 775416;
773512
Fax (263)(4) 751739
Tlx 24626 ZRCS ZW
Tlg. ZIMCROSS
HARARE

The network of International Federation country and regional delegations assists National Societies worldwide.

Christopher Black/International Federation. Democratic Republic of the Congo, 1997.

Chapter

14

International Federation delegation network

Contact details for regional and country delegations of the International Federation of Red Cross and Red Crescent Societies. Information correct as of 31 March 1998.

International Federation of Red Cross and Red Crescent Societies

P.O. Box 372, 1211 Geneva 19
SWITZERLAND
Tel. (41)(22) 730 42 22
Fax (41)(22) 733 03 95
Tlx (045) 412 133 FRC CH
Tlg. LICROSS GENEVA
E-mail secretariat@ifrc.org
WWW http://www.ifrc.org

Red Cross/EU Liaison Bureau

Rue J. Stallaert 1, bte 14
1050 - Bruxelles, BELGIUM
Tel. (32)(2) 3475750
Fax (32)(2) 3474365
E-mail rceulb.brux@infoboard.be

International Federation of Red Cross and Red Crescent Societies at the United Nations

630 Third Avenue, 21st floor, Suite 2104,
New York, NY10017, UNITED STATES
Tel. (1)(212) 3380161; Fax (1)(212) 3389832
E-mail ifrcny@undp.org

International Federation regional delegations

Buenos Aires

Lucio V. Mansilla 2698 2o
1425 Buenos Aires
ARGENTINA
Tel. (54)(1) 9638659;
9638660
Fax (54)(1) 9613320
E-mail
ifrcbue@satlink.com

Yaoundé

c/o Cameroon Red
Cross Society
Rue Henri Dunant
Yaoundé
CAMEROON
Tel. (247) 224177
Fax (247) 1244177

Abidjan

D.P. 2090
Abidjan 04
COTE D'IVOIRE
Tel. (225) 321529;
321202
Fax (225) 328561
Tlx (0983) 22673 LRCS
CI
E-mail
fedecr-r@africaonline.co.
ci

Suva

c/o Fiji Red Cross Society
22 Gorrie Street
Suva
Postal address:
GPO Box 569
Suva
FIJI
Tel. (679) 314133;
314138
Fax (679) 303818
Tlx 2279 Attn: Red Cross
(Public facility)

Guatemala City

19 Calle 1-26, Zona 14
Av. de las Americas, Pl.
Uruguay
Ciudad de Guatemala
GUATEMALA
Tel. (502) 3371686
Fax (502) 3631449
E-mail
fedecruz@guate.net

Budapest

Zolyomi Lepcso Ut 22
1124 Budapest
HUNGARY
Tel. (36)(1) 3193423;
3193425
Fax (36)(1) 3193424
E-mail info@slip.ifrc.hu

New Delhi

F-25A Hauz Khas
Enclave
New Delhi - 110 016
INDIA
Tel. (911)(1) 6858671;
6858672
Fax (911)(1) 6857567
E-mail
fedcross@del2.vsnl.net.in

Kingston

12 Upper Montrose Road
Kingston 6
Postal address:
P.O. Box 1284
Kingston 8
JAMAICA
Tel. (1)(809) 9277971
Fax (1)(809) 9789950

Amman

Al Shmeisani
Maroof Al Rasafi Street
Building No. 19
Amman
Postal address:
P.O. Box 830511 /
Zahran
Amman
JORDAN
Tel. (962)(6) 5681060
Fax (962)(6) 5694556
E-mail ifrc@go.com.jo

Almaty

c/o Red Cross and Red
Crescent Society of
Kazakhstan
86, Kunaeva Street
480100 Almaty
KAZAKHSTAN
Tel. (7)(3272) 542712,
542743
Fax (7)(3272) 541535
Tlx (064) 212378 ifrc su
E-mail
ifrckz@ifrckz.almaty.kz

Nairobi

Chaka Road (off
Argwings Kodhele)
P.O. Box 41275
Nairobi
KENYA
Tel. (254)(2) 714255;
714256
Fax (254)(2) 718415
Tlx (0987) 22622 IFRC
KE
E-mail ifrcke01@ifrc.org
OR ifrcke02@ifrc.org

Kuala Lumpur

c/o Malaysian Red
Crescent Society
32, Jalan Nipah
Off Jalan Ampang
55000 Kuala Lumpur
MALAYSIA
Tel. (60)(3) 4510723;
4524046
Fax (60)(3) 4519359
E-mail
ifrcmy01@ifrc.org

Harare

9, Coxwell Road
Milton Park
Harare
ZIMBABWE
Tel. (263)(4) 720315;
720316
Fax (263)(4) 708784
E-mail ifrchre@harare.iafrica.com

International Federation country delegations

Afghanistan

43 D Jamal-ud-Din
Afghan Road
University Town
Peshawar
PAKISTAN
Tel. (8731) 754374
Fax (8731) 754374

Angola

Rua Emilio M'Bidi 51 -
51A
Bairro Alvalade
Luanda
Postal address:
Caixa Postal 3324
 Luanda
ANGOLA
Tel. (244)(2) 322001
Fax (244)(2) 320648
Tlx 3394 crzver an
E-mail
itrclad@angonet.gn.apc.
org

Armenia

Djrashati Street 96
Yerevan-19
ARMENIA
Tel. (3742) 522253;
561889
E-mail
redplus@arminco.com

Azerbaijan

Niazi Street 11
Baku 370000
AZERBAIJAN
Tel. (99)(412) 925792
Fax (99)(412) 971889
E-mail root@ifrc.baku.az

Bangladesh

c/o Bangladesh Red
Crescent Society
684-686 Bara Magh
Bazar
Dhaka - 1217
BANGLADESH
Tel. (880)(2) 835401;
835402
Fax (880)(2) 834701
E-mail
ifrcbd.hod@pradeshta.net

Belarus

Ulitsa Mayakovkosgo 14
Minsk 220 006
BELARUS
Tel. (375)(172) 217237;
219060
Fax (375)(172) 272620
E-mail
admin@ifrc.minsk.org

Bosnia and Herzegovina

Titova 7
71000 Sarajevo
BOSNIA AND
HERZEGOVINA
Tel. (387)(71) 666009;
666011
Fax (387)(71) 666010
E-mail
ifrc_sarajevo@zamir-tz.
ztn.apc.org

Burundi

Avenue des Etats-Unis
3674A
Bujumbura
Postal address: B.P. 324
Bujumbura
BURUNDI
Tel. (257) 229524;
229525
Fax (257) 229408

Cambodia

53 Deo, Street
Croix-Rouge
Phnom Penh
Postal address: Central
Post Office/P.O. Box 820
Phnom Penh
CAMBODIA
Tel. (855)(23) 362690;
426370
Fax (855)(23) 426599
E-mail ifrckh01@uni.fi

Congo

c/o Comité Croix-Rouge
congolaise
B.P. 650
Pointe-Noire
CONGO
Tel. (242) 945471
Fax (242) 945471

Congo, DR of the

288, avenue des Trois Z
Gombé
Kinshasa
CONGO, THE
DEMOCRATIC
REPUBLIC OF THE
Tel. (243) 1221495
E-mail ifrcd01@ifrc.org

China

c/o Red Cross Society of
China
53 Ganmian Hutong
100010 Beijing
CHINA
Tel. (86)(10) 65124447
Fax (86)(10) 65124169

Croatia

Florijana Andreaseca 14
10000 Zagreb
CROATIA
Tel. (385)(1) 396111
Fax (385)(1) 396254
E-mail ifrc@alf.tel.hr

Eritrea

Andnet Street
Asmara
Postal address:
c/o Red Cross Society
of Eritrea
P.O. Box 575, Asmara
ERITREA
Tel. (291)(1) 181693
Fax (291)(1) 182859

Ethiopia

Ras Desta Damtew
Avenue
Addis Ababa
Postal address:
c/o Ethiopian Red
Cross
P.O. Box 195
Addis Ababa
ETHIOPIA
Tel. (251)(1) 514571
Fax (251)(1) 512888
Tlx 21338 ERCS
E-mail
ifrcet01@padis.gn.apc.
org

Georgia

7, Anton Katalikosi St.
Tbilisi
GEORGIA
Tel. (995)(32) 237176
Fax (995)(32) 985976
E-mail root@ifrc.aod.ge

Guinea

c/o Croix-Rouge de
Guinée
B.P. No 376
Conakry
GUINEA
Tel. (224) 413825;
404344
Fax (224) 414255
E-mail
fedecr-r@mirinet.net.gn

Haïti

18, rue Cheriez (Pont
Morin)
Port-au-Prince
Postal address:
BP 15322
Pétionville
HAITI
Tel. (509) 444868;
455619
Fax (509) 441868

Indonesia

c/o Indonesian Red
Cross Society
P.O. Box 2009
Jakarta
INDONESIA
Tel. (622)(1) 79191841
Fax (622)(1) 79191841

Iraq

c/o Iraqi Red Crescent
Society
Al Mansour
Baghdad
Postal Address:
P.O. Box 6143
Baghdad
IRAQ
Tel. (964)(1) 8862191;
5343922
Fax (964)(1) 8840872
Tlx 213331 HELAL IK

Kenya

South "C" Belle Vue
Off Mombasa Road
Nairobi
Postal address:
P.O. Box 41275
Nairobi
KENYA
Tel. (254)(02) 602468;
602465
Fax (254)(02) 602467
E-mail ifrcke03@ifrc.org

Korea, Democratic People's Republic of

c/o Red Cross Society of
the DPR Korea
Ryonwa 1, Central District
Pyongyang
DPR KOREA
Tel. (850)(2) 3813490;
3814350
Fax (850)(2) 3813490

Korea, Republic of

c/o Republic of Korea
National Red Cross
32-3ka, Namsan/dong
Choong/ku
Seoul 100-043
KOREA, REP. OF
Tel. (82)(2) 7555944
Fax (82)(2) 7579860

Lao People's Democratic Republic

Setthatirath Road
Xiengnhune Vientiane
Postal address:
c/o Lao Red Cross
P.O. Box 2948
Vientiane
LAO PDR
Tel. (856)(21) 215762
Fax (856)(21) 215935

Lebanon

N. Dagher Building
Mar Tacla - Beirut
LEBANON
Tel. (961)(1) 424851;
450781
Fax (961)(1) 429658
E-mail ifrc@cyberia.net.lb

Liberia

107, Lynch Street
Monrovia
Postal address:
c/o Liberian Red Cross
Society
P.O. Box 5081
Monrovia
LIBERIA
Tel. (231) 227485;
226231
Fax (231) 226231

Mongolia

c/o Red Cross Society of
Mongolia
Central Post Office
P.O. Box 537
Ulaan Baatar
MONGOLIA
Tel. (976)(1) 321684
Fax (976)(1) 321684
E-mail
ifrcmongol@magicnet.mn

Mozambique

Avenida 24 de Julho, 641
Maputo
Postal address:
Caixa postal 2488
Maputo
MOZAMBIQUE
Tel. (258)(1) 421210
Fax (258)(1) 423507
E-mail
ifrcpp@zebra.uem.mz

Myanmar

c/o Myanmar Red Cross
Society
Red Cross Building
42 Strand Road
Yangon
MYANMAR
Tel. (95)(1) 297877
Fax (95)(1) 297877

Nigeria

11, Eko Akete Close
Off St. Gregory's Road
South West Ikoyi
Lagos
Postal address:
c/o Nigerian Red Cross
Society
P.O. Box 764
Lagos
NIGERIA
Tel. (234)(1) 2695228;
2695229
Fax (234)(1) 2695229

Pakistan

Hse 2, Str. 55, Sector
F-7/4
Islamabad
PAKISTAN
Tel. (925)(1) 823980
Fax (925)(1) 825808

Papua New Guinea

c/o Papua New
Guinea Red Cross
Society
P.O. Box 6545
Boroko
PAPUA NEW GUINEA
Tel. (675) 3112277
Fax (675) 3230731

Russian Federation

c/o Russian Red Cross
Tcherymomushkinski
Proezd 5
117036 Moscow
RUSSIAN
FEDERATION
Tel. (7)(095) 2306620;
2306621
Fax (7)(095) 2306622
E-mail
rcmos@glas.apc.org

Rwanda

c/o Croix-Rouge
rwandaise
B.P. 425, Nyamirambo
Kigali
RWANDA
Tel. (250) 73232;
73874
Fax (250) 73233

Sierra Leone

6, Liverpool Street
Freetown
Postal address: c/o
Sierra Leone Red
Cross Society
P.O. Box 427
Freetown
SIERRA LEONE
Tel. (232)(22) 227772
Fax (232)(22) 228180

Somalia

Chaka Road/
off Argwings Kodhele
Nairobi
Postal address:
P.O. Box 41275,
Nairobi
KENYA
Tel. (254)(2) 728294;
728299
Fax (254)(2) 729070
Tlx 25436 IFRC KE

Sri Lanka

120 Park Road
Colombo 5
SRI LANKA
Tel. (941) 581903
Fax (941) 583269
E-mail
ifrclk01@srilanka.net

Sudan

Al Mak Nimir
Street/Gamhouria Street
Plot No 1, Block No 4
East Khartoum
Postal address:
P.O. Box 10697
East Khartoum
SUDAN
Tel. (249)(11) 771033
Fax (249)(11) 770484

Tanzania

Ali Hassan Mwinyi
Dar es Salaam
Postal address:
P.O. Box 1133,
Dar es Salaam
TANZANIA, UNITED
REPUBLIC OF
Tel. (255)(51) 116514
Fax (255)(51) 117308

Turkey

Atatürk Bulvari
219/14 Bulvari Apt.
006680 Kavaklidere,
Ankara
TURKEY
Tel. (90)(312) 4672099;
4673349
Fax (90)(312) 4274217
E-mail
ifrc-o@servis2.net.tr

Uganda

Plot 97, Buganda Road
Kampala
Postal address:
c/o Uganda Red Cross
Society
P.O. Box 494
Kampala
UGANDA
Tel. (256)(41) 234968;
343742
Fax (256)(41) 258184

Viet Nam

19 Mai Hac De Street
Hanoï
VIET NAM
Tel. (84)(4) 8252250;
8229283
Fax (84)(4) 8266177
E-mail
ifrcvn@netnam.org.vn

Yugoslavia

Simina Ulica Broj 21
11000 Belgrade
YUGOSLAVIA,
FEDERAL REPUBLIC
OF
Tel. (381)(11)
3282202; 3281376
Fax (381)(11) 3281791
E-mail
ifrcbgd@sezampro.yu

With the support of its 175 National Societies around the world, the **International Federation** *coordinates and provides emergency disaster assistance.*

© Christopher Black/International Federation. Peru, 1998.

Chapter

15
1997 relief operations
and overview maps

In 1997, the International Federation of Red Cross and Red Crescent Societies launched appeals for over 446 million Swiss francs to assist more than 22 million people.

Behind these figures lie an important shift in world disaster trends. For almost a decade, refugee and population movements dominated International Federation operations, claiming between 60 and 70 per cent of all funds raised each year. But there were clear signs, as 1997 drew to a close, that this trend was being reversed.

Refugee operations are declining and emergencies caused by natural events are increasing, both in frequency and in the numbers they affect – essentially local people in their home environment. The chief culprits are world weather changes and a particularly unpredictable *El Niño,* but uncontrolled development and abuse of natural resources are also triggering or aggravating disasters, such as the 1997 Asian smog/haze emergency.

Also growing in importance are public health threats, especially epidemics. This new challenge requires both emergency and long-term preventive action.

The maps in this section summarize the following 1997 operations for which appeals were launched:

- natural disasters, including floods, earthquakes, cyclones and catastrophes caused by the *El Niño* phenomenon;

- population movements;

- socio-economic dislocation;

- others, including food shortages, epidemics and nuclear disaster; and

- regional programmes.

(Maps and the designations used do not imply the expression of any opinion on the part of the International Federation or National Societies concerning the legal status of a territory or of its authorities.)

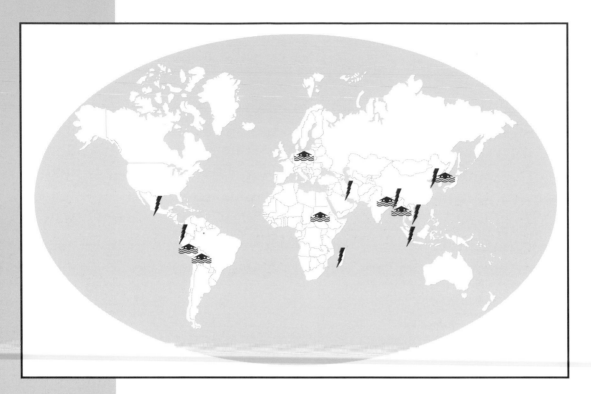

Natural disasters

	Target beneficiaries	Aid sought (CHF)
Natural hazards		
Americas (El Niño)	600,000	13,880,000
Indonesia (haze/smog)	2,000,000	265,000
DPR Korea (tidal wave)	10,000	1,435,000
Viet Nam (typhoon)	150,000	6,750,000
Madagascar (cyclone)	42,000	1,534,000
Bangladesh (cyclone)	50,000	3,000,000
Iran (earthquake)	60,000	9,012,000
Iran (earthquake)	60,000	12,000,000
Mexico (Hurricane Pauline rehabilitation)	10,000	1,010,000
Floods		
Peru	20,000	1,845,000
Central and Eastern Europe	257,000	6,960,000
Myanmar	55,000	1,015,000
Indian subcontinent/South-east Asia	635,000	4,632,000
Bolivia	108,000	2,450,000
Sudan	25,000	800,000
DPR Korea	2,600,000	35,244,000
Total	**6,682,000**	**101,832,000**

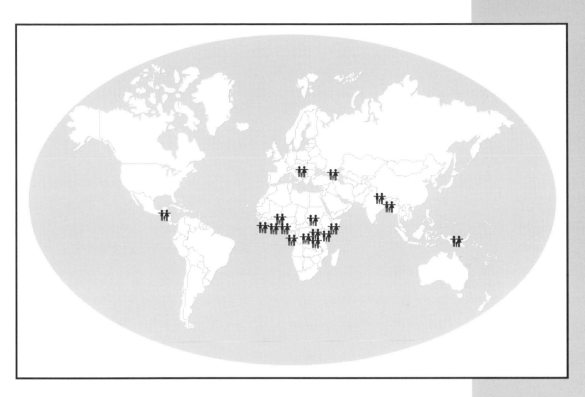

Population movements

	Target beneficiaries	Aid sought (CHF)
The Caucasus	435,000	13,652,000
Congo, PR of	372,500	5,600,000
Kenya	8,000	429,000
Great Lakes region	1,000,000	54,317,000
Former Yugoslavia	808,500	51,156,000
Ghana	11,500	123,000
Benin	9,000	318,000
Nepal	93,000	804,000
Papua New Guinea	120,000	3,799,000
Togo	12,000	87,000
Congo, DR of (formerly Zaire)	23,000	2,575,000
Liberia and region	800,000	12,252,000
Uganda	23,000	2,143,000
Sudan	480,000	1,033,000
Somalia	240,000	4,245,000
Bangladesh	35,000	184,000
Guatemala	200,000	3,995,000
Total	**4,670,500**	**156,712,000**

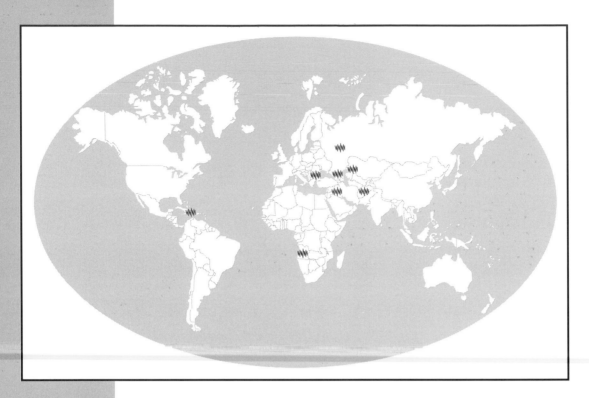

Socio-economic dislocation

	Target beneficiaries	Aid sought (CHF)
Russian Federation	517,000	8,567,000
Iraq	350,000	11,734,000
Kazakhstan	603,600	2,800,000
Angola	365,000	7,690,000
Bulgaria	158,500	8,542,000
Afghanistan	1,500,000	7,800,000
Haiti	128,000	3,690,000
Russian Federation/Moldova/ Ukraine/Belarus	1,057,500	22,742,000
Total	**4,679,600**	**73,565,000**

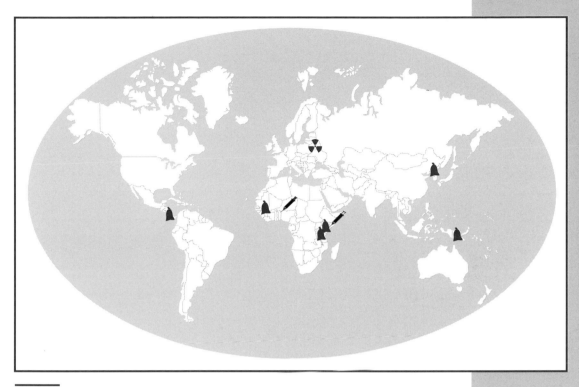

Other

	Target beneficiaries	Aid sought (CHF)
Nuclear disaster		
Chernobyl	200,000	1,300,000
Epidemics		
Kenya (cholera)	240,000	224,000
Africa (meningitis)	–	5,707,000
Food security		
Kenya	100,000	4,739,000
Mauritania/Niger	30,000	2,071,350
Eastern Africa	356,000	12,380,000
DPR Korea	3,500,000	20,011,000
Nicaragua	75,000	1,600,000
Papua New Guinea	160,000	570,000
Total	**4,661,000**	**48,602,350**

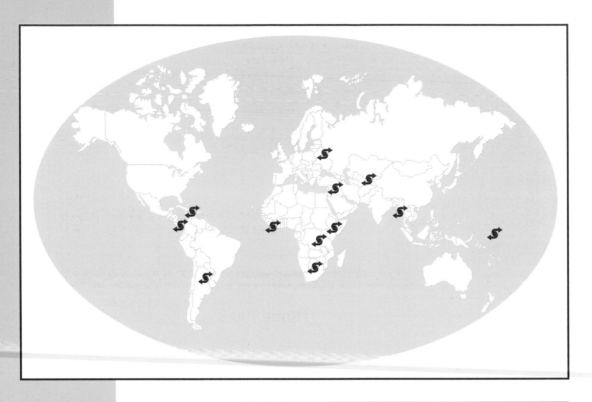

Regional programmes - preparedness and capacity building

	Aid sought (CHF)
West Africa	2,310,000
Central and Eastern Europe	8,949,000
East Africa	1,929,000
Central Africa	3,069,000
Southern Africa	1,823,000
Central Asia	26,223,000
South-east and East Asia	2,578,000
South America	1,345,000
Central America	3,255,000
Pacific	1,363,000
Caribbean	1,622,000
Middle East	630,000
Total	**55,096,000**

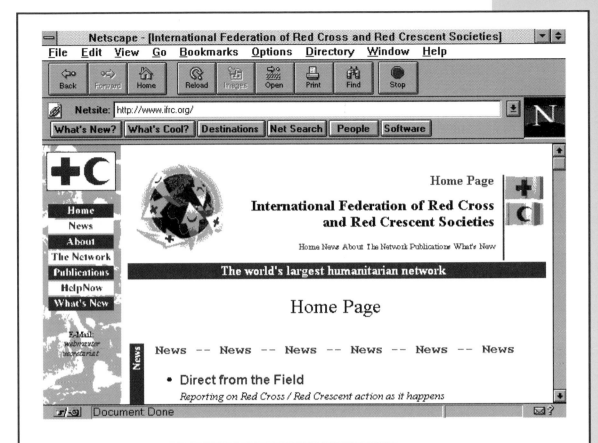

The International Federation on the Internet

A wide range of information, including selected chapters from previous *World Disasters Reports* and the full texts of the 1997 and 1998 editions of the *World Disasters Report,* can be accessed on the International Federation of Red Cross and Red Crescent Societies' website at http://www.ifrc.org

The International Federation web pages also include Direct from the Field – with reports on Red Cross and Red Crescent action as it happens around the world, constantly updated disaster appeals and situation reports from its global network of operations and delegations, as well as links to many disaster-related sites and the web pages of the International Committee of the Red Cross, International Red Cross and Red Crescent Museum, Henry Dunant Institute, and the Asia Pacific region website.

The website is also linked to an ever-increasing number of Red Cross and Red Crescent Societies worldwide, including African and Asian Societies.

To make copies of publications on the International Federation's website or to publish extracts of them, contact the Secretariat (secretariat@ifrc.org) in advance for permission. Full acknowledgement will be required.

If you have any problems connecting or would like more information, please contact the International Federation's Internet manager, Jeremy Mortimer, on webmaster@ifrc.org

The world of disasters in the World Disasters Report 1993-1998

The *World Disasters Report* is the only annual, interdisciplinary report focusing on disasters, from natural hazards to human-induced crises, and the millions of people affected by them.

Published in English and a range of other languages each year since 1993, the *Report* is backed by the expertise and resources of the International Federation of Red Cross and Red Crescent Societies, whose relief operations and National Societies in 175 countries make it the most extensive and experienced humanitarian network.

To order further copies of the *World Disasters Report 1998* – or the 1997 and 1996 editions – in English, use the order form on page 199; for all other languages and years contact the International Federation.

The six-section *World Disasters Report 1998* examines cities and crisis: issues in urban disasters; the toll of traffic accidents; shelter and reconstruction, and psychological support. It also analyses the 1997 Eastern European floods, sanctions and Iraq, rebuilding Sarajevo, refugee camp "cities" and urban Red Cross action in Colombia. Fully illustrated, with maps and index, with new data and full Red Cross/Red Crescent listings.

The *World Disasters Report 1997* includes: NGO futures in a rapidly changing world, the military-humanitarian relationship, information management, epidemiological data collection in disasters, aid trends and standards in disaster response, China's devastating floods, Caribbean natural hazards, the challenge of Somalia, and re-emerging diseases in the former Soviet Union. The *Report* includes a comprehensive 25-year disasters database, and outlines the global activities of the International Federation. Indexed and fully illustrated. Maps.

The five-section *World Disasters Report 1996* includes: global population movements; food security; emergency food aid and nutrition; developmental relief; trends in aid; Kobe earthquake; challenges of Rwanda; Oklahoma's trauma; DPR Korea's food and flood crisis; *Code of Conduct* update; National Society and delegation listings; disasters database. Indexed and fully illustrated.

The four-section *World Disasters Report 1995* includes: UN sanctions and the humanitarian crisis; good disaster-relief practice; early warning systems; the effects of evaluation; listening to the beneficiaries; psychological support; humanitarians in uniform; hate ratio in conflict; cyclones in Bangladesh; Ethiopia; Rwanda; Somalia's grey zone. Fully illustrated.

The three-section *World Disasters Report 1994* includes: drought success in Southern Africa; conflict and progress in Somalia; agency challenges within the former Yugoslavia; Brazil's vulnerability; India's earthquake myths; Caucasus collapse; secrecy's role in disasters; global survey of anti-personnel mines, information and Chernobyl; African peace mechanisms; human rights and disasters; indigenous knowledge and response; and the full text of the *Code of Conduct* for disaster-relief agencies.

The *World Disasters Report 1993* – the pilot issue – includes: humanitarian gap, preparedness versus relief, role of foreign medical teams and military forces, equity in impact, media in disasters, AIDS, famine, flood, high winds, refugees, epidemics, earthquakes, volcanoes. Case histories from: Uganda, Sudan, China, Bangladesh, Afghanistan, Peru, Zambia, Turkey, United States, Philippines. Fully illustrated.

And coming up ...   **World Disasters Report 1999**

The 1999 edition of the *World Disasters Report* will examine environmental hazards and natural disasters, including climate change, *El Niño*, water and sanitation, and fuel for disaster victims. It will also look at the year in disasters 1998, and include: disaster database, aid trends, *Code of Conduct* update, and full listings of National Societies and delegations.

Index

Mozambique 46
Muamilla 110, 111
mudslide(s) 17, 119
Munich Re(-insurance) 75, 123, 129

N

Nairobi 57
National Crash Analysis Center 25
National Red Cross and Red Crescent Societies 17, 33, 36, 37, 84, 128, 168-178
 see also International Committee of the Red Cross
 see also International Federation of Red Cross and Red Crescent Societies
 see also International Red Cross and Red Crescent Movement
 see also Red Cross and Red Crescent
National Road Safety Council 24
National Societies
 see National Red Cross and Red Crescent Societies
National System for Prevention and Attention to Disasters (SNPAD) 116-118, 121
natural disaster(s) 9, 12, 19, 45, 68, 75, 115, 116, 121-123, 128, 129, 131, 135, 137, 185
Neiva 118
Nepal 27
Netherlands 68, 71, 77, 132, 133
 Dutch Road Safety Institute 22
New England Journal of Medicine 30
New Delhi 18, 30
New York 11
New Zealand 68
Ngara 105, 106
Niesse River 123
Nigeria 22
Nile River 111, 113
non-governmental organization(s) (NGOs) 17, 45, 49, 55, 57, 62, 64, 70, 76-80, 85, 87, 88, 111, 116, 119, 128, 133, 134, 138
 NGO Field Cooperation Protocol 62
Norway 68, 70, 72, 79

nutrition 55, 112
Nyiragongo region 105

O

Oceania 28
Oder River 123
official development assistance (ODA) 68, 70, 74
Oklahoma City 35
Omdurman 111
Operation Lifeline Sudan (OLS) 57, 60, 61
Opole 123, 125
Organisation for Economic Co-operation and Development (OECD) 63, 64, 69-71, 73, 74, 77, 132, 134
 Development Assistance Committee (DAC) 64, 69-71, 73, 74, 76-78, 132, 134
 Development Cooperation Report 71, 76
Overseas Development Institute (ODI) 63, 64
 Humanitarian Policy Programme 63
 Relief and Rehabilitation Network 64
Oxfam 75

P

Paez 118
Pakistan 25, 27, 28, 29
Pan-American Health Organization (PAHO) 136
Papua New Guinea 27
Pasto 118
peacekeeping 71, 78, 102
People in Aid 62-64
 People in Aid Code of Best Conduct 64
Pereira 118
Peru 26
Philippines 27
Phoenix 11
PIOOM 132, 133, 138
 Newsletter 138
Poland 123-130
 Central Statistical Office 125
 Institute of Meteorology and Water Resources 125

National Flood Control Committee 124
National Insurance Institute 123
National Programme of Reconstruction and Modernization 126
Polish Psychological Society 124
Supreme Board of Inspection 124
police 13, 24-29, 47, 50, 83, 109, 112, 116
Popayan 118
population movement(s) 34, 47, 49, 185
Portugal 68, 70
post-traumatic stress disorder 33, 124
poverty 68-70, 74, 76, 77, 84, 93, 98, 101, 105, 109, 112, 116
Prague 127, 130, 131
Psychological Support Programme (PSP) 36
psychological support 32-43
 psychological assistance 124
 psychological effects 32, 38, 40, 124
Puerto Rico 26

R

Raciborz 123, 125
ration(s) 95, 97-101
reconstruction 44-53, 69, 85, 88, 125, 126, 128
Red Cross and Red Crescent 36, 78, 84, 102, 108, 118, 121
 Red Cross and Red Crescent symbol(s) 84
 see also International Committee of the Red Cross
 see also International Federation of Red Cross and Red Crescent Societies
 see also International Red Cross and Red Crescent Movement
 see also National Red Cross and Red Crescent Societies
Reference Centre for Psychological Support 36
 Coping with Crisis 36
 see also Danish Red Cross
 see also International Federation of Red Cross and Red Crescent Societies

National Flood Insurance
Program 129
Office of Foreign Disaster
Assistance 125, 135
US Agency for International
Development (USAID) 77, 113,
133
US Centers for Disease Control
(CDC) 41
University of Massachusetts 100
University of Michigan 22
urbanization 9-19,
US Committee for Refugees
(USCR) 132, 133, 137, 138
Refugee Reports 133
World Refugee Survey 133
Uvinza 110

V

Viet Nam 24
Vistula River 123
VOICE 45, 55
volcano(es) 105, 115, 117, 118
volcanic eruption(s) 116, 135
volunteer(s) 36, 41, 42, 84, 106,
108, 110, 116, 118, 120, 121,
128, 135
vulnerability 13, 16, 17, 20, 39,
116

W

Walbrzych 123
war 21, 35, 49, 57, 81, 82, 84,
85, 94, 102, 105, 106, 111, 138,
139
guerrilla war 115
laws of war 93
Warsaw 130, 131
waste 10, 47
waste collection 12
waste disposal 10, 120
water 10, 11, 12, 45, 47-50, 52,
53, 55, 74, 82, 85, 97, 98, 100,
101, 104, 105, 107, 110-114,
119, 125, 128
Wilson, Woodrow 92
World Bank 26, 64, 68, 85, 93,
126
World Disasters Report(s)
see International Federation of
Red Cross and Red Crescent
Societies

World Food Programme (WFP)
93, 96, 100, 101, 113, 132, 134
International Food Aid
Information System
(INTERFAIS) 132, 134
World Health Organization
(WHO) 32, 50, 93, 100, 133
World Meteorological
Organization (WMO) 136
World Vision International 89
World-Wide Web 136
see also Colombian Red Cross
website
see also International Federation
website
Wroclaw 123, 125, 126

Y

Yugoslavia 35, 36, 68, 72, 76,
136

Z

Zaire
see Democratic Republic of the
Congo
Zimbabwe 25, 26, 27, 28
Zurich 12

ow to order the *WORLD DISASTERS REPORT 1998* from Oxford University Press*

REDIT CARD HOTLINE
one OUP's Credit Card Hotline,
en 24 hours a day, quoting the ref.
mber in the bottom right corner:
l.: +44 (0) 1536 454 534

AX ORDERS
ax: +44 (0) 1536 454 518

ELEPHONE ENQUIRIES
l: +44 (0) 1536 741 727

BY E-MAIL
E-mail: book.orders@oup.co.uk

BY POST
From the UK (no stamp required):

CWO Department, OUP, FREEPOST,
NH4051, Corby, Northants, NN18 9BR

From outside the UK:

CWO Department, OUP, Saxon Way
West, Corby, Northants, NN18 9ES

HOW TO ORDER IN THE UNITED STATES
For more information, or to order by credit card, please call:

1-800-451-7556

between the hours of
0900 and 1700
Eastern Standard Time

OUR ORDER

ease supply the following [PLEASE USE BLOCK CAPITALS]:

ty	ISBN	Author	Title	Price[1]
	0-19-829456-5	IFRC	*World Disasters Report 1998*	£ 15.99
				£

EC customers from outside the UK please add VAT[2]
Postage and packing[3]
TOTAL

ELIVERY

ease deliver my goods to:[4]

itle	
irst name	
ast name	
epartment/Faculty	
niversity/Company	
ddress	
ountry	
ost code	
-mail address	

OW TO PAY

ou can pay by: ☐ Credit Card ☐ Cheque from a UK Bank account ☐ Eurocheque

LEASE COMPLETE THE RELEVANT FORM BELOW:

ease charge £_____ to my MasterCard / Visa / American Express / Diners Club account/Switch

ard number ☐☐☐☐ ☐☐☐☐ ☐☐☐☐ ☐☐☐☐ ☐☐☐

xpiry date ____ / ____   Switch issue number ____   Signature _____

redit card account address (if different from delivery address):

_____

_____ I enclose a Eurocheque for £_____

☐ **CHEQUE PAYMENT**
enclose a cheque for £_____
rossed and made payable to **Oxford University Press**,
rawn against a UK Bank.

☐ **EUROCHEQUE PAYMENT**

☐ **PROFORMA INVOICE**
Please send a proforma invoice for £_____
Goods will be despatched on receipt of payment.

Please quote the following code for all telephone or e-mail orders: **VBREDX98Z**

---

[1] Prices and Extents are accurate at the time of going to press, but are liable to alteration without notice.

[2] If you are registered for VAT or a local sales tax, please provide your number here:

[3] Postage and packing charges (including VAT)

UK orders
Up to £50, add £2.50
Over £50, FREE

Non-UK orders
add 10 per cent of the total price of the goods. Minimum charge: £2.50

[4] Please allow 10 days for delivery in the UK; 28 days elsewhere.

☐ Tick here if you do not want to be sent information about OUP titles in the future.

Thank you for your order!

*The *World Disasters Reports* 1996* and *1997* in English can also be ordered through OUP.

For orders and information about 1993, 1994 and 1995 editions in English and all other language versions, please contact:

International Federation of Red Cross and Red Crescent Societies, P.O. Box 372, 1211 Geneva 19, Switzerland.

Tel: +41 22 730 4222;
fax: +41 22 733 0395;
e-mail: guidera@ifrc.org

 # A world of Red Cross Red Crescent news

International Red Cross and Red Crescent Movement

Red Cross, Red Crescent

Red Cross, Red Crescent is a full-colour magazine of the International Red Cross and Red Crescent Movement featuring front line news on conflict and disasters, promoting awareness of urgent social problems, and highlighting the views of opinion-makers working in relief and development.

Published four times a year, in English, French and Spanish, *Red Cross, Red Crescent* uses distinguished writers and photographers to focus attention on the work of volunteers and staff throughout the world and provide analysis on issues of concern within the humanitarian community.

Recent and upcoming topics in *Red Cross, Red Crescent* include: the campaign to ban landmines, return to Rwanda, Asia's growing cities, re-emerging diseases, and street children.

Red Cross, Red Crescent is produced jointly by the International Committee of the Red Cross and the International Federation of Red Cross and Red Crescent Societies.

For more information, or to request a free subscription to *Red Cross, Red Crescent*, please write with your details – title, name, full postal address, phone, fax and e-mail and the language you would prefer, to:

The Editors, *Red Cross, Red Crescent*
PO Box 372, CH 1211 Geneva 19, Switzerland
Fax: +41 22 733 0395; E-mail: rcrc@ifrc.org

International Federation of Red Cross and Red Crescent Societies

Annual Report 1997

Reviews the International Federation Secretariat's work with national Red Cross and Red Crescent societies, through its network of delegations worldwide. The report provides a comprehensive retrospective on the year's activities, highlighting key aspects of governance, humanitarian action and support to National Societies. The *Annual Report* also details initiatives in communications, policy and management and provides a financial overview, complete with audited balance sheets and notes.

To request a free copy in English, French, Spanish or Arabic, send your full details to :

International Federation of Red Cross and Red Crescent Societies
PO Box 372, 1211 Geneva 19, Switzerland
Fax: +41 22 733 0395;
E-mail: guidera@ifrc.org

Direct from the field

Disaster preparedness ... floods ... first aid ... food security ... **want to know more?**
Check out our web site
http://www.ifrc.org
... reporting Red Cross Red Crescent action as it happens around the world.

The Sphere Project

The Humanitarian Charter –
Minimum Standards
in Humanitarian Response

Organizational best practices

Water and sanitation

Nutrition

Food programming

Shelter and site

Health services

Publication: Fall 1998

Updates on the Internet:
http://www.ifrc.org/pubs/sphere

a programme of the
Steering Committee for Humanitarian Response
and **Inter*Action***
with **VOICE - ICRC - ICVA**

OXFORD

Community Development Journal

Published four times a year the **Community Development Journal**
covers political, economic and social programmes that link the
activities of people with institutions and government. Articles
feature community action, village, town and regional planning,
community studies and rural development.
Volume 33, 1998 (4 issues) Institutions: £60/US$105
Individuals: £42/US$75, Developing Countries: US$65

Journal of African Economies

In the last few years there has been a growing output of high quality
economic research on Africa, but until the advent of the **Journal of
African Economies** it was scattered over many diverse publications.
Now this important area of research has its own vehicle to
carry rigorous economic analysis, focused entirely on
Africa, for Africans and anyone interested in the continent
- be they consultants, policymakers, academics, traders,
financiers, development agents or aid workers.
Volume 7, 1998 (3 issues)
Institutions: £84/US$145, Individuals: £43/US$77
Subscribers in Africa: US$50

International Journal of Refugee Law

A journal which aims to stimulate research and thinking on refugee law
and its development, taking account of the broadest range of State and
international organisation practice. It serves as an essential tool for all
engaged in the protection of refugees and finding solutions to their problems,
providing key information and commentary on today's critical issues.
Volume 10, 1998 (4 issues)
Institutions: £85/US$158, Individuals: £39/US$72

African Affairs

African Affairs is one of the oldest journals in the field. It publishes articles on
recent political, social and economic developments in sub-Saharan countries,
and includes historical studies that illuminate current events in the continent.
Volume 97, 1998 (4 issues)
Institutions: £77/US$135, Individuals: £40/US$70, Individuals in Africa: US$28

JOURNALS

Journal of Refugee Studies

The **Journal of Refugee Studies** provides a major focus for research into refugees reflecting the diverse range of issues involved. It aims to promote the theoretical development of refugee studies, and encourages the voice of refugees to be represented by analysis of their experiences.
Volume 11, 1998 (4 issues)
Institutions: £76/US$139, Individuals: £37/US$66
Institutions in Developing Countries: US$57

Refugee Survey Quarterly

RSQ is produced by the Centre for Documentation and Research of the United Nations High Commissioner for Refugees. Published four times a year it serves as an authoritative source for current refugee and country information. Each issue is a combination of country reports, documents, reviews and abstracts of refugee-related literature.
Volume 17, 1998 (4 issues)
Institutions: £68/US$100, Individuals: £42/US$66

International Journal of Epidemiology

Exploring the epidemiology of both infectious and non-infectious disease, including research into health services and medical care, *IJE* encourages communication among those engaged in the research, teaching, and application of epidemiology throughout the world.
Volume 27, 1998 (6 issues)
£205/US$375

Health Policy and Planning

Particularly relevant to those working in international health planning, medical care and public health, *Health Policy and Planning* is concerned with issues of health policy, planning, and management and evaluation, focusing on the developing world.
Volume 13, 1998 (4 issues)
Institutions: £120/US$220, Individuals: £52/US$96

---

nb. £ sterling applies in UK and Europe, US$ elsewhere
Free sample copies are available
Please state your choice (two titles per request only) and send to:
Journals Marketing Department (DR98), Oxford University Press,
Great Clarendon Street, Oxford, OX2 6DP, UK

Refugee Studies from
OXFORD

The State of the World's Refugees, 1997-98
A Humanitarian Agenda
UNITED NATIONS HIGH COMMISSIONER FOR REFUGEES

During the past few years, millions of people have been forced to abandon their homes, fleeing from communal violence, political persecution and other threats to their security. This invaluable book from the UN's refugee agency provides the definitive picture of the world's displaced people, and examines the international community's efforts to respond to their plight.
0-19-829309-7, 310 pages, numerous halftones, line figures, and tables, paperback, £9.99

ALSO AVAILABLE
The State of the World's Refugees 1995
In Search of Solutions
UNITED NATIONS HIGH COMMISSIONER FOR REFUGEES
0-19-828044-0, 264 pages, numerous halftones, figures and tables, £30.00, 0-19-828043-2, Paperback, £9.99

Refugees in Inter-War Europe
The Emergence of a Regime
CLAUDENA SKRAN
'has lessons for anyone concerned with contemporary refugee crises, and the policies currently adopted to deal with their causes and consequences.'
Journal of Refugee Studies
0-19-827392-4, 336 pages, tables, Clarendon Press, £50.00

Available through good bookshops
For further information contact Victoria Bentata, Academic Marketing, Oxford University Press, Great Clarendon Street, Oxford, OX2 6DP
☎ +44 (0) 1865 556767 Ext: 4690
or email: bentatav@oup.co.uk
24 hour credit card hotline ☎ +44 (0) 1536 454534
Booksearch: www.oup.co.uk/catalogue

SECOND EDITION
The Refugee in International Law
Second Edition
GUY S. GOODWIN-GILL
'the second edition has replaced its predecessor as the most authoritative text available on international refugee law.'
Refugee Reports
0-19-826020-2, 624 pages, paperback, £22.50

The Status of Palestinian Refugees in International Law
LEX TAKKENBERG
Lex Takkenberg explores the status of Palestinian refugees in international law, analysing relevant areas of international law and probing their relevance to the provision of international protection for Palestinian refugees in the context of the Middle East peace process.
0-19-826590-5, 448 pages, Clarendon Press, £50.00

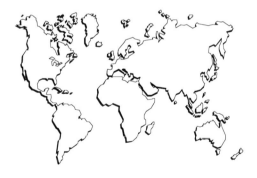

OXFORD
University Press

JOURNALS from FRANK CASS

The Journal of Development Studies

Managing Editors **David Booth, Christopher Colclough** and **Colin Kirkpatrick**

The Journal of Development Studies is one of the best known and well-established international journals in the area of development studies.

ISSN 0022-0388 Volume 34 1997/1998
Six issues per year: October, December, February, April, June, August • Individuals £48/$70 Institutions £195/$260

The European Journal of Development Research
Journal of the European Association for Development Research and Training Institutes (EADI)

Editor **Cristóbal Kay**

This journal aims to achieve the highest standards of debate and analysis on matters of policy, theory and practice, in all aspects of development studies. It exists particularly in order to publish research carried out in Europe or in co-operation with European institutions.

ISSN 0957-8811 Volume 10 1998
Two issues per year: June, December
Individuals £35/$55 Institutions £85/$125

The International Journal of Technical Cooperation

Editor **Gerald E Caiden**

This journal focuses exclusively on international technical cooperation/technical assistance. It is designed to provide a forum and to address the professional needs of practitioners and researchers.

ISSN 1358-8257 Volume 4 1998
Two issues per year: Summer, Winter
Individuals/developing countries £30/$45
Institutions £85/$125

International Peacekeeping

Editor **Michael Pugh**

International Peacekeeping examines the theory and practice of peacekeeping. It reflects the principle that peacekeeping is essentially a political act in which military forces, frequently in a condition of partial demilitarization, are the instruments of policy at an international level.

ISSN 1353-3312 Volume 5 1998
Quarterly: Spring, Summer, Autumn, Winter
Individuals £36/$48 Institutions £125/$190

Civil Wars `new`

Editor **Caroline Kennedy-Pipe**

Civil Wars will bring together academic pieces on all aspects of civil wars, both historical and contemporary. The journal will be required reading for historians, sociologists, political scientists and will be of interest to those in government, international organisations and the military.

ISSN 1369-8249 Volume 1 1998
Quarterly: Spring, Summer, Autumn, Winter
Individuals £35/$45 Institutions £125/$185

The International Journal of Human Rights

Editor **Frank Barnaby**

This covers an exceptionally broad spectrum of human rights issues, in particular those relating to race, religion, gender, children, class, refugees and immigration. It is essential reading for academics and students of political science and international law; officers in relevant NGOs; lawyers; politicians and civil servants; human rights activists; and the interested general public.

ISSN 1364-2987 Volume 2 1998
Quarterly: Spring, Summer, Autumn, Winter
Individuals £35/$45 Institutions £115/$175

FRANK CASS PUBLISHERS
900 Eastern Avenue, Newbury Park, Ilford, Essex, IG2 7HH Tel: +44 (0)181 599 8866 Fax: +44 (0)181 599 0984
North America: c/o ISBS, 5804 NE Hassalo Street, Portland, OR 97213 3644 Tel: 1 800 944 6190 Fax: 503 280 8832
Website: http://www.frankcass.com E-mail: jnlinfo@frankcass.com

Development in Practice

SPECIAL TOPIC ISSUE

During 1998 there will be a special theme issue on *Managing Development*, co-edited with **Tom Hewitt** and **Hazel Johnson** of the Open University, UK.

EDITOR

Deborah Eade,
Oxfam UK and Ireland

Supported by an International Board of Editorial Advisers

Development in Practice is a forum for practitioners, policy makers, and academics to exchange information and analysis concerning the social dimensions of development and humanitarian action. As a multi-disciplinary journal, *Development in Practice* reflects a wide range of institutional and cultural backgrounds and a variety of professional experience. All articles are independently refereed. Each issue offers the following features:

- ◆ Editorial
- ◆ Articles
- ◆ Viewpoints
- ◆ Feedback
- ◆ Practical Notes
- ◆ Research Round-up
- ◆ Conference Reports
- ◆ Book Reviews
- ◆ Book Shelf
- ◆ In Brief
- ◆ Networks in Progress

WORLD WIDE WEB

Full details on *Development in Practice,* including contents pages and Notes for Contributors, can be found on the Carfax Home Page at:
http://www.carfax.co.uk/dip-ad.htm

Abstracts and contents of recent issues may be found on the Oxfam website at:
http://www.oneworld.org.oxfam/

SUBSCRIPTION RATES

Volume 8, 1998,
4 issues, ISSN 0961-4524.

Institutional rate:
£136.00;
North America US$248.00

Personal rate:
£52.00;
North America US$88.00

Subsidised rate:
£25.00; US$39.00
(for individuals and organisations from countries listed in the current UNDP *Human Development Report* as 'developing countries')

Bulk rate (10+ copies):
£48.00;
North America US$80.00

Carfax Publishing Limited
P O Box 25, Abingdon, Oxfordshire OX14 3UE, UK
Tel: +44 (0)1235 401000   *Fax:* +44 (0)1235 401550
E-mail: sales@carfax.co.uk

Online access available to all subscribers in 1998